THE
ABOLITIONISTS

A Collection of Their Writings

By LOUIS RUCHAMES

G. P. Putnam's Sons
New York

TO

Robby and Barbara

© 1963 by Louis Ruchames

*Published simultaneously in the Dominion of
Canada by Longmans Canada Limited, Toronto.*

Library of Congress Catalog
Card Number: 63-16184

MANUFACTURED IN THE UNITED STATES OF AMERICA

Contents

[7

8]   *Contents*

Preface

ࣃ৶

 As the reader will notice, the great majority of selections included in this volume were written during the 1830's and early 1840's. It was during those years that the Abolitionist movement made its greatest contribution to American life and faced its most difficult tasks: to awaken public opinion to the horror of slavery and to stimulate it to take action against the evil. It was during those formative years that the leadership and philosophy of the movement crystallized. On the one hand, issues which were to split the movement into two were born then; on the other, the philosophy and strategy of each of the contending factions took form within that period and were not to undergo any significant change until the Civil War.

 The selections written during the later period have been chosen because they either illuminate the earlier years or, as in the case of William Lloyd Garrison, they are a fitting close to an aspect of history in which Garrison was the overshadowing figure.

 John Brown is not included here because his efforts belong to a much later period and because a large representative sampling of his letters, speeches and other writings is to be found in this writer's volume, *A John Brown Reader,* published by Abelard-Schuman in 1960.

 I am grateful to Prof. Sidney Kaplan, of the University of Massachusetts, for reading the manuscript and offering many valuable suggestions.

Introduction

"The character of a city is determined by the character of the men it crowns," once remarked Wendell Phillips, quoting the Greek orator Aeschines. Applying the lesson to modern times, there are few periods in American history that offer as remarkable an opportunity for the molding of American character to the highest standards of humanity as that in which the men and women known as Abolitionists lived and wrought. Devoted to the ideals of brotherhood and equality of opportunity for all men, their consciences seared by the heartlessness of slavery in the South and racial prejudice in the North, they consecrated their lives to the eradication of both evils. Encompassed by both indifference and hostility, subjected to social ostracism, economic sanctions and physical violence for daring to condemn institutions and customs which were regarded as vital to the welfare of American society and therefore sacrosanct, they stubbornly and heroically continued their efforts until victory in the war against slavery was achieved.

The nature of the revolution wrought by the Abolitionists may best be assessed by placing ourselves in the year 1829, immediately before the rise of the modern Abolitionist movement. In December of that year, the American Convention for Promoting the Abolition of Slavery and Improving the Condition of the African Race held its twenty-first biennial convention at Washington, D. C., with delegates present from New York, Pennsylvania, Maryland, Washington, D. C., and Alexandria, Virginia. Formed thirty-five years earlier in an attempt to unite the efforts of existing state and local anti-slavery groups, the organization's successes and failures during the intervening years were highlighted in three notable reports to the convention.

In the first, Benjamin Lundy, one of the great anti-slavery pioneers, enumerated its successes. These were an increase in the number of anti-slavery advocates from very few to thousands, some of them "among the most influential characters in the nation"; the complete abolition of slavery in certain states, particularly Rhode Island, Connecticut, New York, New Jersey, Pennsylvania, Ohio, Indiana and

Illinois; and the passage of the Missouri Compromise in 1820 which had prohibited the extension of slavery north of 36° 30′.

The failures were detailed in two other reports which noted no visible improvement in the treatment of the slave since 1790, the year of the first census, but rather an alarming increase in the number of slaves from 694,280 to about 2,000,000 and a tripling in the area devoted to slavery from an original 212,000 to nearly 600,000 square miles. Most disturbing, however, one report noted, was the public apathy toward all efforts to help the slave, which "are viewed in the light of encroachment on the established order of society, for so deeply has the system of slavery become rooted in the soil, that even those who are not directly interested in its continuance, are not disposed to aid by their countenance, or afford us assistance in pecuniary manner—and thus our usefulness is checked, and our endeavors to lay before the public the train of evils attendant on a state of slavery are retarded. . . ."

That the anti-slavery movement, in the light of its own statements in 1829, had marched into a cul-de-sac which required heroic efforts on its part to extricate itself, seems evident today. The greatest need was a re-examination of its basic strategy which had been based upon "moderation" and "temperance" in describing the nature of slavery and the responsibility of the slaveholder; the espousal of "gradualism" and colonization of former slaves to areas outside the United States as the most feasible methods of hastening the end of slavery; and an emphasis upon convincing the slaveholder that it was to his economic interest to liberate the slave and utilize free labor instead.

The results of this strategy were the very opposite of what its proponents had intended. The recourse to a very cautious "moderation" in language, and the avoidance of any language likely to antagonize the slaveowner, simply minimized the inherent evils of the institution and the responsibility of the slaveowner for the suffering of the slave and made it more difficult to awaken the public conscience to a recognition of the evil; the appeal to self-interest foundered upon the reality of slavery as a source of wealth to the master and his family; the policy of gradual emancipation provided an excuse for doing nothing immediately and salved the consciences of those who were indisposed to take vigorous action; while colonization, recommended by the American Colonization Society since 1816—and by many who were sincerely interested in helping the slave—actually hindered emancipation and the struggle for equal rights for the Negro. For colonization assumed the inferiority of the Negro and regarded his presence in this country as a danger to white American society and thus reinforced the very arguments which were being used to keep him in slavery and to deprive him, when free, of the rights of a white man.

The resulting situation has been perceptively summarized by Albert Bushnell Hart.[1]

> When Jackson became president, in 1829, anti-slavery seemed, after fifty years of effort, to have spent its force. The voice of the churches was no longer heard in protest; the abolitionist societies were dying out; there was hardly an abolitionist militant in the field; the Colonization Society absorbed most of the public interest in the subject, and it was doing nothing to help either the free Negro or the slave; in Congress there was only one anti-slavery man, and his efforts were without avail. It was a gloomy time for the little band of people who believed that slavery was poisonous to the south, hurtful to the north, and dangerous to the Union.

It was at this point that William Lloyd Garrison appeared with a revolutionary philosophy that challenged every basic assumption of the existing anti-slavery societies, and building upon new foundations, created a movement which ultimately brought about the destruction of slavery. Harriet Martineau, the English author, in her little volume entitled *The Martyr Age of the United States,* has called Garrison "the mastermind of the great revolution." He was indeed that and more. Born in 1805 to a mother who was a pious Baptist and a father who deserted his family when the boy was three years old, Garrison early sought to prepare himself for the profession of writing. A newspaper apprentice at thirteen, he later edited newspapers in Newburyport, Boston and Bennington. In 1827, in Boston, he met Benjamin Lundy, a New Jersey Quaker who had been carrying on a one-man crusade against slavery for more than fifteen years. Lundy had formed anti-slavery societies throughout the country, had promoted schemes for Negro colonization in Mexico and Haiti, and had been editing the

---

[1] Albert Bushnell Hart, *Slavery and Abolition,* 1831–1841 (New York, 1906), p. 165–6.

Genius of Universal Emancipation since 1821. Lundy persuaded Garrison to move to Baltimore in the fall of 1829 and join him is editing his newspaper, which then became a weekly. Several months later the partnership was interrupted when Garrison, convicted of libel by a Baltimore jury for excoriating a Massachusetts shipowner who had been transporting slaves for the South, was jailed upon failure to pay the fine of $50 and costs. Upon his release—the fine having been paid by Arthur Tappan, a New York merchant and anti-slavery philanthropist—he made plans to issue his own newspaper, which he realized with the appearance of the *Liberator* in Boston on January 1, 1831. Starting without capital and aided by Isaac Knapp, a printer, Garrison relied for financial support primarily upon Negro contributions and subscriptions, supplemented by those of a few white sympathizers.

The revolutionary nature of Garrison's thought, made manifest in the first pages of the *Liberator,* was summarized years later by Wendell Phillips in his comment that Garrison "undertook to look at the slave question as the Negro looked at it." Identifying himself completely with the slave, Garrison saw and felt slavery in all its terror and misery, refused to accept as valid any excuse for its continuance, and demanded its immediate and total abolition. Identifying himself, too, with the free Negro, he affirmed the latter's right to complete equality of opportunity and condemned the American Colonization Society for viewing the Negro as a danger to American society, to be freed from slavery only if he left the country. Indeed, within a few years after he had begun to expose the pernicious nature of this philosophy, an anti-slavery man who defended the American Colonization Society became a rarity. One aspect of Garrison's philosophy was his refusal to bate one jot or tittle from the deserved condemnation of either slavery or the slaveholder. Viewing slavery as a crime against millions of human beings which contravened the established moral and religious principles of decent humanity, to Garrison the slaveholder was a criminal whose piety as a Christian and respectability as citizen, husband and father, did not palliate in the slightest the horror of his action toward the slave. So accustomed was American society of that day—including many who were honestly anti-slavery—to speak in soft tones of slavery and the slaveholder, that Garrison's language seemed outlandish and violent. Yet what he wrote was never coarse or vulgar, and to the fair-minded observer today, remembering the villainy that had to be described and the indifference to be overcome, it appears appropriate and necessary.

Through the cogency of his arguments and the sincerity and vitality of his writings and speeches, Garrison soon attracted to himself a varied group of friends and associates.

Harriet Martineau once wrote:

> There is a remarkable set of people now living and vigorously acting in the world, with a consonance of will and understanding which has perhaps never been witnessed among so large a number of individuals of such diversified powers, habits, opinions, tastes and circumstances. The body comprehends men and women of every shade of color, of every degree of education, of every variety of religious opinion, of every gradation of rank, bound together by no vow, no pledge, no stipulation but of each preserving his individual liberty; and yet they act as if they were of one heart and of one soul. Such union could be secured by no principle of worldly interest; nor, for a term of years, by the most stringent fanaticism. A well-grounded faith, directed towards a noble object, is the only principle which can account for such a spectacle as the world is now waking up to contemplate in the abolitionists of the United States.[2]

Among the first to be deeply influenced were Samuel J. May, of Brooklyn, Connecticut, the only Unitarian minister then in the state; May's brother-in-law Bronson Alcott; and Samuel E. Sewall, May's cousin, a young Boston lawyer who was a descendant of Judge Samuel Sewall of Colonial fame and a member of one of the most prominent families of the Commonwealth. The three had attended a lecture by Garrison in Boston in October 1830 at which Garrison had argued the doctrine of immediate emancipation. They had been deeply impressed, had offered Garrison their cooperation, and had invited him to Bronson Alcott's home where they spent several hours. So great was the impact of that meeting that almost forty years later May still retained much of his original fervor when he wrote: "That night my soul was baptized in his spirit, and ever since I have been a disciple and fellow-laborer of William Lloyd Garrison." [3] May helped in the formation of the American Anti-Slavery Society, served

[2] Harriet Martineau, *The Martyr Age of the United States* (Boston, 1839), p. 3.
[3] Samuel J. May, *Some Recollections of Our Antislavery Conflict* (Boston, 1869), p. 19.

as general agent and secretary of the Massachusetts Anti-Slavery Society, and in the midst of a busy ministerial career devoted to many causes, achieved a notable reputation as a reformer and friend of the slave. Others who joined Garrison's standard were John Greenleaf Whittier, whose poems Garrison was the first to publish in the New-buryport *Herald*, and who became an early and devoted friend, though the two later differed on the question of political action; Ellis Gray Loring, a rising young Boston lawyer of a socially prominent family, who took his place as a leader in the Massachusetts Anti-Slavery Society; Oliver Johnson, born and raised in Vermont, who was first influenced by Garrison's *Journal of the Times,* and who later, in 1831, as editor of the *Christian Soldier*—with an office in the building in which the *Liberator* was published—became his devoted friend, collaborator and the author of his first full-length biography; Arnold Buffum, a Quaker hat manufacturer who became the first president of the New England Anti-Slavery Society, although he later left the Garrison camp for political action with the Liberty Party; and David and Lydia Maria Child, husband and wife, the former a journalist, teacher, lawyer and for a short period a member of the Massachusetts legislature, the latter a popular novelist and publicist whose *An Appeal in Favor of that Class of Americans Called Africans,* published in July 1833, gained many new converts for the anti-slavery movement.

The first organizational result of Garrison's teaching was the formation, after several meetings, of the New England Anti-Slavery Society on January 6, 1832. Its constitution, adopted on that day, was the first to avow the principle of immediate emancipation. Among the twelve who signed it were Garrison, Johnson, Buffum, Knapp and Joshua Coffin. Although David Child, Sewall and Loring at first objected to the inclusion of the immediate emancipation clause on grounds of expediency and refused to sign, they did so soon after and assumed leading posts in the organization.

Of great significance to the cause was the publication in 1832 of a pamphlet by Garrison entitled "Thoughts on African Colonization," which exposed the pretensions of the American Colonization Society and condemned it out of the writings and speeches of its leaders as an anti-Negro, pro-slavery organization. The pamphlet had a wide impact, influencing such men as Elizur Wright, Jr. and Beriah Green, two professors at Western Reserve College who were later to play a prominent part in the anti-slavery movement, as well as Lewis and Arthur Tappan, the influential businessmen-philanthropists of New York.

Anti-slavery sentiment now increased in different parts of the country and voices were raised in favor of forming a national anti-slavery organization upon the principles of immediate, unconditional emancipation. The publication in 1833 of Whittier's pamphlet, "Justice and Expediency" and of Lydia Maria Child's *Appeal,* further stirred public opinion and gained new converts. So did the persecution of Prudence Crandall by leading public officials of the State of Connecticut for seeking to educate Negro girls in her school in Canterbury, Connecticut. At this time, too, there emerged in New York City a group of anti-slavery men of ability and vision who began to agitate for the formation of anti-slavery societies in New York City and nationally. These included, along with the Tappans, William Goodell, an editor of the *Genius of Temperance* and later of the *Emancipator,* established in 1833; Isaac T. Hopper, a radical Quaker of Philadelphia who had moved to New York, and who had been helping escaped slaves and free Negroes for many years; Joshua Leavitt, editor of the *Evangelist* and subsequently of the *Emancipator;* and William Jay, author and reformer, the son of Chief Justice John Jay. These took the lead in forming a New York anti-slavery society in October 1833.

On October 29, 1833, a month after Garrison's return from England, where he had spent several months securing the support of English Abolitionists for the American anti-slavery movement and their condemnation of the American Colonization Society, a call for a national convention was issued. According to varying estimates, between 50 and 60 delegates, among whom were several Negroes, met in Philadelphia on three days in early December. Beriah Green, then president of Oneida Institute, acted as president, with Lewis Tappan and Whittier as secretaries. Garrison, May and Whittier were chosen to draw up a declaration of principles. Asked by the other two to write a draft, Garrison wrote through the night at the home of his host, Frederick A. Hinton[4]—a Negro Abolitionist of Philadelphia and

---

[4] It is possible that Garrison's Negro host was James McCrummell. Our primary source, Samuel J. May, is contradictory. In an address delivered in 1853, he names Hinton. In his volume, *Some Recollections of Our Antislavery Conflict,* published in 1869, he names McCrummell.

a delegate to the convention—and completed it by morning. Samuel J. May had this to say about the impact of the declaration upon the delegates: "Never in my life have I seen a deeper impression made by words than was made by that admirable document upon all who were there present . . . We felt that the word had just been uttered which would be mighty, through God, to the pulling down of the strongholds of slavery."[5]

The formation of the national society gave an additional fillip to growing anti-slavery sentiment. From New England to the Mississippi River, anti-slavery organizations mushroomed into being. In 1835, Garrison referred to "our 4 or 500 societies." During that year alone, 328 new societies were formed, 254 of which boasted 27,182 members. By 1838, there were 1,350 societies in the national organization, with a membership of about 250,000. In Massachusetts, in 1837, there were 145 local societies, in New York 274 societies, and in Ohio, the most ardent anti-slavery state in the West, 213.[6]

In 1834, a *cause célèbre* occurred near Cincinnati that proved of immense significance to the anti-slavery movement, especially in the West. The locale was Lane Seminary, which had been founded to prepare young men for the ministry and whose president was the eminent Boston minister, Lyman Beecher. In 1834, as a result of the publication of Garrison's *Thoughts on African Colonization* and the founding of the American Anti-Slavery Society, discussions arose among the students concerning the aims and methods of the anti-slavery enterprise. It was decided to debate two questions: the validity of immediate, unconditional emancipation and the worthwhileness of the American Colonization Society. The upshot was a debate extending over eighteen evenings; the result, the passage of resolutions approving immediate emancipation and condemning the American Colonization Society. Reports of the proceedings were published throughout the country, with ensuing public pressure which impelled the faculty and board of overseers to ban the newly formed student anti-slavery society as well as a previously approved colonization society. Most of the students resigned in protest, and many—including several Southerners—became active Abolitionists and leaders in the American Anti-Slavery Society. Among these were Amos Dresser,

[5] *Ibid.*, p. 88.
[6] See Louis Filler, *The Crusade Against Slavery, 1830–1860* (New York, 1960), pp. 66–67.

who received twenty lashes on his back when found with anti-slavery literature in Tennessee; James A. Thome, son of a Kentucky slave-holder; Henry B. Stanton, who was appointed agent and lecturer for the American Anti-Slavery Society; and most prominent of all, Theodore D. Weld, regarded by the trustees as instigator of the entire episode, of whom Samuel J. May has written that "no one except Garrison and Phillips had done more for the abolition of American slavery." It was partly as a result of the Lane episode, as well as the impact of the formation of the American Anti-Slavery Society, that James G. Birney of Kentucky was led to abandon the American Colonization Society and to participate actively in the anti-slavery movement.

As the Abolitionist movement grew, so did the fears of the friends of slavery and their hatred of the Abolitionists. The outcome included frequent mob riots, beatings and even killings. On October 21, 1835, a Boston mob consisting mostly of "gentlemen of property and in-fluence" broke up a meeting of the Boston Female Anti-Slavery Society, which was to be addressed by George F. Thompson, a well-known English Abolitionist. In the course of the riot, Garrison was almost hanged and was finally saved by being lodged in jail. On the same day, in Utica, a meeting of 600 delegates assembled to form a New York State anti-slavery society was broken up by rioters. It was as a result of this riot that Gerrit Smith, a prominent reformer and philanthropist, joined the American Anti-Slavery Society. Henry B. Stanton is supposed to have been mobbed at least two hundred times, Theodore Weld's speeches were frequently dis-rupted, and in 1837 Owen Lovejoy, the anti-slavery editor, was slain at Alton, Illinois, while trying to prevent the destruction of his fourth newspaper press. It was at a meeting in Boston, called to memorialize Lovejoy's death, that Wendell Phillips, then twenty-six years old, made an impromptu address and began a career which in anti-slavery importance was second perhaps only to Garrison's.

Until 1837, the history of the anti-slavery movement was one of a continuously growing and united movement despite religious, political and social differences among its members. In that year, however, the first of a number of schisms, which ultimately were to lead to a divided movement, appeared. In Massachusetts, an "Appeal of Cler-ical Abolitionists on Anti-Slavery Measures," which criticized some of Garrison's tactics, was followed by another statement by the

Abolitionists of Andover Theological Seminary which objected to
Garrison's language, his attacks upon church ministers who refused
to cooperate with the Abolitionists, and his espousal of public lectures by women.

These attacks soon involved several of the New York anti-slavery
leaders and others of the national organization who refused to come
to Garrison's defense and were therefore, in Garrison's opinion, giving
tacit approval to his critics. These included the Tappans, Birney,
Elizur Wright, Leavitt and others who did not share Garrison's views
on the place of women in the anti-slavery movement, who thought
his attacks on the churches ill-considered, his language abusive and
his negative attitude toward certain kinds of political action a deter-
rent to the further development of the anti-slavery movement. The
conflict came to a head at the annual convention of the national organization in 1840, when Garrison and his followers elected Abby
Kelley to the society's business committee. Thereupon, Lewis Tappan,
who had been the society's president, led his followers from the convention and formed the American and Foreign Anti-Slavery Society.
The *Emancipator,* the official newspaper of the original organization,
had been transferred earlier to the New York Anti-Slavery Society, which was controlled by anti-Garrison forces. In its place,
Garrison and his group established the *National Anti-Slavery Standard* under the aegis of the American Anti-Slavery Society. Lydia M.
Child soon assumed the duties of editor, was followed by her husband
David Lee Child and then by Sydney Gay, who edited the paper
with the help of Edmund Quincy and James Russell Lowell.

It may be noted that while the American Anti-Slavery Society
carried on with undiminished vigor until after the Civil War, the
American and Foreign Anti-Slavery Society, though it held annual
meetings and issued some effective pamphlets, gradually dwindled
in strength and passed out of existence in the 1850's, while the
Emancipator stopped publication even earlier. Years later, Lewis
Tappan, in the biography of his brother Arthur, implied that, judged
by its results, the secession was not as well-advised as it seemed to
be at the time. For though the secessionists adopted "such language
and such measures as Christians could not reasonably object to,
those who had been loudest in their opposition and most offended
with what they termed the unchristian spirit of the Abolitionists,
kept aloof as well from the American and Foreign Anti-Slavery

Society . . ." It seems reasonable to conclude that it was not Garrison's language or his espousal of the rights of women or his attacks upon the churches for their indifference to slavery which brought down upon the Abolitionists the wrath of so many of America's political, economic and religious leaders, but the doctrine of immediate and unconditional emancipation, which was indeed a revolutionary doctrine for its time and represented a threat to what many believed to be the foundation of the existing social and economic order.

The year 1840 marks a watershed in the history of the anti-slavery movement. Besides witnessing the division already mentioned, it also saw the formation of the Liberty Party, with the selection of Birney and Thomas Earle, a Philadelphia Quaker, as the party's candidates for President and Vice-President. The party had been formed by such anti-slavery stalwarts as Myron Holley, who had had a distinguished carreer in public affairs, Joshua Leavitt, Elizur Wright, Henry B. Stanton and Alvan Stewart, a leader in the New York State Anti-Slavery Society. In time it was absorbed by the Free-Soil Party, which in turn gave way to the Republican Party.

A decisive event in Abolitionist history was Garrison's decision, in 1843, that slavery could not be eliminated as long as the North remained in the Government of the United States and thereby co-operated with the South, under the Constitution, in the maintenance of slavery. The Constitution, Garrison came to believe, assumed the existence of slavery, gave the institution its sanction, and could not be changed without the consent of a considerable portion of the slave states themselves, which therefore made the abolition of slavery by constitutional means impossible. The Constitution, he concluded, was —in the words of the prophet Isaiah whom he quoted—"a covenant with death and an agreement with hell." Indeed "the free states," by upholding the Constitution, "are guardians and essential supports of slavery. We are the jailers and constables of the institution." The only moral and just course for the North was disunion or secession, which would ultimately result in the fall of slavery.

Garrison first began to broach this point of view in the *Liberator* in 1842. In the spring of 1843, the Massachusetts Anti-Slavery Society affirmed that "the compact . . . between North and South . . . should be immediately annulled." When the issue was raised in 1844 before the national organization, a long and heated discussion ensued which culminated in a vote of 59 to 21 in favor of disunion. Soon thereafter the entire Garrisonian movement gave its approval to the slogan of "No union with slaveholders" and remained committed to it until the Civil War.

The late 1840's and 50's saw no important changes in anti-slavery theory or practice. The Abolitionists continued their work of arousing public opinion to the increasing advances of slavery, and played a prominent part in the many crises which shook the country to its foundations—the war with Mexico, the Fugitive Slave Law, the Kansas-Nebraska Act and the conflict over control of Kansas, the Dred Scott decision and John Brown's raid on Harpers Ferry. On all of these issues, the Abolitionists acted vigorously to awaken the anti-slavery conscience of America and to convince the North of the imperative necessity of abolishing slavery if the rights of all Americans were to be maintained. They thus helped to mold that public opinion which ultimately resulted in the abolition of slavery in the United States.

On April 6, 1865, in Petersburg, Virginia, Abraham Lincoln spoke with Daniel H. Chamberlain, ex-Governor of North Carolina. In the course of the conversation, Lincoln summed up what he and the entire country owed to Garrison and the anti-slavery movement: "I have been only an instrument," he said. "The logic and moral power of Garrison, and the anti-slavery people of the country and the Army, have done all."

The Abolitionists

BENJAMIN LUNDY

"The Editor to the Public"

ଛ୬

> *In this essay by Benjamin Lundy, which appeared in the* Genius of Universal Emancipation *in April 1830—immediately after he and Garrison had severed their partnership—the great pioneer of the anti-slavery movement evaluates his past efforts and writes of his plans for the future. On receiving the announcement of Lundy's death, which occurred on August 22, 1839, Garrison reprinted the essay in the* Liberator *on September 20, 1839, and wrote as follows about Lundy: "To Benjamin Lundy, more than to any other human being, am I indebted for having my attention called to the wretched condition of the slaves in this liberty-worshipping, slavery-idolizing country. He it was who first informed, quickened, inflamed my mind on the subject of American slavery, and by whom I was induced to consecrate my life to the overthrow of that dreadful system of iniquity."*

The Editor to the Public. Again I find myself, alone, at the editorial desk; and again I resume a *monthly* correspondence with the readers of the *Genius of Universal Emancipation.* I yet hope to have the assistance of an amiable and talented writer, whose services in the cause are invaluable, but the care and responsibility of the publication devolve entirely upon myself.

Nine years have nearly elapsed, since this work first made its appearance. During that period I have witnessed many vicissitudes in the affairs of life; have experienced something of the fickleness of fortune, and a good share of what the world calls hardship and privation. From the commencement until very lately, however, it gradually increased in size, and it is believed in interest. The many difficulties that presented themselves, have occasionally produced some irregularity in its publication; and this, together with the unpopularity of the subject upon which it treats, in a portion of the country, and the general apathy among those who are friendly to the undertaking, have prevented as extensive a circulation as had been anticipated. The strong desire that I have ever felt to contribute my mite towards the promotion of the good cause, has induced me not only to make great exertions to issue a *weekly* publication, devoted to it, but also to render what assistance I could in every other way. But I find that the people are not yet prepared to go with me quite so far. To speak in phrase, *a la militarie,* I am too near to the entrenchment of the enemy—and, of course, like a prudent soldier, must retreat a little, until our troops can "screw up their courage" somewhat more. That they *will,* ere long go much farther, I feel well assured; and I shall still "fight on," and "keep the faith," hoping and believing that a glorious victory will ultimately crown our efforts.

That I shall yet have a severe struggle, for a time, even with the monthly publication, is to be expected—and I submit it to the consideration of those who profess a willingness to aid in promoting the work of emancipation—those who approve the course I have pursued—whether it be reasonable, or just, that I should thus be subjected to the inconveniences and hardships, almost intolerable, when they are equally as much interested in the matter as I am myself, and have it in their power, by giving a little further assistance, to relieve me from a portion of the burden, and enable me to labor much more efficiently for the attainment of our great and important object.

I do not wish to speak boastingly of what I have done, or essayed to do, in advocating the question of African Emancipation: and I detest the idea of making a cringing appeal to the public, for aid in my undertakings. I *am willing to work;* and can support myself and family by my own labor. But after a *ten years' struggle* to promote the cause to the best of my humble abilities, and in every possible manner, it may not be amiss to inform those who take an interest in this publication, that I have (within the period above mentioned) sacrificed several thousand dollars of my own hard earnings; have travelled upwards of five thousand miles on foot, and more than twenty thousand in other ways; have visited nineteen of the States of this Union, and held more than two hundred public meetings, with the view of making known our object, &c—and in addition to this, have performed two voyages to the West Indies, by which means the liberation of a considerable number of slaves has been effected, and I hope the way paved for the enlargement of many more. What effect this work has had, in turning the attention of the public to the subject of the abolition of slavery, it would not become me to say, though I have carefully noted every thing relative thereto that came within the range of my observation. Of this, others, who have acquainted themselves with the matter, must judge. But I am fully persuaded that something of the kind is greatly needed, and may be instrumental in doing much good. *There is not another periodical work, published by a citizen of the United States, whose conductor* DARE *treat upon the subject of slavery as its nature requires, and its importance demands.* And, in viewing the matter in this light, I shall persevere in my efforts, as usual, while the means of doing it are afforded, or until more efficient advocates of the cause shall make themselves known. I shall now devote my undivided attention to this publication, and endeavor to make it as interesting as possible. I will neither be cajoled by the smiles nor awed by the frowns of any to a dereliction of principle, or an abandonment of the cause. My humble exertions shall be directed to the one great end—my whole self shall be devoted to the holy work— my march shall be steadily *onward*—and neither sectarian pride, party zeal, nor even persecution itself, from the "powers that be," or that *may be,* shall turn me to the right hand or the left. If I obtain a reasonable patronage for the work, *it shall go on,* upon the principle that it ever has done, when under my immediate direction, notwithstanding all the opposition that tyranny and malice can array against it.

B. LUNDY.

WILLIAM LLOYD GARRISON

Commencement of the Liberator

ॐ

The Liberator *began publication on January 1, 1831, and carried this statement by Garrison of his aims and purposes.*

To the Public

In the month of August, I issued proposals for publishing the *Liberator* in Washington city; but the enterprise, though hailed in different sections of the country, was palsied by public indifference. Since that time, the removal of the *Genius of Universal Emancipation* to the Seat of Government has rendered less imperious the establishment of a similar periodical in that quarter.

During my recent tour for the purpose of exciting the minds of the people by a series of discourses on the subject of slavery, every place that I visited gave fresh evidence of the fact, that a greater revolution in public sentiment was to be effected in the free States—and particularly in New England—than at the South. I found contempt more bitter, opposition more active, detraction more relentless, prejudice more stubborn, and apathy more frozen, than among slave owners themselves. Of course, there were individual exceptions to the contrary. This state of things afflicted, but did not dishearten me. I determined, at every hazard, to lift up the standard of emancipation in the eyes of the nation, within sight of Bunker Hill, and in the birthplace of liberty. That standard is now unfurled; and long may it float, unhurt by the spoliations of time or the missiles of a desperate foe; yea, till every chain be broken, and every bondman set free! Let Southern oppressors tremble; let their secret abettors tremble; let their Northern apologists tremble; let all the enemies of the persecuted blacks tremble.

I deem the publication of my original prospectus unnecessary, as it has obtained a wide circulation. The principles therein inculcated will be steadily pursued in this paper, excepting that I shall not array myself as the political partisan of any man. In defending the great cause of human rights, I wish to derive the assistance of all religions and of all parties.

Assenting to the "self-evident truth" maintained in the American Declaration of Independence, "that all men are created equal, and endowed by their Creator with certain inalienable rights—among which are life, liberty, and the pursuit of happiness," I shall strenuously contend for the immediate enfranchisement of our slave population. In Park Street Church, on the Fourth of July, 1829, in an address on slavery, I unreflectingly assented to the popular but pernicious doctrine of gradual abolition. I seize this opportunity to make a full and unequivocal recantation, and thus publicly to ask pardon of my God, of my country, and of my brethren, the poor slaves, for having uttered a sentiment so full of timidity, injustice and absurdity. A similar recantation, from my pen, was published in the *Genius of Universal Emancipation,* at Baltimore, in September, 1829. My conscience is now satisfied.

I am aware, that many object to the severity of my language; but is there not cause for severity? I will be as harsh as truth, and as uncompromising as justice. On this subject, I do not wish to think, or speak, or write, with moderation. No! no! Tell a man, whose house is on fire, to give a moderate alarm; tell him to moderately rescue his wife from the hands of the ravisher; tell the mother to gradually extricate her babe from the fire into which it has fallen; but urge me not to use moderation in a cause like the present! I am in earnest. I will not equivocate—I will not excuse—I will not retreat a single inch—AND I WILL BE HEARD. The apathy of the people is enough to make every statue leap from its pedestal, and to hasten the resurrection of the dead.

It is pretended, that I am retarding the cause of emancipation by the coarseness of my invective, and the precipitancy of my measures. The charge is not true. On this question, my influence, humble as it is, is felt at this moment to a considerable extent, and shall be felt in coming years—not perniciously, but beneficially—not as a curse, but as a blessing; and POSTERITY WILL BEAR TESTIMONY THAT I WAS RIGHT. I desire to thank God, that he enables me to disregard "the fear of man which bringeth a snare" and to speak his truth in its simplicity and power. And here I close with this fresh dedication:

"Oppression!" I have seen thee, face to face,
And met thy cruel eye and cloudy brow;
But thy soul-withering glance I fear not now—
For dread to prouder feelings doth give place,
Of deep abhorrence! Scorning the disgrace
Of slavish knees that at thy footstool bow,
I also kneel—but with far other vow
Do hail thee and thy herd of hirelings base:
I swear, while life-blood warms my throbbing veins,
Still to oppose and thwart, with heart and hand,
Thy brutalizing sway—till Afric's chains
Are burst, and Freedom rules the rescued land,
Trampling Oppression and his iron rod:
Such is the vow I take—so help me God!

BOSTON, January 1, 1831.

The New England Anti-Slavery Society

ࡇ

The constitution of the New England Anti-Slavery Society was adopted on January 1, 1832. The preamble was not adopted until January 6. The entire document was first published in the Liberator *on February 18, 1832, and was later published as a pamphlet which also included an* "Address to the Public."

CONSTITUTION

We, the undersigned, hold that every person, of full age and sane mind, has a right to immediate freedom from personal bondage of whatsoever kind, unless imposed by the sentence of the law for the commission of some crime.

We hold that man cannot, consistently with reason, religion, and the eternal and immutable principles of justice, be the property of man.

We hold that whoever retains his fellow man in bondage, is guilty of a grevious wrong.

We hold that a mere difference of complexion is no reason why any man should be deprived of any of his natural rights, or subjected to any political disability.

While we advance these opinions as the principles on which we intend to act, we declare that we will not operate on the existing relations of society by other than peaceful and lawful means, and that we will give no countenance to violence or insurrection.

With these views, we agree to form ourselves into a Society, and to be governed by the rules, specified in the following Constitution, viz.

ARTICLE 1. This Society shall be called the New-England Anti-Slavery Society.

ARTICLE 2. The objects of the Society shall be to endeavor, by all means sanctioned by law, humanity and religion, to effect the Abolition of Slavery in the United States, to improve the character and condition of the free people of color, to inform and correct public opinion in relation to their situation and rights, and obtain for them equal civil and political rights and privileges with the whites.

ARTICLE 3. Any person by signing the Constitution, and paying to the Treasurer fifteen dollars as a life subscription, or two dollars annually, shall be considered a member of the Society, and entitled to a voice and vote in all its meetings, and to a copy of any publications or communications which may be distributed among its members. Honorary members may be chosen by a vote of the Society.

ARTICLE 4. There shall be an annual meeting of the Society on the second Wednesday in January, at which a report of the transactions of the Society for the past year, and of its income, expenditures and funds, shall be presented by the Board of Managers, and the following officers elected by ballot, viz: A President, two Vice Presidents, six Counsellors, a Treasurer, Corresponding Secretary and Recording Secretary, who shall hold their respective offices until the next annual meeting.

ARTICLE 5. The said twelve officers shall together constitute a Board of Managers, to whom shall be entrusted the disposition of the funds, and the management of the concerns of the Society. They shall have power to fill any vacancy, which may occur in their board, until the next meeting of the Society; and it shall be their duty to consider and adopt the means best calculated to promote the objects of the Society, and report the same to the Society.

ARTICLE 6. Meetings of the Managers may be called by the President, or in his absence by either of the Vice Presidents, when they shall judge it necessary, or on application to them from any one of the Managers for any specific purpose; and special meetings of the Society may be called by vote of the Managers, or on application of the members of the Society to the Recording Secretary, and the time and place of the meetings of the Society shall be determined by the Managers.

ARTICLE 7. The President shall preside at all meetings of the Society and of the Managers; in his absence, one of the Vice Presidents; and in their absence, the oldest Manager present.

ARTICLE 8. The Treasurer shall collect the subscriptions and grants to the Society, and hold all its funds, and make payments according to the votes of the Managers; and he shall keep a true account of the same, and render an annual statement to accompany the annual report to the Society.

ARTICLE 9. The Corresponding Secretary shall receive and keep all communications or publications directed to the Society, and transmit those issued by them, and shall correspond with the agents, or any other bodies or individuals according to the directions of the Society or the Managers.

ARTICLE 10. The Recording Secretary shall notify all meetings of the Society, and of the Board of Managers, and shall keep the Records of the same and of the transactions of the Society, and shall furnish copies of any votes to any persons, when required by the President, or a Vice President.

ARTICLE 11. The Board of Managers may appoint an agent or agents, to be employed in any part of the United States, in obtaining or communicating intelligence, in the publication or distribution of tracts, books, or. papers, or in the execution of any measure, which may be adopted, to promote the objects of the Society. The compensation of the agents shall be determined by the Board of Managers.

ARTICLE 12. Any Anti-Slavery Society, or any association founded on kindred principles in the New-England States, may become auxiliary to this Society, by contributing to its funds, and by sending a delegate, or delegates, to attend its meetings.

ARTICLE 13. There shall be a regular meeting of the Society on the last Monday of every month.

ARTICLE 14. The Constitution may be altered at any annual meeting, by a vote of two thirds of those present.

Letter from Beriah Green to Reverend S. S. Jocelyn

ಶಿ

> *Beriah Green (1795–1874) was at this time professor of sacred literature at Western Reserve College, a position he had held since 1830. He later became president of Oneida Institute and presided at the convention which formed the American Anti-Slavery Society in December 1833. Reverend Simeon Smith Jocelyn (1799–1879), who had been born in New Haven, was a white minister of a colored church in New Haven, and helped to found the American Anti-Slavery Society. The letter indicates Garrison's strong impact upon anti-slavery sentiment in Ohio even at that early date. The letter was printed in the* Abolitionist: or Record of the New-England Anti-Slavery Society *(February 1833), Vol. I, p. 29.*

HUDSON, (PORT. CO. O.) Nov. 5, 1832.

REV. AND DEAR SIR:

A great change has, within a few months, been wrought in the views and movements of some of the gentlemen connected with this College, both as instructors and students, respecting the ground occupied by the American Colonization Society, and the tendency of the principles avowed, and the course pursued, by that institution. In a single word, the President of the College, *Rev. Charles B. Storrs,* a gentleman well known and highly esteemed on many accounts in New-England as well as in Ohio, *Elizur Wright, Jr.* Professor of Mathematics and Natural Philosophy, whose reputation as a gentleman, a scholar, and a christian, is elevated, if I mistake not, at Yale College; *Elizur Wright, Esq. of Tallmadge,* a Trustee of this College, and an early graduate of Yale, whose reputation as a scholar and a christian I need not describe, and some others, have, upon examining the matter in discussion between the abolitionists and anti-abolitionists, yielded to the conviction that the former occupy the only ground, which the Bible can justly be regarded as approving and sustaining. These gentlemen have been brought to this conviction, not without many struggles and much reluctance. They had been ardent friends and prompt patrons of the American Colonization Society; had labored to sustain its claims to public patronage by their authority, their eloquence, and their purses. They now feel, and feel very deeply too, that they had been blinded by a strange prejudice, which had the effect of infatuation on their minds. They have opened their eyes upon an object which has taken fast hold of their whole souls. They feel themselves impelled by motives which they cannot and would not resist, to give "arm and soul" to the cause of African emancipation. They are now making the inquiry with unwonted solicitude—"Lord, what wilt thou have us to do?"

A good deal of interest has been awakened in the College among the students, on the subject of African emancipation. The matter has, in different forms and on various occasions, been pretty thoroughly discussed. A number of the students take the ground maintained by the New-England Anti-Slavery Society. We hope the number may increase. Mr. Storrs has been almost universally— perhaps I need not qualify the expression by any such word as *almost* —regarded as preeminent for soundness of judgment, warmth of piety, force of mind, and general attractiveness of character. The posture which he has taken on the subject of this letter cannot, we think, fail of setting hundreds a-thinking. Professor Wright has written a good many very able columns for the *Observer & Telegraph*—the religious paper of the Western Reserve; and would have continued to write, had he not been denied the farther use of this medium of working on the public mind. He is an attractive, powerful writer. His whole soul is engaged; and I think no human agency can beat him off the ground which he has taken. We need the sympathy and aid of the friends of this good cause in New-England. We want facts —*facts*—FACTS.

One copy of Mr. Garrison's "Thoughts" has reached us, and we take a few copies of his admirable paper. Charles Stuart's last pamphlet on Colonial Slavery in the West Indies, we have; and the African Repository, and the Colonization Society Reports and Speeches, which we find may be made directly and powerfully subservient to the cause of African emancipation. Every fact on this subject will be estimated here at its full worth. Will you, as the friend of poor, persecuted, trodden down Africa, help us? We much wish to know the history of the efforts which you have made in the cause of wretched humanity in New-Haven and elsewhere.

Your letter to Mr. Gurley I thank you for, and wish I had 500 or 1,000 copies of it for circulation. Things in Maine and Massachusetts, I should think, were assuming a brighter aspect. Mr. Garrison's reception in Maine could not but have been highly encouraging. Our British brethren, too, the Lord Jesus bless them.

We have here a great struggle to go through with, if the Saviour will help us. The strength of public *prejudice, as such openly avowed!* is awaking. We have, however, a calm and deep conviction that we are right, and that God will help us. This hope we cling to as the anchor of our souls. O, may we not forfeit its high consolations—its sustaining, exhilarating influence! We hope before many days to bring our little forces together in the form of an Anti-Slavery Society. Pray for us, dear brethren, as I hope we do for you—and for all who are consecrated to the great and glorious design, to which, "after so long a time," we are beginning to awake.

Yours in the Lord Jesus,
BERIAH GREEN.

WILLIAM LLOYD GARRISON

"Words of Encouragement to the Oppressed"

ε∾

Garrison left New York for Europe in May 1833. The following address was presumably delivered to an audience of colored people before his departure and was included in the volume entitled Selections from the Writings and Speeches of William Lloyd Garrison, *published in Boston in 1852. Actually, as edited by Garrison for that volume, it is a composite of three addresses. Its opening paragraphs are from an address delivered in June 1831; its central portions are from the address he delivered before his departure for England in April 1833; and its final paragraphs are from an address of July 16, 1832.*

I never rise to address a colored audience, without feeling ashamed of my own color; ashamed of being identified with a race of men, who have done you so much injustice, and who yet retain so large a portion of your brethren in servile chains. To make atonement, in part, for this conduct, I have solemnly dedicated my health, and strength, and life, to your service. I love to plan and to work for your social, intellectual, and spiritual advancement. My happiness is augmented with yours: in your sufferings I participate.

Henceforth I am ready, on all days, on all convenient occasions, in all suitable places, before any sect or party, at whatever peril to my person, character or interest, to plead the cause of my colored countrymen in particular, or of human rights in general. For this purpose, there is no day too holy, no place improper, no body of men too inconsiderable to address. For this purpose, I ask no church to grant me authority to speak—I require no ordination—I am not careful to consult Martin Luther, or John Calvin, or His Holiness the Pope. It is a duty, which, as a lover of justice, I am bound to discharge; as a lover of my fellow-men, I ought not to shun; as a lover of Jesus Christ, and of his equalizing, republican and benevolent precepts, I rejoice to perform.

Your condition, as a people, has long attracted my attention, secured my efforts, and awakened in my breast a flame of sympathy, which neither the winds nor waves of opposition can ever extinguish. It is the lowness of your estate, in the estimation of the world, which exalts you in my eyes. It is the distance that separates you from the blessings and privileges of society, which brings you so closely to my affections. It is the unmerited scorn, reproach and persecution of your persons, by those whose complexion is colored like my own, which command for you my sympathy and respect. It is the fewness of your friends—the multitude of your enemies—that induces me to stand forth in your defense.

Countrymen and Friends! I wish to gladden your hearts, and to invigorate your hopes. Be assured, your cause is going onward, right onward. The signs of the times do indeed show forth great and glorious and sudden changes in the condition of the oppressed. The whole firmament is tremulous with an excess of light; the earth is moved out of its place; the wave of revolution is dashing in pieces ancient and mighty empires; the hearts of tyrants are beginning to fail them for fear, and for looking forward to those things which are to come upon the earth. There is:

> A voice on every wave,
> A sound on every sea!
> The watchword of the brave,
> The anthem of the free!
> Where'er a wind is rushing,
> Where'er a stream is gushing,
> The swelling sounds are heard,
> Of man to freeman calling,
> Of broken fetters falling—
> And, like the carol of a cageless bird,
> The bursting shout of Freedom's rallying word!

Let this be an occasion of joy. Why should it not be so? Is not the heaven over your heads, which has so long been clothed in sackcloth, beginning to disclose its starry principalities, and illumine your pathway? Do you not see the pitiless storm, which has so long been pouring its rage upon you, breaking away, and a bow of promise, as glorious as that which succeeded the ancient deluge, spanning the sky—a token that, to the end of time, the billows of prejudice and oppression shall no more cover the earth, to the destruction of your race; but seed-time and harvest shall never fail, and the laborer shall eat the fruit of his hands? Is not your cause developing like the spring? Yours has been a long and rigorous winter. The chill of contempt, the frost of adversity, the blast of persecution, the storm of oppression—all have been yours. There was no sustenance to be found— no prospect to delight the eye, or inspire the drooping heart—no golden ray to dissipate the gloom. The waves of derision were stayed by no barrier, but made a clear breach over you. But, now—thanks be to God! that dreary winter is rapidly hastening away. The sun of humanity is going steadily up, from the horizon to its zenith, growing larger and brighter, and melting the frozen earth beneath its powerful rays. The genial showers of repentance are softly falling upon the barren plain; the wilderness is budding like the rose; the voice of joy succeeds the notes of wo [*sic*]; and hope, like the lark, is soaring upwards, and warbling hymns at the gate of heaven.

And this is but the outbursting of spring. What, think you, shall be the summer and autumn?

> Then shall the trembling mourner come,
> And bind his sheaves, and bear them home;
> The voice, long broke with sighs, shall sing,
> And heaven with hallelujahs ring!

This is but "the twilight, the dim dawn" of day. What, then, shall be the brightness of the day itself? These are but a few drops of mercy. What shall be the full shower, the rolling tide? These are but crumbs of comfort, to prevent you wholly from perishing. What shall be the bountiful table?

Why should this not be an occasion of joy, instead of sorrow? Listen to those trumpet tones which come swelling on the winds of the Atlantic, and which shall bring an echo from every harp in heaven! If there is joy in that blissful abode over one sinner that repenteth, how mighty and thrilling must it be over a repentant nation! And Great Britain is that nation. Her people are humbling themselves before God, and before those whom they have so long held in bondage. Their voices are breaking, in peals of thunder, upon the ear of Parliament, demanding the immediate and utter overthrow of slavery in all the colonies; and in obedience to their will, the mandate is about being issued by Parliament, which shall sever at a blow the chains of eight hundred thousand slaves! What heart can conceive, what pen or tongue describe, the happiness which must flow from the consummation of this act? That cruel lash, which has torn so many tender bodies, and is dripping with innocent blood; that lash, which has driven so many human victims, like beasts, to their unrequited toil; that lash, whose sounds are heard from the rising of the sun to its decline, mingled with the shrieks of bleeding sufferers; that lash is soon to be cast away, never again to wound the flesh, or degrade those who are made in the image of God. And those fetters of iron, which have bound so many in ignominious servitude, and wasted their bodies, and borne them down to an untimely grave, shall be shivered in pieces, as the lightning rends the pine, and the victims of tyranny leap forth, "redeemed, regenerated, and disenthralled, by the irresistible genius of universal emancipation." And that darkness, which has for so many generations shrouded the minds of the slaves—making them like the brutes that perish—shall give way to the light of freedom and religion. O, how transforming the change! In contemplating it, my imagination overpowers the serenity of my soul, and makes language seem poor and despicable.

Cheers for Great Britain! Cheers for her noble men and women! Cheers for the bright example which they are setting to the world! Cheers for their generous sympathy in the cause of the oppressed in our own country!

Why should we not rejoice this evening, brethren? Find we nothing at home to raise our drooping spirits, to invigorate our hopes, and to engage our efforts? Have we made no progress, either in self-improvement, or in the cause of bleeding humanity? Are there no cheering signs of the times, in our moral sky, upon which we may fix our joyful gaze?

Look, in the first place, at the abolition standard—more gorgeous and spirit-stirring than the Star-Spangled Banner—floating high in the air! Fresh is the breeze that meets it! Bright are the sunny rays which adorn it! Around it thousands are gathering, with high and holy courage, to contend, not with carnal but spiritual weapons, against the powers of darkness. O, the loftiness of that spirit which

animates them! It towers above the Alps, it pierces beyond the clouds.
O, the intensity of that flame of brotherly love which burns within
their breasts! It never can burn out—nor can many waters extinguish
it. O, the stability of that faith which sustains them under all their toils
and trials! It is firmer than the foundations of the earth—it is strong
as the throne of God. O, the generous daring of that moral principle
which inspires their hearts and governs their actions! Neither reproach
nor persecution, neither wealth nor power, neither bolts nor bars,
neither the gibbet nor the stake, shall be able to subdue it. Yes, my
colored countrymen, these are the men—ay, and the women, too,
who have espoused your cause. And they will stand by it, until life
be extinct. They will not fail in strength, or faith, or courage, or
zeal, or action. Loud as the tempest of oppression may rage around
them, above it shall their rallying cry be heard in the thunder-tone
of heaven. Dark as their pathway may be, it shall blaze with the
light of truth in their possession. Numberless as may be the enemies
who surround them, they will not retreat from the field; for He who
is mightier than legions of men and devils is the captain of their
salvation, and will give them the victory. I know your advocates well
—I know the spirit which actuates them. Whether they reside in the
East, or West, or North, they have but one object—their hearts are
stirred with the same pulsation; their eye is single, their motives are
pure. Tell me not of the bravery and devotedness of those whose
life-blood reddened the plains of Marathon, poured out in defence
of liberty. Tell me not of the Spartan band, with Leonidas at their
head, who defended the pass of Thermopylae against a Persian host.
I award to them the meed of animal courage; but the heroism of
blood and carnage is as much below the patient endurance of wrong,
and the cheerful forgiveness of injury, as the earth is below the sky—
it is as often displayed by brute animals as by men. With infinitely
higher satisfaction, with a warmer glow of emulation, with more intense admiration, do I contemplate the abolition phalanx in the
United States, who are maintaining your cause, unflinchingly, through
evil report—for the good report is yet to come—and at the imminent
peril of their lives; and, what is dearer than life, the sacrifice of their
reputation. If ever there was a cause which established the disin-
terestedness and integrity of its supporters, yours is that cause. They
who are contending for the immediate abolition of slavery, the destruction of its ally, the American Colonization Society, and the

bestowal of equal rights and privileges upon the whole colored population, well knew what would be the consequences of their advocacy to themselves. They knew that slander would blacken their characters with infamy; that their pleadings would be received with ridicule and reproach; that persecution would assail them on the right hand and on the left; that the dungeon would yawn for their bodies; that the dagger of the assassin would gleam behind them; that the arm of power would be raised to crush them to the earth; that they would be branded as disturbers of the peace, as fanatics, madmen and incendiaries; that the heel of friendship would be lifted against them, and love be turned into hatred, and confidence into suspicion, and respect into derision; that their worldly interests would be jeoparded, and the honor and emoluments of office would be withheld from their enjoyment. Knowing all this, still they dare all things, in order to save their country by seeking its purification from blood. Will the base and the servile accuse them of being actuated by a hope of reward? Reward! It is the reward which calumny gives to virtue—the reward which selfishness bestows upon benevolence; but nothing of worldly applause, or fame, or promotion. Yet they have a reward—and who will blame them for coveting it? It is the gratitude of the suffering and the oppressed—the approbation of a good conscience—the blessing of the Most High.

> Tempt them with bribes, you tempt in vain;
> Try them with fire, you'll find them true.

To deter such souls from their purposes, or vanquish them in combat, is as impossible as to stop the rush of the ocean when the spirit of the storm rides upon its mountain billows. They are hourly increasing in number and strength, and going on from conquering to conquer. Convert after convert, press after press, pulpit after pulpit, is subdued, and enlisted on the side of justice and freedom.

A grave charge is brought against me, that I am exciting your rage against the whites, and filling your minds with revengful feelings? Is this true? Have not all my addresses and appeals to you had just the contrary effect upon your minds? Have they not been calculated to make you bear all your trials and difficulties in the spirit of Christian resignation, and to induce you to return good for evil? Where is the calumniator who dares to affirm that you have been turbulent and quarrelsome since I began my labors in your behalf? Where is the man who is so ignorant as not to know or perceive that, as a people, you are constantly improving in knowledge and virtue? No, brethren; you will bear me a unanimous testimony, that I have not implanted in your minds any malice towards your persecutors, but, on the contrary, forgiveness of injuries. And I can as truly aver that, in all my intercourse with you as a people, I have not seen or heard any thing of a malignant or revengeful spirit. No: yours has been eminently a spirit of resignation and faith, under the most aggravating circumstances.

I will notice but one other charge which the enemies of our cause have brought against me. It is, that I am unduly exciting your hopes, and holding out to your view prospects of future happiness and respectability which can never be realized in this country. Pitiful complaint! Because I have planted a solitary rose, as it were, in the wilderness of suffering in which your race has so long wandered, to cheer your drooping hearts, I am sharply reproved for giving even this little token of good things to come—by those, too, who make loud professions of friendship for you, that is, if you will go to Liberia, but who are constantly strewing in your path briars and thorns, and digging pits into which you may stumble to rise no more. These querulous complainants, who begrudge every drop of comfort which falls upon your thirsty lips, as a miser mourns the loss of a penny, seem to forget or discard the promise of Jehovah, that "the wilderness shall bud and blossom like the rose." I have faith to believe that this promise will ultimately be fulfilled, even in this land of republicanism and Christianity. Surely I may be pardoned, when so many are endeavoring to break down all your rising hopes and noble aspirations, if I urge you not to despair, for the day of redemption will assuredly come. Nay, I may still be forgiven, if I transcend the limits of probability, and suffer my imagination to paint in too glowing colors the recompense which is to be yours; since, strive as I may, I can scarcely hope to equalize the heart-crushing discouragements and assaults made by your enemies.

All things considered, you have certainly done well, as a body. There are many colored men whom I am proud to rank among my friends; whose native vigor of mind is remarkable; whose morals are unexceptionable; whose homes are the abode of contentment, plenty and refinement. For my own part, when I reflect upon the peculiarities of your situation; what indignities have been heaped upon your heads; in what utter dislike you are generally held even by those who profess to be the ministers and disciples of Christ; and how difficult has been your chance to arrive at respectability and affluence, I marvel greatly, not that you are no more enlightened and virtuous, but that you are not like wild beasts of the forests. I fully coincide with the sentiment of Mr. Jefferson, that the men must be prodigies who can retain their manners and morals under such circumstances. Surely, you have a right to demand an equal position among mankind.

O, if those whose prejudices against color are deeply rooted—if the asserters of the natural inferiority of the people of color, would but even casually associate with the victims of their injustice, and be candid enough to give merit its due, they could not long feel and act as they now do. Their prejudices would melt like frost-work before the blazing sun; their unbelief would vanish away, their contempt be turned into admiration, their indifference be roused to benevolent activity, and their dislike give place to friendship. Keeping aloof from your society, ignorant of the progress which you are making in virtue, knowledge and competence, and believing all the aspersions of malice which are cast upon your character, they at length persuade themselves that you are utterly worthless, and nearly akin to the brute creation. Cruel men! Cruel women! Thus hastily and blindly to pass condemnation upon those who deserve your compassion, and are worthy of your respect!

Be this your encouragement, in view of our separation. Although absent from you in body, I shall still be with you in spirit. I go away, not to escape from toil, but to labor more abundantly in your cause. If I may do something for your good at home, I hope to do more abroad. In the mean time, I beseech you fail not, on your part, to lead quiet and orderly lives. Let there be no grounds whatever for the charge which is brought against you by your enemies, that you are turbulent and rude. Let all quarrelling, all dram-drinking, all profanity, all violence, all division, be confined to the white people. Imitate them in nothing but what is clearly good, and carefully shun even the appearance of evil. Let them, if they will, follow the devices and perform the drudgery of the devil; but be ye perfect, even as your heavenly Father is perfect. Conquer their aversion by moral excellence; their proud spirit by love; their evil acts by acts of goodness; their animosity by forgiveness. Keep in your hearts the fear of God, and rejoice even in tribulation; for the promise is sure, that all things shall work together for good to those who love His name.

As for myself, whatever may be my fate—whether I fall in the spring-time of manhood by the hand of the assassin, or be immured in a Georgia cell, or be permitted to live to a ripe old age—I know that the success of your cause is not dependent upon my existence. I am but as a drop in the ocean, which, if it be separated, cannot be missed.

My own faith is strong—my vision, clear—my consolation, great. "Who art thou, O great mountain? Before Zerubbabel thou shalt become a plain: and he shall bring forth the headstone thereof with shoutings, crying, Grace, grace unto it." Let us confidently hope, that the day is at hand, when we shall be enabled to celebrate not merely the abolition of the slave trade by law but in fact, and the liberation of every descendant of Africa, wherever one exists in bondage under the whole heavens.

Whittier on "Justice and Expediency"

ह‌ॐ

> *John Greenleaf Whittier (1807–1892) was not only an outstanding poet and man of letters but also a prominent reformer and Abolitionist. He was one of the founders of the American Anti-Slavery Society and remained a friend of the slave and of the free Negro throughout his life. In May 1833, he published at his own expense a pamphlet entitled* "Justice and Expediency," *in which he called for immediate emancipation. In this pamphlet was reflected the deep influence upon him of Garrison, who was the first editor to print Whittier's verse, and who then helped to convert him to the idea of*

immediate and unconditional emancipation. Although the pamphlet was first published in only 500 copies, it was later reprinted in an edition of 5,000 by Arthur Tappan, and appeared also in the September 1833 issue of the American Anti-Slavery Reporter. *The selections presented here are from Volume III of* The Prose Works of John Greenleaf Whittier *(Boston and New York, 1892), pp. 9–57.*

JUSTICE AND EXPEDIENCY:
or, Slavery Considered With a View to Its Rightful and Effectual Remedy, Abolition.

———

[The opening paragraph, consisting of a quotation from Lord Brougham, has been omitted.]

It may be inquired of me why I seek to agitate the subject of Slavery in New England, where we all acknowledge it to be an evil. Because such an acknowledgment is not enough on our part. It is doing no more than the slave-master and the slave-trader. "We have found," says James Monroe, in his speech on the subject before the Virginia Convention, "that this evil has preyed upon the very vitals of the Union; and has been prejudicial to all the states in which it has existed." All the states in their several Constitutions and declarations of rights have made a similar statement. And what has been the consequence of this general belief in the evil of human servitude? Has it sapped the foundations of the infamous system? No. Has it decreased the number of its victims? Quite the contrary. Unaccompanied by philanthropic action, it has been in a moral point of view worthless, a thing without vitality, sightless, soulless, dead.

But it may be said that the miserable victims of the system have our sympathies. Sympathy! the sympathy of the Priest and the Levite, looking on, and acknowledging, but holding itself aloof from mortal suffering. Can such hollow sympathy reach the broken of heart, and does the blessing of those who are ready to perish answer it? Does it hold back the lash from the slave, or sweeten his bitter bread? One's heart and soul are becoming weary of this sympathy, this heartless mockery of feeling; sick of the common cant of hypocrisy, wreathing the artificial flowers of sentiment over unutterable pollution and unimaginable wrong . . .

No! let the truth on this subject, undisguised, naked, terrible as it is, stand out before us. Let us no longer seek to cover it; let us no longer strive to forget it; let us no more dare to palliate it. It is better to meet it here with repentance than at the bar of God. The cry of the oppressed, of the millions who have perished among us as the brute perisheth, shut out from the glad tidings of salvation, has gone there before us, to Him who as a father pitieth all His children. Their blood is upon us as a nation; woe unto us, if we repent not, as a nation, in dust and ashes . . .

But it may be urged that New England has no participation in slavery, and is not responsible for its wickedness.

Why are we thus willing to believe a lie? New England not responsible! Bound by the United States Constitution to protect the slave-holder in his sins, and yet not responsible! Joining hands with crime, covenanting with oppression, leaguing with pollution, and yet not responsible! Palliating the evil, hiding the evil, voting for the evil,[1] do we not participate in it?

Slavery is protected by the constitutional compact, by the standing army, by the militia of the free states.[2] Let us not forget that should the slaves, goaded by wrongs unendurable, rise in desperation, and pour the torrent of their brutal revenge over the beautiful Carolinas, or the consecrated soil of Virginia, New England would be called upon to arrest the progress of rebellion—to tread out with the armed heel of her soldiery that spirit of freedom, which knows no distinction of caste or color; which has been kindled in the heart of the black as well as in that of the white.

And what is this system which we are thus protecting and upholding? A system which holds two millions of God's creatures in bondage, which leaves one million females without any protection save their own feeble strength, and which makes even the exercise of that strength in resistance to outrage punishable with death! which considers rational, immortal beings as articles of traffic, vendible commodities, merchantable property—which recognizes no social obligations, no natural relations—which tears without scruple the

[1] Messrs. Harvey of New Hampshire, Mallary of Vermont, and Ripley of Maine, voted in the Congress of 1829 against the consideration of a Resolution for inquiring into the expediency of abolishing slavery in the District of Columbia.

[2] J. Q. Adams is the only member of Congress who has ventured to speak plainly of this protection.

infant from the mother, the wife from the husband, the parent from the child . . .

I come now to the only practicable, the only just scheme of emancipation: Immediate abolition of slavery; an immediate acknowledgment of the great truth, that man cannot hold property in man; an immediate surrender of baneful prejudice to Christian love; an immediate practical obedience to the command of Jesus Christ: "Whatsoever ye would that men should do unto you, do ye even so to them."

A correct understanding of what is meant by immediate abolition must convince every candid mind that it is neither visionary nor dangerous; that it involves no disastrous consequences of bloodshed and desolation; but, on the contrary, that it is a safe, practicable, efficient remedy for the evils of the slave system.

The term immediate[3] is used in contrast with that of gradual. Earnestly as I wish it, I do not expect, no one expects, that the tremendous system of oppression can be instantaneously overthrown. The terrible and unrebukable indignation of a free people has not yet been sufficiently concentrated against it. The friends of abolition have not forgotten the peculiar organization of our confederacy, the delicate division of power between the states and the general government. They see the many obstacles in their pathway; but they know that public opinion can overcome them all. They ask no aid of physical coercion. They seek to obtain their object not with the weapons of violence and blood, but with those of reason and truth, prayer to God, and entreaty to man.

They seek to impress indelibly upon every human heart the true doctrines of the rights of man; to establish now and forever this great and fundamental truth of human liberty, that man cannot hold property in his brother; for they believe that the general admission of this truth will utterly destroy the system of slavery, based as that system is upon a denial or disregard of it . . .

The friends of emancipation would urge in the first instance an

[3] Rev. Dr. Thomson, of Edinburgh, thus speaks of it: "Were I to treat the term gradual as some of our enemies have the term immediate, I could easily, by the help of a little quibbling, bring you to the conclusion that, as hitherto employed, it means that the abolition of slavery will never take place." "The meaning of the word as used by us is perfectly clear; it is to be considered and understood under the direction of common sense, and as modified and expounded by the statements with which it is associated."

immediate abolition of slavery in the District of Columbia, and in the Territories of Florida and Arkansas. . . .

Here, then, are twenty-six thousand human beings, fashioned in the image of God, the fitted temples of His Holy Spirit, held by the government in the abhorrent chains of slavery. The power to emancipate them is clear. It is indisputable.[4] It does not depend upon the twenty-five slave votes in Congress. It lies with the free states.[5] Their duty is before them: in the fear of God, and not of man let them perform it.

Let them at once strike off the grievous fetters. Let them declare that man shall no longer hold his fellow-man in bondage, a beast of burden, an article of traffic, within the governmental domain . . . If our fathers intended that slavery should be perpetual, that our practice should forever give the lie to our professions, why is the great constitutional compact so guardedly silent on the subject of human servitude? If state necessity demanded this perpetual violation of the laws of God and the rights of man, this continual solecism in a government of freedom, why is it not met as a necessity, incurable and inevitable, and formally and distinctly recognized as a settled part of our social system? State necessity, that imperial tyrant, seeks no disguise . . .

What, then, is our duty?

To give effect to the spirit of our Constitution; to plant ourselves upon the great declaration and declare in the face of all the world that political, religious, and legal hypocrisy shall no longer cover as with loathsome leprosy the features of American freedom; to loose at once the bands of wickedness; to undo the heavy burdens, and let the oppressed go free.

We have indeed been authoritatively told in Congress and elsewhere that our brethren of the South and West will brook no further agitation of the subject of slavery. What then! Shall we heed the unrighteous prohibition? No; by our duty as Christians, as politicians, by our duty to ourselves, to our neighbor, and to God, we are called

[4] The report of Mr. Alexander in the Congress of 1829, unfavorable to the prayer of the petition for abolishing slavery in the District of Columbia, may be referred to as a specimen of the veriest sophistry which ever supplied the place of argument.

[5] "Trust not," said the illustrious Canning, "the masters of slaves in what concerns legislation for slavery. Let the evil be remedied by a government of free people, and not by the masters of slaves."

upon to agitate this subject; to give slavery no resting-place under the hallowed aegis of a government of freedom; to tear it root and branch, with all its fruits of abomination, at least from the soil of the national domain . . .

I deny the right of the slave-holder to impose silence on his brother of the North in reference to slavery. What! Compelled to maintain the system, to keep up the standing army which protects it, and yet be denied the poor privilege of remonstrance! Ready, at the summons of the master to put down the insurrections of his slaves, the outbreaking of that revenge which is now, and has been, in all nations, and all times, the inevitable consequence of oppression and wrong, and yet like automata to act but not speak! Are we to be denied even the right of a slave, the right to murmur?

I am not unaware that my remarks may be regarded by many as dangerous and exceptionable; that I may be regarded as a fanatic for quoting the language of eternal truth, and denounced as an incendiary for maintaining, in the spirit as well as the letter, the doctrines of American Independence. But if such are the consequences of a simple performance of duty, I shall not regard them. If my feeble appeal but reaches the hearts of any who are now slumbering in iniquity; if it shall have power given it to shake down one stone from that foul temple where the blood of human victims is offered to the Moloch of slavery; if under Providence it can break one fetter from off the image of God, and enable one suffering African

> To feel
> The weight of human misery less, and glide
> Ungroaning to the tomb,

I shall not have written in vain; my conscience will be satisfied.

Far be it from me to cast new bitterness into the gall and wormwood waters of sectional prejudice. No; I desire peace, the peace of universal love, of catholic sympathy, the peace of a common interest, a common feeling, a common humanity. But so long as slavery is tolerated, no such peace can exist. Liberty and slavery cannot dwell in harmony together . . . Peace! There can be no peace between justice and oppression, between robbery and righteousness, truth and falsehood, freedom and slavery.

The slave-holding states are not free. The name of liberty is there, but the spirit is wanting. They do not partake of its invaluable blessings. Wherever slavery exists to any considerable extent, with the exception of some recently settled portions of the country, and which have not yet felt in a great degree the baneful and deteriorating influences of slave labor, we hear at this moment the cry of suffering. We are told of grass-grown streets, of crumbling mansions, of beggared planters and barren plantations, of fear from without, of terror within. The once fertile fields are wasted and tenantless, for the curse of slavery, the improvidence of that labor whose hire has been kept back by fraud, has been there, poisoning the very earth beyond the reviving influence of the early and the latter rain. A moral mildew mingles with and blasts the economy of nature. It is as if the finger of the everlasting God had written upon the soil of the slave-holder the language of His displeasure.

Let, then, the slave-holding states consult their present interest by beginning without delay the work of emancipation. If they fear not, and mock at the fiery indignation of Him, to whom vengeance belongeth, let temporal interest persuade them. They know, they must know, that the present state of things cannot long continue. Mind is the same everywhere, no matter what may be the complexion of the frame which it animates: there is a love of liberty which the scourge cannot eradicate, a hatred of oppression which centuries of degradation cannot extinguish. The slave will become conscious sooner or later of his brute strength, his physical superiority, and will exert it. His torch will be at the threshold and his knife at the throat of the planter. Horrible and indiscriminate will be his vengeance. Where, then, will be the pride, the beauty, and the chivalry of the South? The smoke of her torment will rise upward like a thick cloud visible over the whole earth.

> Belie the Negro's powers: in headlong will,
> Christian, thy brother thou shalt find him still.
> Belie his virtues: since his wrongs began,
> His follies and his crimes have stamped him man.[6]

Let the cause of insurrection be removed, then, as speedily as possible. Cease to oppress. "Let him that stole steal no more." Let the laborer have his hire. Bind him no longer by the cords of slavery,

[6] Montgomery.

but with those of kindness and brotherly love. Watch over him for his good. Pray for him; instruct him; pour light into the darkness of his mind.

Let this be done, and the horrible fears which now haunt the slumbers of the slave-holder will depart. Conscience will take down its racks and gibbets, and his soul will be at peace. His lands will no longer disappoint his hopes. Free labor will renovate them.

Historical facts; the nature of the human mind; the demonstrated truths of political economy; the analysis of cause and effect, all concur in establishing:

1. That immediate abolition is a safe and just and peaceful remedy for the evils of the slave system.

2. That free labor, its necessary consequence, is more productive, and more advantageous to the planter than slave labor.

In proof of the first proposition it is only necessary to state the undeniable fact that immediate emancipation, whether by an individual or a community, has in no instance been attended with violence and disorder on the part of the emancipated; but that on the contrary it has promoted cheerfulness, industry, and laudable ambition in the place of sullen discontent, indolence, and despair . . .

Yes, putting aside altogether the righteous law of the living God—the same yesterday, today, and forever—and shutting out the clearest political truths ever taught by man, still, in human policy selfish expediency would demand of the planter the immediate emancipation of his slaves:

Because slave labor is the labor of mere machines; a mechanical impulse of body and limb, with which the mind of the laborer has no sympathy, and from which it constantly and loathingly revolts.

Because slave labor deprives the master altogether of the incalculable benefit of the negro's will. That does not cooperate with the forced toil of the body. This is but the necessary consequence of all labor which does not benefit the laborer. It is a just remark of that profound political economist, Adam Smith, that "a slave can have no other interest than to eat and waste as much, and work as little, as he can." . . . .

Let us look at this subject from another point of view. The large sum of money necessary for stocking a plantation with slaves has an inevitable tendency to place the agriculture of a slave-holding community exclusively in the hands of the wealthy, a tendency at war with practical republicanism and conflicting with the best maxims of political economy.

Two hundred slaves at $200 per head would cost in the outset $40,000. Compare this enormous outlay for the labor of a single plantation with the beautiful system of free labor as exhibited in New England, where every young laborer, with health and ordinary prudence, may acquire by his labor on the farms of others, in a few years, a farm of his own, and the stock necessary for its proper cultivation; where on a hard and unthankful soil independence and competence may be attained by all . . .

Emancipation would reform this evil. The planter would no longer be under the necessity of a heavy expenditure for slaves. He would only pay a very moderate price for his labor; a price, indeed, far less than the cost of the maintenance of a promiscuous gang of slaves, which the present system requires.

In an old plantation of three hundred slaves, not more than one hundred effective laborers will be found. Children, the old and superannuated, the sick and decrepit, the idle and incorrigibly vicious, will be found to constitute two thirds of the whole number. The remaining third perform only about one third as much work as the same number of free laborers.

Now disburden the master of this heavy load of maintenance; let him employ free, able, industrious laborers only, those who feel conscious of a personal interest in the fruits of their labor, and who does not see that such a system would be vastly more safe and economical than the present?

The slave states are learning this truth by fatal experience. Most of them are silently writhing under the great curse. Virginia has uttered her complaints aloud. As yet, however, nothing has been done even there, save a small annual appropriation for the purpose of colonizing the free colored inhabitants of the state. Is this a remedy?

But it may be said that Virginia will ultimately liberate her slaves on condition of their colonization in Africa, peacefully if possible, forcibly if necessary.

Well, admitting that Virginia may be able and willing at some remote period to rid herself of the evil by commuting the punishment of her unoffending colored people from slavery to exile, will her fearful remedy apply to some of the other slave-holding states?

It is a fact, strongly insisted upon by our Southern brethren as a reason for the perpetuation of slavery, that their climate and peculiar agriculture will not admit of hard labor on the part of the whites; that amidst the fatal malaria of the rice plantations the white man is almost annually visited by the country fever; that few of the white overseers of these plantations reach the middle period of ordinary life; that the owners are compelled to fly from their estates as the hot season approaches, without being able to return until the first frosts have fallen. But we are told that the slaves remain there, at their work, mid-leg in putrid water, breathing the noisome atmosphere, loaded with contagion, and underneath the scorching fervor of a terrible sun; that they indeed suffer; but that their habits, constitutions, and their long practice enable them to labor, surrounded by such destructive influences, with comparative safety.

The conclusive answer, therefore, to those who in reality cherish the visionary hope of colonizing all the colored people of the United States in Africa or elsewhere, is this single, all-important fact: The labor of the blacks will not and cannot be dispensed with by the planter of the South.

To what remedy, then, can the friends of humanity betake themselves but to that of emancipation?

And nothing but a strong, unequivocal expression of public sentiment is needed to carry into effect this remedy, so far as the general government is concerned.

And when the voice of all the non-slave-holding states shall be heard on this question, a voice of expostulation, rebuke, entreaty— when the full light of truth shall break through the night of prejudice, and reveal all the foul abominations of slavery, will Delaware still cling to the curse which is wasting her moral strength, and still rivet the fetters upon her three or four thousand slaves?

Let Delaware begin the work, and Maryland and Virginia must follow; the example will be contagious; and the great object of universal emancipation will be attained.

Freeman, Christians, lovers of truth and justice! Why stand ye idle? Ours is a government of opinion, and slavery is interwoven with it. Change the current of opinion, and slavery will be swept away. Let the awful sovereignty of the people, a power which is limited only by the sovereignty of Heaven, arise and pronounce judgment against the crying iniquity . . .

The conflicting interests of free and slave labor furnish the only ground for fear in relation to the permanency of the Union. The line of separation between them is day by day growing broader and deeper; geographically and politically united, we are already, in a moral point of view, a divided people. But a few months ago we were on the very verge of civil war, a war of brothers, a war between the North and the South, between the slave-holder and the free laborer. The danger has been delayed for a time; this bolt has fallen without mortal injury to the Union, but the cloud from whence it came still hangs above us, reddening with the elements of destruction . . .

To counteract the dangers resulting from a state of society so utterly at variance with the great Declaration of American freedom should be the earnest endeavor of every patriotic statesman. Nothing unconstitutional, nothing violent, should be attempted; but the true doctrine of the rights of man should be steadily kept in view; and the opposition to slavery should be inflexible and constantly maintained. The almost daily violations of the Constitution in consequence of the laws of some of the slave states, subjecting free colored citizens of New England and elsewhere, who may happen to be on board of our coasting vessels, to imprisonment immediately on their arrival in a Southern port should be provided against. Nor should the imprisonment of the free colored citizens of the Northern and Middle states, on suspicion of being runaways, subjecting them, even after being pronounced free, to the costs of their confinement and trial, be longer tolerated; for if we continue to yield to innovations like these upon the Constitution of our fathers, we shall erelong have the name only of a free government left us.

Dissemble as we may, it is impossible for us to believe, after fully considering the nature of slavery, that it can much longer maintain a peaceable existence among us. A day of revolution must come, and it is our duty to prepare for it. Its threatened evil may be changed into a national blessing. The establishment of schools for the instruction of the slave children, a general diffusion of the lights of Christianity, and the introduction of a sacred respect for the social obligations of marriage and for the relations between parents and children, among our black population, would render emancipation not only perfectly safe, but also of the highest advantage to the country. Two millions of freemen would be added to our population, upon whom in the hour of danger we could safely depend; "the domestic foe" would be changed into a firm friend, faithful, generous, and ready to encounter all dangers in our defence. It is well known that during the last war with Great Britain, wherever the enemy touched upon our Southern coast, the slaves in multitudes hastened to join them. On the other hand, the free blacks were highly serviceable in repelling them. So warm was the zeal of the latter, so manifest their courage in the defense of Louisiana, that the present Chief Magistrate of the United States publicly bestowed upon them one of the highest eulogiums ever offered by a commander to his soldiers . . . .

. . . An intense and powerful feeling is working in the mighty heart of England; it is speaking through the lips of Brougham and Buxton and O'Connell, and demanding justice in the name of humanity and according to the righteous law of God. The immediate emancipation of eight hundred thousand slaves is demanded with an authority which cannot much longer be disputed or trifled with. That demand will be obeyed; justice will be done; the heavy burdens will be unloosed; the oppressed set free. It shall go well for England.

And when the stain on our own escutcheon shall be seen no more; when the Declaration of our Independence and the practice of our people shall agree; when truth shall be exalted among us; when love shall take the place of wrong; when all the baneful pride and prejudice of caste and color shall fall forever; when under one common sun of political liberty the slave-holding portions of our republic shall no longer sit, like the Egyptians of old, themselves mantled in thick darkness, while all around them is glowing with the blessed light of freedom and equality, then, and not till then, shall it go well for America!

ELIZUR WRIGHT

The Sin of Slavery and Its Remedy; Containing Some Reflections on the Moral Influence of American Colonization

ॐ

> *At the time of the appearance of this pamphlet of fifty-two pages, Elizur Wright (1804–1885) was professor of mathematics and natural philosophy at Western Reserve College. With the formation of the American Anti-Slavery Society, he became its corresponding secretary. In 1835–37, he edited the* Quarterly Anti-Slavery Magazine, *wrote the society's reports and supervised its agents in the field. He later disagreed with Garrison, especially on political action, and in 1839 edited the* Massachusetts Abolitionist, *an organ of Garrison's opponents. Soon thereafter he dropped out of the anti-slavery movement.*
>
> *The pamphlet was published in New York, during the middle of 1833. The following extracts are from the introduction and from Chapter V.*

INTRODUCTION

The American revolution was incomplete. It left one sixth part of the population the victims of a servitude immeasurably more debasing, than that from which it delivered the rest. While this nation held up its Declaration of Independence—its noble bill of human rights, before an admiring world, in one hand; it mortified the friends of humanity, by oppressing the poor and defenceless with the other. The progress of time has not lessened the evil. There are now held in involuntary and perpetual slavery, in the southern half of this republic, more than 2,000,000 of men, women, and children, guarded with a vigilance, which strives, and with success appalling as it is complete, to shut out every ray of knowledge, human and divine, and reduce them as nearly as possible to a level with the brutes. These miserable slaves are not only compelled to labor without choice and without hire, but they are subjected to the cruelty and lust of their masters to an unbounded extent. In the northern states there is very generally a sympathy with the slave-holders, and a prejudice against the slaves, which shows itself in palliating the crime of slave-holding, and in most unrighteously disregarding the rights, and vilifying the characters of the free colored men.

At the same time, slavery, as a system, is (in a certain sense) condemned. It is confessed to be a great evil, "a moral evil," and when the point is urged, *a sin.* The slaves, it is admitted, have rights —every principle of honesty, justice, and humanity, *"in the abstract,"* calls aloud that they should be made free. The word of God is in their favour. Indeed, there is no ground claimed by the abettors of slavery, on which they pretend to justify it for a moment, but a supposed—a begged—*expediency,* baseless as the driven clouds. I say baseless, for while not a single fact has ever been produced, going to show the danger of putting the slaves, all at once, under the protection of law, and employing them as free laborers, there have been produced, on the other side, varied and fair experiments showing, that it is altogether safe and profitable. . . .

IMMEDIATE ABOLITION

. . . Under the government of God, as exhibited in this world, there is but one remedy for sin, and that is available only by a *repentance,* evidenced by reformation. There is no such thing as holding on to sin with safety. It is not only to be renounced, but the very occasions of it are to be avoided at whatever sacrifice. If thy right hand cause thee to offend, cut it off—if thy right eye, pluck it out. The dearest human relationships are to be broken through when they interfere with the relation which a man bears to God, and through him to his rational creatures. This being the case, we might naturally expect that the entire agency which God has provided to reclaim the world should be adapted to produce *immediate repentance.* It certainly is so if we take the testimony of the Bible . . . The doctrine of the immediate abolition of slavery asks no better authority than is offered by scripture. It is in perfect harmony with the letter and spirit of God's word.

The doctrine may be thus briefly stated. It is the duty of the holders of slaves immediately to restore to them their liberty, and to extend to them the full protection of law, as well as its control. It is their duty equitably to restore to them those profits of their labor, which have been wickedly wrested away, especially by giving them that moral and mental instruction—that education, which alone can render any considerable accumulation of property a blessing. It is their duty to employ them as voluntary laborers, on equitable wages. Also, it is the duty of all men to proclaim this doctrine—to urge upon slave-holders *immediate emancipation,* so long as there is a slave—to agitate the consciences of tyrants, so long as there is a tyrant on the globe.

Though this doctrine does not depend, in regard to the slave-holder, upon the safety of immediate emancipation, nor, in regard to the non-slave-holder, on the prospect of accomplishing any abolition at all, but upon the commands of God, yet I shall attempt to establish it upon those lower grounds. I am willing to rest the cause on the truth of the following propositions.

1. The instant abolition of the whole slave system is safe, and the substitution of a free labor system is safe, practicable and profitable.

2. The firm expression of an enlightened public opinion, on the part of non-slave-holders, in favor of instant abolition, is an effectual, and the only effectual means of securing abolition in any time whatsoever. . . .

An Abolitionist Novelist, Lydia M. Child, Protests Slavery and Segregation

ह≫

Lydia Maria Child (1802–1880) was a popular novelist when she wrote An Appeal in Favor of That Class of Americans Called Africans, *which was published in July 1833, in Boston, by Allen and Ticknor. Though her popularity dimin-*

*ished in some quarters with the publication of her book—
which was widely read and made many converts for the anti-
slavery movement—she continued her anti-slavery writings
until the end of the Civil War and the liberation of the slaves.
Among her other works were* Isaac T. Hopper: A True Life
(1853); The Patriarchal Institution, as Described by Members
of Its Own Family *(1860);* The Right Way the Safe Way,
Proved by Emancipation in the British West Indies, and Elsewhere *(1860); and* Correspondence Between Lydia Maria
Child and Gov. Wise and Mrs. Mason of Virginia *(1860),
concerning John Brown and his raid on Harpers Ferry. The
selection printed here is from Chapter VIII, pp. 208–232, of*
An Appeal.

PREJUDICES AGAINST PEOPLE OF COLOR,
AND OUR DUTIES IN RELATION TO THIS SUBJECT

While we bestow our earnest disapprobation on the system
of slavery, let us not flatter ourselves that we are in reality any better
than our brethren of the South. Thanks to our soil and climate, and
the early exertions of the Quakers, the *form* of slavery does not exist
among us; but the very *spirit* of the hateful and mischievous thing is
here in all its strength. The manner in which we use what power we
have, gives us ample reason to be grateful that the nature of our
institutions does not intrust us with more. Our prejudices against
colored people is even more inveterate than it is at the South. The
planter is often attached to his negroes, and lavishes caresses and
kind words upon them, as he would on a favorite hound: but our
cold-hearted, ignoble prejudice admits of no exception—no inter-
mission.

The Southerners have long continued habit, apparent interest and
dreaded danger, to palliate the wrong they do; but we stand without
excuse. They tell us that Northern ships and Northern capital have
been engaged in this wicked business; and the reproach is true.
Several fortunes in this city have been made by the sale of negro
blood. If these criminal transactions are still carried on, they are done
in silence and secrecy, because public opinion has made them disgraceful. But if the free States wished to cherish the system of slavery
forever, they could not take a more direct course than they now do.

Those who are kind and liberal on all other subjects, unite with the selfish and the proud in their unrelenting efforts to keep the colored population in the lowest state of degradation; and the influence they unconsciously exert over children early infuses into their innocent minds the same strong feelings of contempt.

The intelligent and well informed have the least share of this prejudice; and when their minds can be brought to reflect upon it, I have generally observed that they soon cease to have any at all. But such a general apathy prevails and the subject is so seldom brought into view, that few are really aware how oppressively the influence of society is made to bear upon this injured class of the community. When I have related facts, that came under my own observation, I have often been listened to with surprise, which gradually increased to indignation. In order that my readers may not be ignorant of the extent of this tyrannical prejudice, I will as briefly as possible state the evidence, and leave them to judge of it, as their hearts and consciences may dictate.

In the first place, an unjust law exists in this Commonwealth, by which marriages between persons of different color are pronounced illegal. I am perfectly aware of the gross ridicule to which I may subject myself by alluding to this particular; but I have lived too long, and observed too much, to be disturbed by the world's mockery. In the first place, the government ought not to be invested with power to control the affections, any more than the consciences of citizens. A man has at least as good a right to choose his wife, as he has to choose his religion. His taste may not suit his neighbors; but so long as his deportment is correct, they have no right to interfere with his concerns. In the second place, this law is a *useless* disgrace to Massachusetts. Under existing circumstances, none but those whose condition in life is too low to be much affected by public opinion, will form such alliances; and they, when they choose to do so, *will* make such marriages, in spite of the law. I know two or three instances where women of the laboring class have been united to reputable, industrious colored men. These husbands regularly bring home their wages, and are kind to their families. If by some of the odd chances, which not unfrequently occur in the world, their wives should become heirs to any property, the children may be wronged out of it, because the law pronounces them illegitimate. And while this injustice exists with regard to *honest,* industrious individuals, who are merely guilty of differing from us in a matter of taste, neither the legislation nor customs of slave-holding States exert their influence against *immoral* connexions . . .

There is another Massachusetts law, which an enlightened community would not probably suffer to be carried into execution under any circumstances; but it still remains to disgrace the statutes of this Commonwealth. — It is as follows:

> No African or Negro, other than a subject of the Emperor of Morocco, or a citizen of the United States (proved so by a certificate of the Secretary of the State of which he is a citizen), shall tarry within this Commonwealth longer than two months; and on complaint a justice shall order him to depart in ten days; and if he do not then, the justice may commit such African or Negro to the House of Correction, there to be kept at hard labor; and at the next term of the Court of C. P., he shall be tried, and if convicted of remaining as aforesaid, shall be whipped not exceeding ten lashes; and if he or she shall not *then* depart such process shall be repeated and punishment inflicted *tolies quoties*. Stat. 1788, Ch. 54.

An honorable Haytian or Brazilian, who visited this country for business or information, might come under this law, unless public opinion rendered it a mere dead letter.

There is among the colored people an increasing desire for information, and a laudable ambition to be respectable in manners and appearance. Are we not foolish as well as sinful, in trying to repress a tendency so salutary to themselves, and so beneficial to the community? Several individuals of this class are very desirous to have persons of their own color qualified to teach something more than mere reading and writing. But in the public schools, colored children are subject to many discouragements and difficulties; and into the private schools they cannot gain admission. A very sensible and well-informed colored woman in a neighboring town, whose family have been brought up in a manner that excited universal remark and approbation, has been extremely desirous to obtain for her eldest daughter the advantages of a private school; but she has been resolutely repulsed, on account of her complexion. The girl is a very light mulatto, with great modesty and propriety of manners; perhaps no young person in the Commonwealth was less likely to have a bad influence on her associates. The clergyman respected the family, and he remonstrated with the instructor; but while the latter admitted the injustice of the thing, he excused himself by saying such a step would occasion the loss of all his white scholars . . .

The attempt to establish a school for African girls at Canterbury, Connecticut, has made too much noise to need a detailed account in this volume. I do not know the lady who first formed the project, but I am told that she is a benevolent and religious woman. It certainly is difficult to imagine any other motives than good ones, for an undertaking so arduous and unpopular. Yet had the Pope himself attempted to establish his supremacy over that Commonwealth, he could hardly have been repelled with more determined and angry resistance . . . Town meetings were held, the records of which are not highly creditable to the parties concerned. Petitions were sent to the Legislature, beseeching that no African school might be allowed to admit individuals not residing in the town where said school was established; and strange to relate, this law, which makes it impossible to collect a sufficient number of pupils, was sanctioned by the State. A colored girl, who availed herself of this opportunity to gain instruction, was warned out of town, and fined for not complying; and the instructress was imprisoned for persevering in her benevolent plan.

It is said, in excuse, that Canterbury will be inundated with vicious characters, who will corrupt the morals of the young men; that such a school will break down the distinctions between black and white; and that marriages between people of different colors will be the probable result. Yet they seem to assume the ground that colored people *must* always be an inferior and degraded class—that the prejudice against them *must* be eternal; being deeply founded in the laws of God and nature . . . Finally, they endeavored to represent the school as one of the *incendiary* proceedings of the Anti-Slavery Society; and they appeal to the Colonization Society, as an aggrieved child is wont to appeal to its parent.

The objection with regard to the introduction of vicious characters into a village, certainly has some force; but are such persons likely to leave cities for a quiet country town, in search of moral and intellectual improvement? Is it not obvious that the best portion of the colored class are the very ones to prize such an opportunity for instruction? Grant that a large proportion of these unfortunate people *are* vicious—is it not our duty, and of course our wisest policy, to try to make them otherwise? And what will so effectually elevate their character and condition, as knowledge? I beseech you, my countrymen, think of these things wisely, and in season.

As for intermarriages, if there be such a repugnance between the two races, founded in the laws of *nature,* methinks there is small reason to dread their frequency . . .

A similar, though less violent opposition arose in consequence of the attempt to establish a college for colored people at New Haven. A young colored man, who tried to obtain education at the Wesleyan college in Middleton, was obliged to relinquish the attempt on account of the persecution of his fellow students. Some collegians from the South objected to a colored associate in their recitations; and those from New England promptly and zealously joined in the hue and cry. A small but firm party were in favor of giving the colored man a chance to pursue his studies without insult or interruption; and I am told that this manly and disinterested band were all Southerners. As for those individuals, who exerted their influence to exclude an unoffending fellow-citizen from privileges which ought to be equally open to all, it is to be hoped that age will make them wiser—and that they will learn, before they die, to be ashamed of a step attended with more important results than usually belong to youthful follies.

It happens that these experiments have all been made in Connecticut; but it is no more than justice to that State to remark that a similar spirit would probably have been manifested in Massachusetts, under like circumstances. At our debating clubs and other places of public discussion, the demon of prejudice girds himself for the battle, the moment negro colleges and high schools are alluded to . . .

Let us seriously consider what injury a negro college could possibly do us. It is certainly a fair presumption that the scholars would be from the better portion of the colored population; and it is an equally fair presumption that knowledge would improve their characters. There are already many hundreds of colored people in the city of Boston . . . In the street they generally appear neat and respectable; and in our houses they do not "come between the wind and our nobility." Would the addition of one or two hundred more even be perceived? As for giving offence to the Southerners by allowing such establishments—they have no right to interfere with our internal concerns, any more than we have with theirs . . . Why should they not give up slavery to please us, by the same rule that we must refrain from educating the negroes to please them? If they are at liberty to do wrong, we certainly ought to be at liberty to do right. They may talk and publish as much about us as they please; and we ask for no other influence over them . . .

In Boston there is an Infant School, three Primary Schools, and a Grammar School. The two last, are I believe supported by the public; and this fact is highly creditable. A building for the colored Grammar School is not supplied by the city, though such provision is always made for similar institutions for white boys . . . The apartment is close and uncomfortable, and many pupils stay away, who would gladly attend under more convenient circumstances. There ought likewise to be a colored teacher instead of a white one. Under the dominion of existing prejudices, it is difficult to find a white man, well qualified to teach such a school, who feels the interest he ought to feel, in these Pariahs[1] of our republic. The parents would repose more confidence in a colored instructor; and he, both from sympathy and pride, would be better fitted for his task.

It is peculiarly incumbent on the city authorities to supply a commodious building for the colored grammar school, because public prejudice excludes these oppressed people from all lucrative employments, and they cannot therefore be supposed to have ample funds of their own.

I was much pleased with the late resolution awarding Franklin medals to the colored pupils of the grammar school; and I was still more pleased with the laudable project, originated by Josiah Holbrook, Esq. for the establishment of a colored Lyceum. Surely a better spirit *is* beginning to work in this cause; and when once begun, the good sense and good feeling of the community will bid it go on and prosper. How much this spirit will have to contend with is illustrated by the following fact. When President Jackson entered this city, the white children of all the schools were sent out in uniform, to do him honor. A member of the Committee proposed that the pupils of the African schools should be invited likewise; but he was the only one who voted for it. He then proposed that the yeas and nays should be recorded; upon which, most of the gentlemen walked off, to prevent the question from being taken. Perhaps they felt an awkward

---

[1] The Pariahs are the lowest and most degraded caste in Hindostan. The laws prevent them from ever rising in their condition, or mingling with other castes.

consciousness of the incongeniality of such proceedings with our republican institutions. By order of the Committee the vacation of the African schools did not commence until the day after the procession of the white pupils; and a note to the instructor intimated that the pupils were not expected to appear on the Common. The reason given was because "their numbers were so few"; but in private conversation, fears were expressed lest their sable faces should give offence to our slave-holding President. In all probability the sight of the colored children would have been agreeable to General Jackson, and seemed more like home, than anything he witnessed.

In the theatre, it is not possible for respectable colored people to obtain a decent seat. They must either be excluded, or herd with the vicious.

A fierce excitement prevailed, not long since, because a colored man had bought a pew in one of our churches. I heard a very kind-hearted and zealous democrat declare his opinion that "the fellow ought to be turned out by constables, if he dared to occupy the pew he had purchased." Even at the communion-table, the mockery of human pride is mingled with the worship of Jehovah. Again and again have I seen a solitary negro come up to the altar, meekly and timidly, after all the white communicants had retired. One Episcopal clergy-man of this city, forms an honorable exception to this remark. When there is room at the altar, Mr. —— often makes a signal to the colored members of his church to kneel beside their white brethren; and once, when two white infants and one colored one were to be baptized, and the parents of the latter bashfully lingered for behind the others, he silently rebuked the unchristian spirit of pride, by first administering the holy ordinance to the little dark-skinned child of God.

An instance of prejudice lately occurred, which I should find it hard to believe, did I not positively know it to be a fact. A gallery pew was purchased in one of our churches for two hundred dollars. A few Sabbaths after, an address was delivered at that church, in favor of the Africans. Some colored people, who very naturally wished to hear the discourse, went into the gallery; probably because they thought they should be deemed less intrusive there than else-where. The man who had recently bought a pew, found it occupied by colored people, and indignantly retired with his family. The next day, he purchased a pew in another meeting-house, protesting that nothing would tempt him again to make use of seats, that had been occupied by negroes.

A well known country representative, who makes a very loud noise about his democracy, once attended the Catholic church. A pious negro requested him to take off his hat, while he stood in the presence of the Virgin Mary. The white man rudely shoved him aside, saying, "You son of an Ethiopian, do you dare to speak to me!" I more than once heard the hero repeat this story; and he seemed to take peculiar satisfaction in telling it. Had he been less ignorant, he would not have chosen "son of an Ethiopian" as an *ignoble* epithet; to have called the African his own equal would have been abundantly more sarcastic. The same republican dismissed a strong, industrious colored man, who had been employed on the farm during his absence. "I am too great a democrat," quoth he, "to have any body in my house, who don't sit at my table; and I'll be hanged, if I ever eat with the son of an Ethiopian." . . .

A worthy colored woman, belonging to an adjoining town, wished to come into Boston to attend upon a son, who was ill. She had a trunk with her, and was too feeble to walk. She begged permission to ride in the stage. But the passengers with *noble* indignation, declared they would get out, if she were allowed to get in. After much entreaty, the driver suffered her to sit by him upon the box. When he entered the city, his comrades began to point and sneer. Not having sufficient moral courage to endure this, he left the poor woman, with her trunk, in the middle of the street, far from the place of her destination; telling her, with an oath, that he would not carry her a step further . . .

Every year a colored gentleman and scholar is becoming less and less of a rarity—thanks to the existence of the Haytian Republic, and the increasing liberality of the world! Yet if a person of refinement from Hayti, Brazil, or other countries, which we deem less enlightened than our own, should visit us, the very boys of this republic would dog his footsteps with the vulgar outcry of "Nigger! Nigger!" I have known this to be done, from no other provocation than the sight of a colored man with the dress and deportment of a gentleman. Were it not that republicanism, like Christianity, is often perverted from its true spirit by the bad passions of mankind, such things as these would make every honest mind disgusted with the very name of republics.

I am acquainted with a gentleman from Brazil who is shrewd, enterprising, noble-spirited, and highly respectable in character and manners; yet he has experienced almost every species of indignity on account of his color . . .

Will any candid person tell me why respectable colored people should not be allowed to make use of public conveyances, open to all who are able and willing to pay for the privilege? Those who enter a vessel, or a stagecoach, cannot expect to select their companions. If they can afford to take a carriage or boat for themselves, then, and then only, they have a right to be exclusive . . .

Stage-drivers are very much perplexed when they attempt to vindicate the present tyrannical customs; and they usually give up the point, by saying they themselves have no prejudice against colored people—they are merely afraid of the public. But stage-drivers should remember that in a popular government, they, in common with every other citizen, form a part and portion of the dreaded public.

The gold was never coined for which I would barter my individual freedom of acting and thinking upon any subject, or knowingly interfere with the rights of the meanest human being. The only true courage is that which impels us to do right without regard to consequences. To fear a populace is as servile as to fear an emperor. The only salutary restraint is the fear of doing wrong.

Our representatives to Congress have repeatedly rode in a stage with colored servants at the request of their masters. Whether this is because New Englanders are willing to do out of courtesy to a Southern gentleman, what they object to doing from justice to a colored citizen—or whether those representatives, being educated men, were more than usually divested of this absurd prejudice—I will not pretend to say.

The state of public feeling not only makes it difficult for the Africans to obtain information, but it prevents them from making profitable use of what knowledge they have. A colored man, however intelligent, is not allowed to pursue any business more lucrative than that of a barber, a shoe-black, or a waiter. These, and all other employments, are truly respectable, whenever the duties connected with them are faithfully performed; but it is unjust that a man should, on account of his complexion, be prevented from performing more elevated uses in society. Every citizen ought to have a fair chance to try his fortune in any line of business, which he thinks he has ability to transact. Why should not colored men be employed in the manufactories of various kinds? If their ignorance is an objection, let them be enlightened, as speedily as possible. If their moral character is not sufficiently pure, remove the pressure of public scorn, and thus supply them with motives for being respectable. All this can be done. It merely requires an earnest wish to overcome a prejudice, which has "grown with our growth and strengthened with our strength," but which is in fact opposed to the spirit of our religion, and contrary to the instinctive good feelings of our nature. When examined by the clear light of reason, it disappears. Prejudices of all kinds have their strongest holds in the minds of the vulgar and the ignorant. In a community so enlightened as our own, they must gradually melt away under the influence of public discussion . . .

Mr. Garrison was the first person who dared to edit a newspaper, in which slavery was spoken of as altogether wicked and inexcusable. For this crime the Legislature of Georgia have offered five thousand dollars to any one who will "arrest and prosecute him to conviction *under the laws of that State.*" An association of gentlemen in South Carolina have likewise offered a large reward for the same object. It is, to say the least, a very remarkable step for one State in this Union to promulgate such a law concerning a citizen of another State, merely for publishing his opinions boldly. The disciples of Fanny Wright promulgate the most zealous and virulent attacks upon Christianity, without any hindrance from the civil authorities; and this is done upon the truly rational ground that individual freedom of opinion ought to be respected—that what is false cannot stand, and what is true cannot be overthrown. We leave Christianity to take care of itself; but slavery is a "delicate subject"—and whoever attacks that must be punished. Mr. Garrison is a disinterested, intelligent, and remarkably pure-minded man, whose only fault is that he cannot be moderate on a subject which it is exceedingly difficult for an honest mind to examine with calmness. Many, who highly respect his character, and motives, regret his tendency to use wholesale and unqualified expressions; but it is something to have the truth told, even if it be not in the most judicious way. Where an evil is powerfully supported by the self-interest and prejudice of the community, none but an ardent individual will venture to meddle with it. Luther was deemed indiscreet even by those who liked him best; yet a more prudent man would never have given an impetus sufficiently powerful to heave the great mass of corruption under which the church was buried. Mr. Garrison has certainly the merit of having first called public attention to a neglected and very important subject. I believe whoever fairly and dispassionately examines the question, will be more than disposed to forgive the occasional faults of an ardent temperament, in consideration of the difficulty of the undertaking, and the violence with which it has been opposed. . . .

Amherst College Forms an Anti-Slavery Society

ક્રે

The following notice appeared in the August 1833, issue of the Abolitionist, *a monthly publication issued in 1833 by the New England Anti-Slavery Society, Vol. 1, pp. 124–5.*

ANTI-SLAVERY SOCIETY AT AMHERST COLLEGE

We have lately received the following interesting communication from this institution. It gives us the highest gratification to find good principles gaining ground so rapidly among the young men of our country.

TO THE EDITOR OF THE ABOLITIONIST

AMHERST COLLEGE, July 25, 1833.

SIR: It affords us pleasure to inform you, that an Auxiliary to the New England Anti-Slavery Society, has recently been formed in this Institution. The number of its members, though at present comparatively small, is increasing. All other circumstances connected with the progress of the Society thus far, have been peculiarly auspicious and animating. If a thorough understanding of the cause we plead—deep felt sympathies for the suffering slave—a perfect unity of feeling and effort—and "a mind to work" may constitute strength—then we are strong. We have adopted a constitution fundamentally the same with that of the Parent Society. The noble cause of Immediate Emancipation—advocated by your Society, has been rapidly gaining ground in this College for a few months past. Three of our number listened to the recent public debate in Boston, between Messrs. Wright and Finley. Previously they had been zealous defenders of the *principles* of African Colonization—and by education were strongly prejudiced in their favor; but by that discussion they were led to an examination of the *principles* of the two Societies, which resulted in the firm persuasion that the cause of *"immediate* abolition" was the cause of God and humanity—and that the advocates of *gradual* emancipation were but dallying with the sin of slavery—while the influence of their measures was to render more hopeless the condition of the slave. Among other resolutions submitted at our last meeting were the following:

1. *Resolved,* That the *principles* of the New England Anti-Slavery Society harmonize with the plainest precepts of Patriotism, Philanthropy and Religion.

2. *Resolved,* That we cordially approve the plan adopted by the New England Anti-Slavery Society to establish an Institution for the instruction of colored youth—and as a Society, pledge ourselves to raise for so benevolent an object, such sums as our means, from time to time will admit—and also to exert ourselves to elevate and enlighten the colored population of our own vicinity, as well as abroad.

3. *Resolved,* That we view with unqualified disapprobation and utter abhorrence the barbarous treatment of Miss Crandall, and that she is justly entitled to the prayers and sympathies of the Christian community while suffering persecution for her laudable and Christian efforts to instruct the ignorant and oppressed.

The above resolutions were accompanied by interesting remarks, and unanimously adopted.

A Petition to Abolish Slavery in the District of Columbia

ु

> *The effort to bring about the abolition of slavery in the District of Columbia was perhaps the earliest form of anti-slavery activity in the United States. The following petition is but one of many, variously worded, which circulated almost constantly. The petition, with the accompanying remarks, appeared in the* Abolitionist, *September 1833, Vol. 1, pp. 139–140.*

SLAVERY IN THE DISTRICT OF COLUMBIA

The abolition of the slave-trade and slavery in this District ought to be constantly kept in mind by all the friends of the colored race. In this object thousands will unite who are opposed to Anti-Slavery Societies. Few men, we believe can be found at the north, who do not regard the toleration of slavery at the seat of our national government as disgraceful to the country; and, even at the South, many persons who are not prepared to exert themselves to put down this system in their own States, will readily admit that no just cause exists for perpetuating it in the District of Columbia. Nothing, we are confident, is necessary, in order to abolish the national sin and shame, but resolution and activity in the friends of the measure. If all who really have this cause at heart would but put their names to petitions to Congress in favor of the object, they would be astonished at their own numbers, and Congress would not dare refuse to perform a great work of justice and humanity, which was demanded by the great mass of the people.

The following is a petition which is now circulating in this vicinity. It has already received numerous and respectable signatures:

To the Honorable Senate and House of Representatives of the United States of Amreica in Congress Assembled, the petition of the undersigned, citizens of the United States, respectfully represents—

That your petitioners are deeply impressed with the evils arising from the existence of Slavery in the District of Columbia. The Constitution of the United States provides that Congress shall have power, "to exercise exclusive legislation in all cases whatsoever, over such district (not exceeding ten miles square), as may, by the cession of particular States, and the acceptance of Congress, become the seat of government of the United States." In pursuance of this provision, the States of Maryland and Virginia respectively ceded portions of their territories, which being accepted by Congress, now compose the District of Columbia. By the plain words of the constitution Congress has the power to abolish slavery in this District, and no other body can legislate on the subject.

While our Declaration of Independence boldly proclaims as self-evident truths "that all men are created equal, that they are endowed by their Creator with certain inalienable rights, that among these are life, liberty, and the pursuit of happiness"; at the very seat of government human beings are born almost daily, whom the laws pronounce to be from their birth not equal to other men, and who are for life, deprived of liberty and the free pursuit of happiness.

In addition to the other evils flowing from slavery, both moral and political, which it is needless to specify, circumstances have rendered this District a great market for traders in human flesh. The unhappy victims of this traffic, are brought into this District in chains, and then lodged in private jails and other places of confinement, from whence they are carried to the markets of the south and west.

The toleration of slavery and the slave trade at the seat of Government not only produces the most cruel sufferings to those who are legally slaves, but also frequently leads to the enslaving of free people of color, citizens of the United States, some of whom are kidnapped by violence, and others of whom are reduced to hopeless bondage under the forms of law.

From the small number of slaves in the District of Columbia, and the moderate proportion which they bear to the free population there, the difficulties which in most of the slaveholding States, oppose the restoration of this degraded class of men to their natural rights, do not exist in this place. Your petitioners, therefore, pray that Congress will, without delay, enact laws for the abolition of slavery in the District of Columbia, and for preventing the bringing of slaves into that District for the purpose of traffic, in such mode as may be thought advisable, and, whatever measures may be adopted, will also make suitable provision for the education of all free black and colored children in the District, thus to preserve them from continuing even as free men, an unenlightened and degraded caste.

We earnestly entreat all persons who wish slavery in the District to be abolished, to exert themselves in preparing petitions for this object to be presented at the next session of Congress. Even if the measure should then fail, they will have the satisfaction of having done their duty, and having assisted, in some degree, to effect a great moral reform which must sooner or later be accomplished.

Lewis Tappan Speaks of William Lloyd Garrison

ε∾

> *Lewis Tappan (1788–1873), philanthropist, businessman and anti-slavery leader, was the brother of Arthur Tappan and a founder of the American Anti-Slavery Society. On December 5, 1833—the second day of the society's founding convention in Philadelphia—Lewis Tappan rose and made the following remarks, which were reprinted in the* Abolitionist, *December 1833, pp. 181–2.*

Some men, Mr. President, are frightened at a name. There is good evidence to believe that many professed friends of abolition would have been here, had they not been *afraid* that the name of WILLIAM LLOYD GARRISON would be inserted prominently in our proceedings. Sir, I am ashamed of such friends. We ought to place that honored name in the forefront of our ranks. The cause is under obligations to him, which such an evidence of respect will but poorly repay.

The first time I ever heard of him was when he was in jail in Baltimore, where he was incarcerated like a felon, for pleading the cause of the oppressed, and rebuking iniquity. When I saw him, appearing so mild and meek as he does, shortly after he was liberated by a gentleman in New-York, I was astonished. Is this the renegade Garrison? thought I, as I grasped his open hand. Is this the enemy of our country? I shall never forget the impression which his noble countenance made on me at that time, as long as I live.

An anecdote is related of a gentleman—a Colonizationist—which is worth repeating in this Convention. That gentleman had purchased, without knowing who it represented, a portrait of Mr. Garrison, and after having it encased in a splendid gilt frame, suspended it in his parlor. A friend calling in observed it, and asked the purchaser if he knew who he had honored so much? He was answered "No—but it is one of the most godlike looking countenances I ever beheld." "That, sir," resumed the visitor, "is a portrait of the fanatic, the incendiary William Lloyd Garrison!" "Indeed!" concluded the gentleman, evidently much disconcerted. "But, sir, it shall remain in its place. I will never take it down."

Who that is familiar with the history of Mr. Garrison does not remember the determination expressed in the first number of his paper—the *Liberator*—to sustain it *as long as could live on bread and water?* And, sir, I am informed that he has really practised what he so nobly resolved on the beginning.

Look at his course during his recent mission to England. He has been accused of slandering his country. Sir, he has vindicated the American name. He has *not* slandered it. He has told the whole truth, and put hypocrites and dough faces to open shame. He has won the confidence of the people of England. They saw him attached to his country by the dearest ties; but loathing her follies and abhorring her crimes. He has put the Anti-Slavery movement forward a quarter of a century.

A fellow passenger with Mr. Garrison from Europe—a clergyman of much intelligence—on arriving in this country heard that he was called a fanatic and a madman. "What," said he, "do you call such a man a fanatic? Do you deem such a man insane? For six weeks have I been with him, and a more discreet, humble and faithful christian I never saw."

Sir, we should throw the shield of our protection and esteem around Mr. Garrison. His life is exposed at this moment. At the door of this saloon, a young man from the South said to-day that if he had opportunity, he would dip his hands in his heart's blood. And, sir, there must be martyrs in this cause. We ought to feel this moment that we are liable to be sacrificed. But when I say this, I know that we are not belligerants. We would die in such a cause, only as martyrs to the truth. In this, our blessed Saviour has set the example.

I did not contemplate delivering a eulogy on Mr. Garrison, when I rose to speak to this resolution. I wish simply to express my heart-felt sympathy with an injured and persecuted man. Be it the honor-able object of the members of this Convention to show to our country-men that they have misunderstood the character, and misconceived the plans, of William Lloyd Garrison. He is said to be imprudent. What is prudence? Is it succumbing to a majority of our frail fellow mortals? Is it holding back a faithful expression of the whole truth, until the people are ready to say *amen*? Was that the prudence of the Apostle Paul, when he stood before the Roman Governor? Was that the prudence of William Penn, when he poured contempt on the regalia of Kings, by wearing before the king of England his broad beaver? Imprudence is moral timidity. That man is imprudent who is afraid to speak as God commands him to speak, when the hour of danger is near. If this reasoning be correct, Mr. Garrison is one of the most *prudent* men in the nation!

He is not perfect. He is frail, like the rest of human flesh. But if God had not endowed him as He has, and smiled propitiously on his imprudencies, we should not now be engaged in the deliberation of this most interesting and important Convention. God has raised up just such a man as William Lloyd Garrison, to be a pioneer in this cause. Let each member present feel solemnly bound to vindicate the character of Mr. Garrison. Let us not be afraid to go forward with him even into the "imminent breach," although there may be pro-fessed friends who stand back because of him.

I coincide with the views of another gentleman, and hope that the name of Benjamin Lundy will not be forgotten. It is a name dear to every one engaged in this cause.

In a recent conversation which I had with a distinguished civilian of New-York—he informed me that he was a subscriber to Lundy's paper, the *Genius of Universal Emancipation,* and that he had the highest opinion of his talents and devotedness to the cause of the slave. He said that he had been roused by Lundy's appeals, and induced to examine the bearing the Constitution had on Slavery. The result is a conviction that *a slave should not be given up* who has fled from the South to the North, and dared to assert his claim to his own body. He now contends that the Constitution does not recognize slavery: that the framers of that Instrument had in view the final destruction of our greatest national sin. And he argues that the laws which grow out of the construction of the Constitution to uphold slavery, are contrary to the highest of all laws, and the genius of our republican government. Benjamin Lundy, sir, is the man, under God, who has thus affected the heart of that celebrated individual.

Posterity should know, that their fathers held such men as are contemplated in the resolution now before this body, as men to be highly esteemed. Although they are held accursed by those who know them not, and who seek to impeach their motives and to destroy their lives, yet the coming generation shall hallow their memories, and rise up to call them blessed.

Declaration of Sentiments of the American Anti-Slavery Society

ঌ

As has already been mentioned in the introduction, it was Garrison who wrote this statement which was adopted by the American Anti-Slavery Society at its first convention in December 1833, in Philadelphia.

DECLARATION OF SENTIMENTS
OF THE AMERICAN ANTI-SLAVERY CONVENTION
———

The Convention assembled in the city of Philadelphia, to organize a National Anti-Slavery Society, promptly seize the opportunity to promulgate the following Declaration of Sentiments, as cherished by them in relation to the enslavement of one-sixth portion of the American people.

More than fifty-seven years have elapsed, since a band of patriots convened in this place, to devise measures for the deliverance of this country from a foreign yoke. The corner-stone upon which they founded the Temple of Freedom was broadly this—"that all men are created equal; that they are endowed by their Creator with certain inalienable rights; that among these are life, LIBERTY, and the pursuit of happiness." At the sound of their trumpet-call, three millions of people rose up as from the sleep of death, and rushed to the strife of blood; deeming it more glorious to die instantly as freemen, than desirable to live one hour as slaves. They were few in number—poor in resources; but the honest conviction that Truth, Justice and Right were on their side, made them invincible.

We have met together for the achievement of an enterprise, without which that of our fathers is incomplete; and which, for its magnitude, solemnity, and probable results upon the destiny of the world, as far transcends theirs as moral truth does physical force.

In purity of motive, in earnestness of zeal, in decision of purpose, in intrepidity of action, in steadfastness of faith, in sincerity of spirit, we would not be inferior to them.

Their principles led them to wage war against their oppressors, and to spill human blood like water, in order to be free. Ours forbid the doing of evil that good may come, and lead us to reject, and to entreat the oppressed to reject, the use of all carnal weapons for deliverance from bondage; relying solely upon those which are spiritual, and mighty through God to the pulling down of strong holds.

Their measures were physical resistance—the marshalling in arms —the hostile array—the mortal encounter. Ours shall be such only as the opposition of moral purity to moral corruption—the destruction of error by the potency of truth—the overthrow of prejudice by the power of love—and the abolition of slavery by the spirit of repentance.

Their grievances, great as they were, were trifling in comparison with the wrongs and sufferings of those for whom we plead. Our fathers were never slaves—never bought and sold like cattle—never shut out from the light of knowledge and religion—never subjected to the lash of brutal taskmasters.

But those, for whose emancipation we are striving—constituting at the present time at least one-sixth part of our countrymen—are recognized by law, and treated by their fellow-beings, as marketable commodities, as goods and chattels, as brute beasts; are plundered daily of the fruits of their toil without redress; really enjoy no constitutional nor legal protection from licentious and murderous outrages upon their persons; and are ruthlessly torn asunder—the tender babe from the arms of its frantic mother—the heart-broken wife from her weeping husband—at the caprice or pleasure of irresponsible tyrants. For the crime of having a dark complexion, they suffer the pangs of hunger, the infliction of stripes, the ignominy of brutal servitude. They are kept in heathenish darkness by laws expressly enacted to make their instruction a criminal offence.

These are the prominent circumstances in the condition of more than two millions of our people, the proof of which may be found in thousands of indisputable facts, and in the laws of the slaveholding States.

Hence we maintain—that, in view of the civil and religious privileges of this nation, the guilt of its oppression is unequalled by any other on the face of the earth; and, therefore, that it is bound to repent instantly, to undo the heavy burdens, and to let the oppressed go free.

We further maintain—that no man has a right to enslave or imbrute his brother—to hold or acknowledge him, for one moment, as a piece of merchandise—to keep back his hire by fraud—or to brutalize his mind, by denying him the means of intellectual, social and moral improvement.

The right to enjoy liberty is inalienable. To invade it is to usurp the prerogative of Jehovah. Every man has a right to his own body—to the products of his own labor—to the protection of law—and to the common advantages of society. It is piracy to buy or steal a native African, and subject him to servitude. Surely, the sin is as great to enslave an American as an African.

Therefore we believe and affirm—that there is no difference, in principle, between the African slave trade and American slavery;

That every American citizen, who detains a human being in involuntary bondage as his property, is, according to Scripture (Ex. xxi, 16), a man-stealer;

That the slaves ought instantly to be set free, and brought under the protection of law;

That if they had lived from the time of Pharaoh down to the present period, and had been entailed through successive generations, their right to be free could never have been alienated, but their claims would have constantly risen in solemnity;

That all those laws which are now in force, admitting the right of slavery, are therefore, before God, utterly null and void; being an audacious usurpation of the Divine prerogative, a daring infringement on the law of nature, a base overthrow of the very foundations of the social compact, a complete extinction of all the relations, endearments and obligations of mankind, and a presumptuous transgression of all the holy commandments; and that therefore they ought instantly to be abrogated.

We further believe and affirm—that all persons of color, who possess the qualifications which are demanded of others, ought to be admitted forthwith to the enjoyment of the same privileges, and the exercise of the same prerogatives, as others; and that the paths of preferment, of wealth, and of intelligence, should be opened as widely to them as to persons of a white complexion.

We maintain that no compensation should be given to the planters emancipating their slaves;

Because it would be a surrender of the great fundamental principle, that man cannot hold property in man;

Because slavery is a crime, and therefore is not an article to be sold;

Because the holders of slaves are not the just proprietors of what they claim; freeing the slave is not depriving them of property, but restoring it to its rightful owner; it is not wronging the master, but righting the slave—restoring him to himself;

Because immediate and general emancipation would only destroy nominal, not real property; it would not amputate a limb or break a bone of the slaves, but by infusing motives into their breasts, would make them doubly valuable to the masters as free laborers; and

Because, if compensation is to be given at all, it should be given to the outraged and guiltless slaves, and not to those who have plundered and abused them.

We regard as delusive, cruel and dangerous, any scheme of expatriation which pretends to aid, either directly or indirectly, in the emancipation of the slaves, or to be a substitute for the immediate and total abolition of slavery.

We fully and unanimously recognise the sovereignty of each State, to legislate exclusively on the subject of the slavery which is tolerated within its limits; we concede that Congress, under the present national compact, has no right to interfere with any of the slave States, in relation to this momentous subject:

But we maintain that Congress has a right, and is solemnly bound, to suppress the domestic slave trade between the several States, and to abolish slavery in those portions of our territory which the Constitution has placed under its exclusive jurisdiction.

We also maintain that there are, at the present time, the highest obligations resting upon the people of the free States to remove slavery by moral and political action, as prescribed in the Constitution of the United States. They are now living under a pledge of their tremendous physical force, to fasten the galling fetters of tyranny upon the limbs of millions in the Southern States; they are liable to be called at any moment to suppress a general insurrection of the slaves; they authorize the slave owner to vote for three-fifths of his slaves as property, and thus enable him to perpetuate his oppression; they support a standing army at the South for its protection; and they seize the slave, who has escaped into their territories, and send him back to be tortured by an enraged master or a brutal driver. This relation to slavery is criminal, and full of danger: IT MUST BE BROKEN UP.

These are our views and principles—these our designs and measures. With entire confidence in the overruling justice of God, we plant ourselves upon the Declaration of our Independence and the truths of Divine Revelation, as upon the Everlasting Rock.

We shall organize Anti-Slavery Societies, if possible, in every city, town and village in our land.

We shall send forth agents to lift up the voice of remonstrance, of warning, of entreaty, and of rebuke.

We shall circulate, unsparingly and extensively, anti-slavery tracts and periodicals.

We shall enlist the pulpit and the press in the cause of the suffering and the dumb.

We shall aim at a purification of the churches from all participation in the guilt of slavery.

We shall encourage the labor of freemen rather than that of slaves, by giving a preference to their productions; and

We shall spare no exertions nor means to bring the whole nation to speedy repentance.

Our trust for victory is solely in God. We may be personally defeated, but our principles never! Truth, Justice, Reason, Humanity, must and will gloriously triumph. Already a host is coming up to the help of the Lord against the mighty, and the prospect before us is full of encouragement.

Submitting this Declaration to the candid examination of the people of this country, and of the friends of liberty throughout the world, we hereby affix our signatures to it; pledging ourselves that, under the guidance and by the help of Almighty God, we will do all that in us lies, consistently with this Declaration of our principles, to overthrow the most execrable system of slavery that has ever been witnessed upon earth; to deliver our land from its deadliest curse; to wipe out the foulest stain which rests upon our national escutcheon; and to secure to the colored population of the United States, all the rights and privileges which belong to them as men, and as Americans —come what may to our persons, our interests, or our reputation— whether we live to witness the triumph of Liberty, Justice and Humanity, or perish untimely as martyrs in this great, benevolent, and holy cause.

Done at Philadelphia, December 6th, A. D. *1833*

A Negro Writes of Racial Intermarriage

ૄ๛

David Ruggles (1810–1849), the author of the following selection, was an author, editor and bookseller who lived in New York City. He published, over a period of years, The Mirror of Liberty, *a quarterly magazine that advocated the rights of Negroes. In 1834, Dr. David M. Reese, a New York physician, wrote a pamphlet entitled* "A Brief Review of the First Annual Report of the American Anti-Slavery Society," *in which he attacked the Abolitionists and defended white racial superiority. Ruggles replied in a forty-eight page pamphlet, published in New York during the same year, which he entitled,* "The 'Extinguisher' Extinguished! or David M. Reese, M. D. 'Used Up.'"

Abolitionists do not wish "amalgamation." I do not wish it, nor does any colored man or woman of my acquaintance, nor can instances be adduced where a desire was manifested by any colored person; but I deny that "intermarriages" between the "whites and blacks are unnatural," and hazard nothing in giving my opinion that if *"amalgamation"* should become popular Dr. R. would not be the last to vindicate it, practically too if *expedient* . . .

Now "that no white person never did consent to marry a negro without having previously forfeited all character with the respectable and virtuous among the whites," *is not true,* unless it is true that a man's "character" depends upon the color of his skin; if it does, which of the two races would "forfeit all character" by intermarrying, the white or the colored? The whites have robbed us (the blacks) for centuries—they made Africa bleed rivers of blood!—they have torn husbands from their wives—wives from their husbands—parents from their children—children from their parents—brothers from their sisters—sisters from their brothers, and bound them in chains—forced them into holds of vessels—subjected them to the most unmerciful tortures: starved and murdered, and doomed them to endure the horrors of slavery! Still, according to Dr. Reese's logic, the whites have virtuous "characters" and we are *brutes!*

Deem our nation brutes no longer,
Till some reason you can find,
Worthier to regard, and stronger,
Than the color of our kind!
Slaves of gold! whose sordid dealings
Tarnish all your boasted powers,
Prove that *ye* have human feelings,
Ere ye proudly question ours!

. . . What is the reason that a white man cannot marry a female of a different hue without expecting the execration of the majority of the whites? Prejudice is against it; we are human. Why is it argued that our elevation "to an equality" with other "Americans is incongruous and unnatural"? Simply because public opinion is against it. Now we don't wish to alter public opinion respecting intermarriages, but *we do* respecting our "equality" . . . Now we are degraded and ground to the very dust by prejudice. But does it follow from the fact that prejudice *exists,* that "equality in any aspect in this country is neither practicable nor desirable"? If so, it would prove too much. *First,* it would prove that the removal of the prejudice that exists against the religion of Jesus Christ "is neither practicable nor desirable," a parallel case exactly. Why does Dr. Reese preach the gospel? Popular feeling is against it, to a majority (and a majority constitutes the popular opinion)—to a majority it is unwelcome news; and its success upon this principle "is neither practicable nor desirable." But has the Dr. never read of nations who had a prejudice against a white skin? Prejudice is not so much dependent upon a natural antipathy as upon education. What then will become of all the frothy expressions or rather execrations against amalgamation?

"Would you be willing to marry a black wife?" is a question often asked by colonizationists to members of the A. S. Society. Were I a white man, or was the question reversed and put to me, my reply would be—you had better put your question to colonizationists at the south, who have been so long in a process of training. Why insult gentlemen with a silly, "quirkish," nonsensical interrogative, loped off from the fag ends of extremity. Every man that can read and has sense sufficient to put two ideas together without losing one, knows what the abolitionists mean when they speak of elevating us "according to our equal rights." But why is it that it seems to you so "repugnant" to marry your sons and daughters to colored persons? Simply because public opinion is against it. *Nature* teaches no such "repugnance," but experience has taught me that education only does. Do children feel and exercise that prejudice towards colored persons? Do not colored and white children play together promiscuously until the white is taught to despise the colored? How old are children, I mean white children, before this *"natural repugnance"* shows itself?

Just old enough to receive the elements of an inculcated repugnance from five to fifteen years of age. In *by-gone* days in New England, the land of steady habits, where my happiest hours were spent with my play mates, in her schools—in her churches—treading my little pathway over her broad hills, and through her deep valleys. When we waded and swam her beautiful silver streams—when we climbed her tall pines and elms and oaks—when we rambled her fine orchards, and partook of sweet fruits—when we followed our hoops and our balls—when we wended our way from the top of the snowy white hills to the valley. When on the icy pond we did skate—till the school-bell would bid us "retire"! Then—then, her morals were rich—she taught us sweet virtue! Then Connecticut, indeed, was the queen of our land!—then *nature,* never, *never!* taught us such sinful "repugnance"! She was *strong* to the contrary. It took the most powerful efforts of a sophisticated education to weaken her hold:

> "Fleecy locks and black complexion"
> Did not forfeit nature's claim;
> "Skins" did "differ," but affection
> Dwelt "in black and white the same."

How could "nature" excite such a repugnance, and uneducated children know it not? The southern infant, I mean the white infant, "is suckled at slavery's breast, and dandled on black slavery's knee," and if it was here that nature excited a "repugnance" in the whites against the colored child, could they both suck at one breast? Now all this "repugnance" about which such repugnant ideas are entertained, is identified with public opinion. Let it become fashionable (God grant it never may) for white and colored persons to intermarry and the "repugnance" will vanish like dew before the rising sun; and those who were loudest in the cry against "amalgamation" will be first to advocate it both by precept and example. In south America, white and colored persons live together on terms of perfect equality, no "repugnance" exists natural or artificial; and certainly nature is true to herself. If the "repugnance" of N. America is natural, why is it not natural in S. America? The Dr.'s logic on this subject is as false as I believe his heart to be, and just so far as such logic excludes the offices of christian benevolence, it is sinful in the sight of God. . . .

REVEREND AMOS PHELPS

Lectures on Slavery and Its Remedy

&

Reverend Amos Phelps (1804–1847) was pastor of the Pine Street Congregational Church in Boston. The publication of his book was an important contribution to the anti-slavery cause. Oliver Johnson, Garrison's biographer, calls it "of equal power and value with Mrs. Child's Appeal." *Its value was enhanced by the addition of a declaration of anti-slavery sentiment signed by 124 clergymen of Maine, New Hampshire, Vermont, Massachusetts, Rhode Island, Connecticut, New York, New Jersey and Ohio. Phelps was one of the founders of the American Anti-Slavery Society. He was general agent of the Massachusetts Anti-Slavery Society from June 1837 to December 1838. While a close friend of Garrison's for several years, the two quarreled bitterly in 1838 and 1839 over the admission of women to the Massachusetts and American Anti-Slavery societies. "Lectures on Slavery and Its Remedy" was published in 1834, in Boston, by the New England Anti-Slavery Society. The "Address to Clergymen" consists of pages 13–24.*

ADDRESS TO CLERGYMEN

———

To the Ministers of the Gospel of Every Denomination of Christians:

BRETHREN AND FRIENDS:

You will doubtless be ready to ask, why I should dedicate these lectures to you. It is not, I assure you, that I would presume to "rebuke," or set myself up as an instructor of those, who, in knowledge and in years both, are my elders. Far otherwise. I am governed in the matter by other and very different reasons. Permit me to state them. I dedicate these lectures to you then,

1. *Because Slavery in our land is a great and threatening* NA-
TIONAL *evil.* The guilt and the danger involved in it are therefore
in an eminent degree, a common guilt and a common danger; and the
responsibilities and duties growing out of it are, to the same extent,
common responsibilities and common duties imposed on all, but
specially on ministers of the gospel, and others, who, like them, exert
an extensive influence in swaying the public mind and controlling
public sentiment.

2. *I dedicate to you, because this subject has been woefully and
criminally overlooked and forgotten by ministers, who, of all other
men, ought ever to be alive to it.* I appeal to your own consciences.
Who of you prays for the emancipation of the slave, the extinction
of slavery, and the pardon of our *sin* in the matter, as often as *once
in four Sabbaths*? Who of you preaches *one* sermon a year for the
express purpose of arousing the public mind to the *sin* of this thing?
Nay, who of you has taken the pains to *investigate* the subject even?

3. *I dedicate to you because it is specially true in respect to ministers, that every man, who adopts opinions or pursues practices,
which, adopted and pursued by all others, would go to perpetuate this
sin, does* THEREBY *become personally guilty in respect to it.* He
does so, because such opinions and practices are an *abetting* of the
sin; and indifference, silence, affected neutrality, &c., are such practices; and those, therefore, who cherish them do but *abet* the sin and
involve themselves in personal guilt. This is a case in which *silence
gives consent.*

4. *I dedicate these lectures to you, because I think you will be
more likely to read them than you otherwise would.* The extensive
change, which has recently taken place in the minds of ministers in
respect to the sin of present slaveholding and its proper remedy,
justifies the belief, that, if we can only get other ministers to read
and investigate the subject, their opinions will undergo a similar
change.

But the chief reason of this dedication is this: *Ministers are, in an
eminent degree, the* HINGES *of public sentiment in respect to all
prevailing sins.* Once get the public sentiment of the ministry right,
and then inspire them with courage to speak that sentiment out, and
you revolutionize the public sentiment of the community in a trice.

I know that ministers, like other men, are sometimes turned aside from duty by fear, or self-interest, or some other sinister motive; that, too often, they are *covetous of a good living*—looking "to their own way, every one for his gain from his quarter"; or *lazy*—"sleeping, lying down, loving to slumber"; or *cowardly*—mere dumb dogs that dare not bark; and that this is specially apt to be true, when duty calls them to encounter a vitiated public sentiment, which tolerates and gives respectability to some prevalent sin. Still these same ministers are the *hinges* of public sentiment. Let them get right, and then, let them muster the courage to meet that vitiated sentiment, and, with all its blustering, it will soon yield. And this is as true of slavery as of any other sin.

I am aware indeed, that the feeling is very prevalent, among ministers as well as others, that ministers ought to let this subject alone; that it is a political subject; a subject that touches the South in a very delicate and tender point; that the discussion of it in northern pulpits and by northern ministers especially, is fraught with most fearful danger to the South and to the nation; that northern ministers have not been on the ground, do not and cannot know the true state of the case, are therefore most unfit to discuss the matter or devise a remedy; and that, for these and other reasons, our mouths and our pulpits ought to maintain a studied silence—scarcely presuming to "mutter" or "peep" even, lest the Union should fly to atoms, or some more direful calamity befal us.

To such sentiments as these, I, for one, cannot subscribe. So far from it, I feel bound to protest against them, and pronounce them nothing better than those cries of "peace, peace," which are the earnest of "sudden destruction." Pray, brethren and friends, when was there ever a time, in which the pulpit gave signs of awaking from its guilty slumbers, to the discussion of any prevailing sin, that the cry of "hush, hush—it's a delicate subject—you'll make disturbance," &c., was not heard?

The truth is, prevailing sins, sanctioned and made popular as they are by the practice of large classes of the community, are the *strong holds of Satan.* They especially, are *the* means by which he maintains his cruel sway on earth. These demolished, and the strength of his kingdom is demolished. Of course, when one of these strong holds is seriously assailed, it is to be expected, that he, and all who are personally implicated in the matter, as well as all others under their

influence, will be very sensitive on the point, and withal very delicate in their feelings; and ten to one, if they do not make a "fuss"
about this impertinent intermeddling. But what then? Shall the minister of Christ hold his peace? It is his peculiar business, as a minister,
to wield, in every possible way, those spiritual weapons, which,
through God, are mighty to the *pulling down* of strong holds. Shall
he forget his business or be frightened out of it? Rather, let him cry
aloud and spare not, let him lift up his voice like a trumpet, and
show the people their transgression; and if they complain, as did the
Jews of Jeremiah, that "he weakeneth the hands of the men of war,"
and "seeketh not the welfare of the people but the hurt," so be it.
The plea is false, and theirs is the guilt of making it.

This is a world lying in wickedness. The public sentiment of it,
therefore, is in favor of wickedness. Of course, in respect to all prevailing sins that sentiment is utterly wrong. It is a sentiment which
tolerates and sanctions their existence. And now, it is the grand and
special business of the ministry—their *professional* business—to see
to it, that this wrong sentiment is righted. But how can the ministry
ever do this, if they descend from the high ground of gospel truth,
and, falling in with this vitiated sentiment, and reechoing its stale
pleas of "necessity," "expediency," &c., presume to "call evil," in
present circumstances, "good, and good," in present circumstances,
"evil," and thus really take sides *with* the very sentiment they propose
to correct, and *against* themselves? Plainly this is no way to set a
wrong public sentiment right. The high and uncompromising principles of the gospel must be brought to bear on the subject, and the
ministry, instead of waiting for public sentiment to change itself,
on its own principles of expediency, or to be changed by others,
ought to put on the whole "armor of God," and having "no fellowship
with the unfruitful works of darkness," lead the way, in every species
of moral reform. They ought ever to be ahead of public sentiment,
and, instead of strengthening the "hands of evil doers," by their
silence even, stand in the counsel of the Lord, and cause the people
to hear *his* words; then shall they turn them from their evil way,
and from the evil of their doings.[1]

To all this, I doubt not, every minister of Christ will give his hearty
Amen, at least in theory. Let us come to practice then. Let us give

[1] Jeremiah XXIII. 22.

our theories and abstractions some practical, tangible form. And here, brethren, with all due deference to the better judgment of those who may differ from me, allow me to say, that these remarks apply in all their force, to the sin of slavery; and to northern ministers as well as southern. Why not? Indeed, they apply to the former most emphatically. If slavery is ever to be remedied, it is to be done by the omnipotence of a correct public sentiment. And if that sentiment is ever to be gotten up, and its energies made to bear on the subject, the work of getting it up must begin at the North, with northern men, and especially northern ministers. They, of all others, are the men, whose special business it is to lead the way in this thing; not indeed as a political, but as a moral and religious matter. They are bound to go ahead of the public sentiment on this subject as well as others, and let in upon it all the light of the gospel, and all the influence and authority of the pulpit. Let me illustrate . . .

Northern men and northern ministers, then, must awake to this subject. Sooner or later it must be discussed; and, from the very nature of the case, that discussion must and will begin with non-slaveholders. Is there danger in discussion? Will the South get angry? Will the Union fly to atoms? Will the slaves—the poor ignorant slaves, that cannot read and do not know enough to take care of themselves—*"poor brutes—mere animals—that are so comfortable and love their masters so"!!!*—will they get hold of the newspapers, turn politicians, "organize an army of outlaws," [2] and declare a war of independence, &c. &c.? Grant it, absurd as is the plea, grant it. Still, sooner or later, these dangers, or others greater, must be met. The war of argument must come, or in its stead will come the war

[2] Dr. Porter, Andover. The Dr. in giving his views on "several important topics" connected with Slavery, begins by saying, "In all my intercourse with the South, I have rather *avoided* than invited discussion on the subject of slavery, because the *intrinsic difficulties* of the subject are great, and because the interference of northern, or of any foreign influence respecting it, is *attended with peculiar delicacy.*" Indeed! This then is the way that going among slavery qualifies one to judge of it and its remedy! "Avoid" the discussion of a subject because of its "intrinsic difficulties" and "peculiar delicacy," and then, very gravely give one's opinion upon it, as if the whole matter had been sifted to the bottom! A very summary way this, to dispose of difficult matters. Dr. P. is worthy of all respect, but if this is the way he forms his opinions he must not expect that those who think, will place much confidence in them. And, if this is the way one gets qualified to judge of slavery and its remedy by going into the midst of it, I, for one, am in favor of staying at home.

of arms. Is discussion, free, frank, and unrestricted, fraught with danger? Discussion smothered, rely upon it, is fraught with ten-fold danger.

Has it indeed come to this, that, while men have slept, an evil has grown up, in the midst of us, to such rank maturity, and embodied in itself such elements of destruction, that we cannot touch it, even with the power of sober argument, without uncapping a volcano and whelming ourselves in utter ruin? Has it come to this? Then let us know it. It is time we knew it, and governed ourselves accordingly. If this is our real condition, why be ignorant of it? And if it is not, why not awake to timely discussion, and search out thereby a timely remedy? Silence will never mend the matter. The very evil, that threatens us with such ruin, is itself the creature of silence. It sprang up "while men slept"; and while men have slept it has been putting on maturity and strength. Every day's silence hitherto has only been making the matter worse and worse. Shall we then go silently on to certain and not distant destruction, or shall we break the silence and commence discussion now, at the risk of all the evils attendant on it, and with the hope of averting greater evils? Plainly there is no other alternative. One or the other we must do. For, disguise or forget the matter as we may, slavery is one element in our political fabric. It is the element of discord; and already, on more occasions than one, it has shaken the whole fabric and set it a-jar. And it will do so, in time to come, just so long as it exists. There is no avoiding it. Undiscussed and perpetuated, it will originate collisions without end, and work out certain, if not speedy destruction to the Union and the nation. Liberty and slavery are, from their nature, discordant elements. They can never harmonize. They can never, for any length of time, co-exist in the same political fabric. Sooner or later they will fly asunder. "Every kingdom divided against itself is brought to desolation, and every city or house divided against itself shall not stand." And where I ask was there ever a kingdom more palpably divided against itself, than that, which attempts to incorporate in its political fabric, the two discordant elements of freedom and bondage? It is plain, then, that free, unfettered discussions must go on, enlightening the public mind and arousing the public conscience, even if evils do attend it, or we must make up our minds for evils still more dreadful.

For one, however, I anticipate no danger whatever, from discussion. It will indeed create some excitement and call forth some hard speeches, and give occasion to some threatening. But all this will amount to little or nothing. The great source of danger, after all, is silence.

With these remarks, brethren and friends, I affectionately commend these lectures to your attentive perusal. Read them, for my sake, your fellow servant in the ministry of the gospel. Read them, for the sake of Jesus Christ, whose special errand to earth, was among other things, "to preach deliverance to the captives—to set at liberty them that are bruised." Read them for the sake of two millions of your fellow beings, pining in cruel bondage at your very door. Read them; then read something better on the subject; ponder, pray, act, plead the cause of the oppressed, and the blessing of him that is ready to perish shall come upon you.

Yours with great respect and affection,
AMOS A. PHELPS.

An Anti-Slavery Agent

ह∾

Samuel J. May (1797–1871) writes of his experiences as general agent of the Massachusetts Anti-Slavery Society. The following selection is from the Liberator, *April 18, 1835, p. 62.*

REV. MR. MAY

Our devoted brother seems to have entered upon the duties of his office with great zeal and activity, as General Agent of the Massachusetts Anti-Slavery Society. He has gone to labor in Bristol county for a short time. From a letter addressed by him to Mr. B. C. Bacon, dated Fall River, April 13th, we make the following extract:

We reached Fall River at 4—and after divesting myself of some of the dust collected on the way, I called on Rev. Asa Bronson, the Corresponding Secretary of the Anti-Slavery Society, who gave me a hearty welcome, and informed me he had appointed a meeting for me at his Meeting House (the Baptist), to be held Sunday afternoon at five o'clock. I then called upon Rev. Mr. Fowler (Orthodox congregationalist), who expressed an interest in the cause of the oppressed, but seemed to be in doubt as to the expediency of taking a decided stand on their behalf at present.

I took up my abode in the family of Nathaniel Borden, Esq., President of the Anti-Slavery Society, and lately chosen representative of this District to the next Congress.

Yesterday, I preached in the Unitarian Meeting House in the forenoon—and in the afternoon at five o'clock went to the Baptist House, where I found an audience of 900 or more, who listened to me with great attention for an hour and a half. I then appointed a meeting for the ladies, to be held this afternoon at the same place at 2 o'clock. Thus far the prospect here is encouraging. You shall be informed from time to time of whatever may transpire where I am, that will interest you and our fellow-laborers in this righteous cause.

Since the foregoing was in type, we have received the following letter from Mr. May:

FALL RIVER, April 14, 1835.

MY DEAR GARRISON—I sent a hasty letter yesterday to Brother Bacon, which will give you an account of my doings up to Sunday evening. Immediately after closing my letter, I went to Mr. Bronson's office to attend a meeting of the managers of the Anti-Slavery Society. Eight or nine were present—and they all appeared to be faithful men, and true. They were members of four different religious denominations, which is another illustration of the power of our holy cause (like true religion) to unite all hearts in love and good works. I learnt from them that the Society which they conduct, embraces 80 members, about half of whom are females. Their organization, which took place last July, was at first seriously opposed, owing to the excitement of this community caused by the accounts of the outrages in New York. One meeting at which they attempted to organize, was dissolved, because of the riotous behavior of a number, who had gone there to prevent the accomplishment of their purpose. They have not done so much since their formation as they have been disposed to do—not having been able to obtain lecturers—But they now show a determination to avail themselves of all the assistance I can give them. The Board of Managers appointed a committee to collect subscriptions for the Massachusetts Anti-Slavery Society from those who are known to be friendly to it; and agreed with me that it would also be well to take up a contribution at one of the last public meetings I may hold in this place.

Yesterday afternoon at half past 2, I delivered an address in the Baptist Meeting House, designed particularly for the ladies. A heavy rain, which fell about the time of assembling, deterred many who meant to have attended. The whole audience comprised about a hundred, who gave me their undivided attention for more than an hour.

Last evening at half past 7, I met in the same place about 250 people, to whom I spoke as I was able for more than an hour—their attention bearing me witness that I was not spending my strength for nought.

This morning I am to meet by appointment a company of "the Friends" at the house of one of their Society, that I may open my mind to them respecting their duty in reference to the abolition of Slavery. They are timid and inactive.

This afternoon at half past 2, am engaged to deliver an address in the orthodox Congregational Meeting House. And this evening another address in the new Unitarian House. I feel well and in good spirits, but I do not think it will be prudent for me to continue laboring so abundantly in other places as I have done here. Having made an appointment to lecture in Taunton next Wednesday evening, I am restricted to three days in this town, and finding the harvest here so ripe, I have determined to gather in all I can, even though I faint a little in the effort.

Yours affectionately,
S. J. MAY.

William Jay Denies That Abolitionists Are Fanatics

ક≫

William Jay (1789–1858) was a son of John Jay, the first Chief Justice of the United States Supreme Court, and an early Abolitionist. He was a member of the American Anti-Slavery Society and was for many years a member of its executive committee. With the division in Abolitionist ranks in 1840, Jay left the society and helped to form the anti-Garrisonian American and Foreign Anti-Slavery Society. For many years he was a member of its executive committee.

Jay's writings played an important part in awakening the public conscience to the evils of slavery. His volume, An Inquiry into the Character and Tendency of the American Colonization, and American Anti-Slavery Societies, *was first published in 1835, in New York, by the American Anti-Slavery Society, and went through ten editions. The following selection is from Chapter III, pp. 145–149.*

CHAPTER III. FANATICISM OF ABOLITIONISTS

One of the most usual terms by which Abolitionists are designated by their opponents is, "the Fanatics." It seems they are fanatics, because they believe slavery to be sinful. The grounds for this belief, have been already stated. But is the sinfulness of slavery a *new* doctrine; or has it been held only by weak and misguided men? Is Wilberforce to be denounced as a "wretched fanatic" because he declared, "slavery is the full measure of pure unsophisticated wickedness, and scorning all competition or comparison, it stands alone without a rival, in the secure, undisputed possession of its detestable pre-eminence."

Was Jonathan Edwards a poor "misguided" man, for thus addressing slaveholders? "While you hold your negroes in slavery, you do wrong, exceedingly wrong—you do not, as you would men should do to you; you commit sin in the sight of God; you daily violate the plain rights of mankind, and that in a higher degree than if you committed theft or robbery." Were Porteus, Horseley, Fox, Johnson, Burke, Jefferson, and Bolivar, "miserable enthusiasts"? Yet hear their testimonies.

"The Christian religion is opposed to slavery, in its spirit and in its principles; it classes men-stealers among murderers of fathers and of mothers, and the most profane criminals upon earth."—*Porteus.*

"Slavery is injustice, which no consideration of policy can extenuate."—*Horseley.*

"Personal freedom is the right of every human being. It is a right of which he who deprives a fellow creature, was absolutely criminal in so depriving him; and which he who withheld, was no less criminal in withholding."—*Fox.*

"No man is by nature the property of another. The rights of nature must be some way forfeited, before they can be justly taken away."—*Johnson.*

"Slavery is a state so improper, so degrading, and so ruinous to the feelings and capacities of human nature, that it ought not to be suffered to exist."—*Burke.*

"The Almighty has no attribute which can take sides with *us,* in such contest." (A contest with insurgent slaves.)—*Jefferson.*

"Slavery is the infringement of all laws—a law having a tendency to preserve slavery, would be the grossest sacrilege."—*Bolivar.*

We would take the liberty of recommending to the consideration of certain Methodist Colonizationists, the following language of John Wesley:

"Men-buyers, are exactly on a level with men-stealers. Indeed, you say, I pay honestly for my goods, and am not concerned to know how they are come by. Nay, but you are—you are deeply concerned to know that they are honestly come by. Otherwise, you are a partaker with a thief, and are not a jot honester than him. But you know they are not honestly come by; you know they are procured by means nothing so innocent as picking of pockets, or robbery on the highway. Perhaps you will say, I do not buy my negroes, I only use those left me by my father. So far is well, but is it enough to satisfy your conscience? Had your father, have you, has any man living a right to use another as a slave? It cannot be, even setting Revelation aside."

But Abolitionists are fanatics, not merely because they believe slavery sinful, but also because they contend it ought *immediately* to be abolished. In their fanaticism on this point, as well as on the

other, they are kept in countenance by a host of divines and statesmen, and by the unanimous opinion of thousands, and tens of thousands of Christians. Men of all ranks and characters, from John
Wesley to Daniel O'Connell, have exhibited this fanaticism—it has
been borne by the republicans of France, the Catholics of South
America, the people of England, Scotland and Ireland.

So long ago as 1774, John Wesley declared: "It cannot be that
either war or contract can give any man such a property in another,
as he has in his sheep and oxen. Much less is it possible that any
child of man should ever be *born a slave*. If, therefore, you have any
regard to justice (to say nothing of mercy, nor the revealed will of
God), render unto all their due. Give liberty to whom liberty is due,
that is, to every child of man, to every partaker of human nature."

Jonathan Edwards was fanatic enough to assert: "Every man, who
cannot show that his negro hath, by his voluntary conduct, forfeited
his liberty, is obligated *immediately* to manumit him."

One million five hundred thousand persons petitioned the British
Parliament for the total and immediate abolition of slavery. Indeed,
Mr. O'Connell expressed the nearly unanimous sentiment of the
whole nation, when he exclaimed:

"I am for speedy, immediate abolition. I care not what creed or
color slavery may assume, I am for its total, its *instant* abolition."

We have not yet exhausted the proofs of the alleged fanaticism of
Abolitionists. It seems they are fanatics, for wishing to elevate the
blacks to a civil and religious equality with the whites. Certain
Colonization editors deny to Abolitionists, as we have seen, the constitutional right of freedom of speech, the press, and pulpit, and even
of peaceably assembling together; and multitudes seem to think that
they have forfeited the protection of the ninth commandment. Men
of all ranks have united in charging upon them designs which they
indignantly disclaim, and in support of which, not a particle of evidence has been, or can be adduced. One of the designs falsely im-
puted to them, is that of bringing about an amalgamation of colors
by intermarriages. In vain have they again and again denied any
such design; in vain have their writings been searched for any recom-
mendation of such amalgamation. No Abolitionist is known to have
married a negro, or to have given his child to a negro; yet has the
charge of amalgamation been repeated, and repeated, till many have,
no doubt, honestly believed it.

During the very height of the New-York riots, and as if to excite the mob to still greater atrocities, the editor of the *Commercial Advertiser* asserted, that the Abolitionists had "*sought* to degrade" the identity of their fellow citizens, as a "nation of white men, by reducing it to the condition of MONGRELS."—*Com. Adv.* 11th *July,* 1834.

No one, in the possession of his reasoning faculties, can believe it to be the duty of white men to select black wives; and Abolitionists have given every proof the nature of the case will admit, that they countenance no such absurdity.

But most true it is, that the Anti-Slavery Society avows its intention to labor for the civil and religious equality of the blacks. It has been found *expedient* to accuse it of aiming also at their *social* equality. He must be deeply imbued with fanaticism, or rather with insanity, who contends, that *because* a man has a dark skin, he is, *therefore,* entitled to a reception in our families, and a place at our tables.

We all know white men whose characters and habits render them repulsive to us, and whom no consideration would induce us to admit into our social circles; and can it be believed, that Abolitionists are willing to extend to negroes, merely on account of their color, courtesies and indulgences, which, in innumerable instances, they withhold, and properly withhold, from their white fellow citizens? But who pretends that, because a man is so disagreeable in his manners and person that we refuse to associate with him, that *therefore* he ought to be denied the right of suffrage, the privilege of choosing his trade and profession, the opportunities of acquiring knowledge, and the liberty of pursuing his own happiness? Yet such is our conduct towards the free blacks, and it is this conduct which the Society aims at reforming. The Society does contend, that no man ought to be punished for the complexion God has given him. And are not black men *punished* for the color of their skin? Read the laws of the slave States relative to free negroes; alas! read the laws of Ohio, and Connecticut; read the decision of Judge Daggett; behold them deprived of the means of education, and excluded from almost every trade and profession; see them *compelled* to wander in poverty and in ignorance. Now, all this, Abolitionists contend is *wrong,* and their opposition to this system of persecution and oppression is fanaticism! Be it so, but it is only *modern* fanaticism, and it was not so regarded when in 1785, JOHN JAY declared: "I wish to see all unjust and unnecessary discriminations every where abolished, and that the time may soon come, when all our inhabitants, of every COLOR and denomination, shall be free and EQUAL PARTAKERS OF OUR POLITICAL LIBERTY."

It requires no great exercise of candor, to admit, that the prejudices existing against the blacks are sinful, whenever they lead us to treat those unhappy people with injustice and inhumanity. They have their rights as well as ourselves. They have no right to associate with us against our will, but they have a right to acquire property by lawful industry; they have a right to participate in the blessings of education and political liberty. When, therefore, our prejudices lead us to *keep* the blacks in poverty, by restricting their industry,[1] to *keep* them in ignorance, by excluding them from our seminaries, and preventing them from having seminaries of their own; to *keep* them in a state of vassalage by denying them any choice in their rulers; our prejudices are so far sinful, and so far only does the Anti-Slavery Society aim at removing them.

Address of the Boston Female Anti-Slavery Society to the Women of Massachusetts

ह्≈

> *This communication was printed in the* Liberator *on August 13, 1836.*

ADDRESS OF THE BOSTON FEMALE ANTI-SLAVERY SOCIETY TO THE WOMEN OF MASSACHUSETTS:

SISTERS AND FRIENDS:

As *immortal souls,* created by God to know and love him with all our hearts, and our neighbor as ourselves, we owe immediate obedience to his commands, respecting the sinful system of Slavery,

---

[1] As one instance among the innumerable restrictions on the industry of these people, we may mention, that no free black, however moral and intelligent, can obtain a license in the city of New-York to drive a cart!

beneath which, 2,500,000 of our Fellow-Immortals, children of the same country, are crushed, soul and body, in the extremity of degradation and agony.

As *women,* it is incumbent upon us, instantly and always, to labor to increase the knowledge and the love of God, that such concentrated hatred of his character and laws may no longer be so intrenched in *men's* business and bosoms, that they dare not condemn and renounce it.

As *wives* and *mothers,* as *sisters* and *daughters,* we are deeply responsible for the influence we have on the human race. We are bound to exert it; we are bound to urge men to cease to do evil, and learn to do well. We are bound to urge them to regain, defend, and preserve inviolate the rights of all, especially those whom they have most deeply wronged. We are bound to the constant exercise of the only right we ourselves enjoy—the right which our physical weakness renders peculiarly appropriate—the right of petition. We are bound to try how much it can accomplish in the District of Columbia, or we are as verily guilty touching slavery as our brethren and sisters in the slaveholding States: for Congress possesses power "to exercise exclusive legislation over the District of Columbia in all cases whatsoever," by a provision of the Constitution; and by an *act* of the *First* Congress, the right of petition was secured to us.

By a *resolution* of the *Last* Congress, that no petition respecting slavery, shall be printed for the information of the members, and that no vote shall be taken on it, by which we may know whether the men we call our representatives are truly such, the whole nation is made to feel the slaveholder's scourge. The best and noblest of our countrymen, thus seeing, and thus feeling these things, have spoken and acted like freemen—Oh, let us aid them to rouse the slumbering manhood of the rest! Let us rise in the moral power of womanhood; and give utterance to the voice of outraged mercy, and insulted justice, and eternal truth, and mighty love, and holy freedom; in the name and for the sake of our Saviour; and in the mountain-moving faith, that we can do all things, Christ strengthening us.

Let us petition—petition, till, even for our importunity, we cannot be denied. Let us know no rest till we have done our utmost to convince the mind, and to obtain the testimony of every woman, in every town, in every county of our Commonwealth, against the horrible Slave-traffic, which makes the District of Columbia a disgrace to the earth, and exhibits in the centre of a Christian country, an un-rebuked wickedness, for which no other spot on earth affords a parallel.

To facilitate this, we annex a form of petition, and entreat the aid of every woman whose hand it reaches, to circulate it (or a better) rapidly, faithfully and thoroughly, and to transmit the signatures, as soon as possible, to 46, Washington Street, Boston, addressed to the person whose name, as a member of our Executive Committee, shall be affixed to this address.

A detail of the mere physical particulars involved in the arrangements of a single Slave-dealer, would show the abolition of Slavery in the ten miles square, to be "a cause worth dying for": but while our whole country, by deliberately sanctioning such atrocities, stands before God and the world, as the strong hold of Slavery, while the institutions of the free are daily breaking down under the operation of the Slave system; while in the best regulated parts of our country, the lives of the free are endangered by an avowal of the principles of the Declaration of Independence; and freedom itself embittered because honorable and dignifying industry is stigmatized as *slavish*—while these things are, we must devote ourselves to avert the fearful crisis to which these things are leading. Weak and wicked is the idea, that union in oppression is possible. Every nation that attempts it, "God beholds, and drives asunder"; and has done from the foundation of the world.

Christian friends, again we conjure you, by all that woman holds dear and holy, to labor as woman has never yet done, in view of the unutterable destruction which waits visibly round about, to make our land a perpetual desolation, unless the people repent.

Leave no energy unemployed, no righteous means untried. Grudge no expense—yield to no opposition—forget fatigue—till, by the strength of prayer and sacrifice, the spirit of love shall have overcome sectional jealousy, political rivalry, prejudice against color, cowardly concession of principle, wicked compromise with sin, devotion to gain, and spiritual despotism, which now bear with a mountain's weight upon the Slave. Let but each *woman* in the land do a Christian womans' duty, and the result cannot fail to be his instant, peaceful, unconditional deliverance . . . Thus, and thus only can we hope to deliver our own souls. Only in thus doing, can we hope to hear the voice of Jesus, saying unto us, "Come, ye blessed of my Father!—

Inasmuch as ye have done it unto the least of these my brethren, ye have done it unto me"!

By Order of the Boston Female Anti-Slavery Society,

M. W. CHAPMAN)
M. AMMIDON)   *Cor. Secretaries.*

July 13, 1836.

PETITION

TO THE HONORABLE SENATE AND HOUSE OF REPRESENTATIVES, IN CONGRESS ASSEMBLED:

The undersigned, women of —— deeply convinced of the sinfulness of Slavery, and keenly aggrieved by its existence in a part of our country over which Congress possesses exclusive jurisdiction in all cases whatsoever, do most earnestly petition your honorable body, immediately to abolish Slavery in the District of Columbia, and to declare every human being free, who sets foot upon its soil.

We also respectfully announce our intention, to present the same petition, yearly, before your honorable body, that it may at least be a "memorial of us," that in the holy cause of Human Freedom, "We have done what we could."

An Abolitionist Condemns the Attempt to Seize Texas from Mexico

ε⋟

> *As mentioned in the Introduction, David L. Child (1794–1874) was an early Garrisonian and anti-slavery leader. The following letter appeared in the* Liberator *on August 13, 1836. Child later wrote a pamphlet entitled "The Taking of Naboth's Vineyard; or, History of the Texas Conspiracy, and an examination of the Reasons Given by the Hon. J. C. Calhoun,*

Hon. R. J. Walker, and Others, for the Dismemberment and Robbery of the Republic of Mexico," *which was published in New York, in 1845.*

LETTER FROM MR. CHILD

WEST BOYLSTON, Aug. 8th, 1836.

DEAR GARRISON:

I see by the last newspaper, which has reached me, that our President, assuming at last the power of the *sword* as he did several years back, that of the purse, has actually commenced a war with a neighboring and friendly people. It seems that Gen. Gaines, having obtained a reinforcement, consisting of *volunteers* from each of the States of Mississippi, Louisiana, Kentucky, and Tennessee, has invaded Mexico, upon the pretext of the killing by Indians of some white person or persons in a distant and *interior* part of that country. It is suggested, that he may have taken this unlawful step under old orders received from the President last winter, the same I suppose alluded to in Mr. Adams' eloquent speech at the late session of Congress. It is of no importance whether the orders are old or new. Judging from the circumstances of the case, and from the habits of the President, I have no doubt that he is the author of the measure. Gen. Gaines is too prudent and politic to expose himself, by undertaking, on his own responsibility, so dangerous an enterprise. It would, if the laws were duly executed, cost him his commission, and subject him to fine and imprisonment.

And what authority has the President to commence this war? Not a jot more than Gen. Gaines. His power, in respect to making war upon a foreign nation, is restricted by the Constitution to the *repelling of invasions;* and he cannot, without a violation of the Constitution, and his oath, march a man beyond the limits of the Union. If it be true, as there appears no reason to doubt, that he has done this, he ought by law to be impeached, and expelled from office, and then punished by fine and imprisonment, or given up to the injured nation to be punished by them for any *murder or robbery,* which the troops may commit in pursuing his orders. He has no more right to enter Mexico, seize property, and slay inhabitants, whether Indians or others, than any citizen of the United States has to go into Great Britain and do it. Such acts will be robbery, piracy, or murder, and ought to be punished accordingly.

The power of declaring war is vested exclusively in the Congress of the United States; and there cannot be a lawful war, and one which shall confer upon those taking part in it, *the rights of war,* without such declaration. Supposing Com. Porter, when he entered the town of Foxardo, in the Island of Porto Rico—or Aaron Burr, when he entered Texas, thirty years ago, had been taken with their officers and men; would they not have been put to death agreeably to the law of nations? So would Gen. Jackson and his men, when, in two instances, they deliberately marched into Florida, and seized the towns and possessions of Spain. If the Constitution had been supported, and the laws of the land faithfully executed, on either of those occasions, we should not now have had a President who would have ventured to issue an order to invade a friendly country and begin a war; nor a general who would dare to obey it, nor a subordinate officer, who would not throw up his commission, nor a soldier who would not throw down his arms at the frontier, and refuse, as they might lawfully and dutifully do, to be the instruments of usurpation, and the perpetrators of crime. This I acknowledge is too much to expect of common soldiers, when such corruption and subserviency prevail among their superiors; but it was not too much to expect, that in the army of our republic, there would be *some* officers who would have had intelligence, firmness, and patriotism enough to have acted this noble and useful part. But they have all gone over like sheep, but without their innocence, after the bell-wether. They have committed a great crime against the Constitution, against liberty, and our country. I cannot but hope, for the sake of the future peace of this continent, that they will meet in Mexico the fate which they deserve. If *successful* in doing wrong, there is no hope of their meeting with just punishment here. This nation has grown too familiar with unlawful violence and unpunished usurpa-tions to think of bringing any man to a reckoning for new ones, whatever consequences they may involve. There needs to be cited no other proof that the moral sense of this nation is dead, than that knell which the voice of a Northern Senator lately sounded in our ears, by proposing an appropriation of half a million for slaughtering the persecuted and helpless children of the forest, and replying to a demand of the *cause of the war,* that really he did not know what was the cause of the war—but he knew that war existed and must be prosecuted! It was a good commentary on this detestable text, that the cause finally turned out to be an order from the President to *kidnap* Indian babes and make slaves of them! If the principle be approved, that an existing war is to be carried on *Because* it exists, without inquiry into the justice of it, or the original act of aggression; what a felonious and bloody career are we about to run! My friend, did not that annunciation shock you? I cannot think of it now without shuddering. It appears, however, to have met the approbation of both Houses of Congress. The money was voted, and as I believe, without opposition.

And is this nation, "exalted to Heaven" in point of privileges, to be dragged "down to hell," by corrupt rulers and selfish politicians? Is the old course of brutal rapine, lust, and havoc, to be the result of all our boasted intelligence, republicanism, and Christianity? Yes, it is just what might be expected from Christianity and intelligence, *boasted* of. Writers who assiduously watch the popular vane, boldly announce, that thus the wind sets, and that this is our *destiny*. If I were to undertake to *vaticinate,* I should say that it was the destiny of such audacious pimps to the public vices, to commit highway robbery and be hanged for it.

And where are the remonstrances of the press, and the meetings of the people? Where are the friends of universal peace, and above all, where is the Christian priesthood? And you merchants, ship-owners, and underwriters, where are you? Know you not that this presidential measure is fatally opposed to the purest devotion to self-interest that ever chilled a halfpenny heart? Awake, arise; it is not a breach of the Constitution. There is a breach in the strong-box.

It is of no use to remonstrate. Tears of blood would not turn a single office-seeker or office-holder, or land speculator, or politician. Our course is to tumble "onward." Providence will probably leave us to the natural consequences of our own misconduct. It cannot inflict a severer punishment. For a war with *Great Britain,* and, if necessary, for the protection of the Mexican territory and Gulf, with *France,* also, will, in my opinion, inevitably result from the recent invasion, if is be not promptly abandoned, disavowed, and the authors and agents properly punished. Mr. Adams, in his admirable and timely warning, has said all that need be said on the subject.

Woe, unto thee, Columbia, "It shall be more tolerable for Sodom in the Day of Judgment than for thee."

If any circumstance could enhance the intrinsic wickedness of the Executive proceedings, it is the end and object at which they are aiming. It is to PROPAGATE SLAVERY, or in other words, *perpetual robbery, rapine, and murder throughout a vast and beautiful region, now, by the laws of Mexico, perfectly free. It is to open a new and interminable slave-market to the old slave-breeding sinners of Maryland, Virginia, North and South Carolina, and other old slave States, and to flesh mongers every where. It is to bring into this Union, for the benefit of NULLIFIERS, FIVE TO TEN new slave States, each with a Constitution, not only establishing slavery, but also forbidding their own legislatures ever to abolish it.* This is a provision of the new Constitution of Texas, formed since the struggle for *liberty* commenced! The old or Mexican Constitution of Texas abolished slavery forever!

And the free States are willing to pay three fourths of the taxes (as they ever must so long as they are raised on *consumption*) to support a war for these objects; for, remember if war *exists,* "appropriations *must* be made to carry it on." But I have done.

Unpromising as the prospect is of effecting any good, I feel impelled to contribute all in my power to open the eyes of our countrymen to the true origin and outrageous intent of this invasion. For this purpose I request you to publish the enclosed copy of a letter, written, as you will perceive, almost a year ago. The person addressed, was a distinguished officer in the Mexican army.

———

NEW ROCHELLE, Sept. 15th, 1835.

SIR—You will receive herewith two letters from ——, now residing in Philadelphia. I should have had the pleasure of delivering them personally, but not knowing your lodgings, and having little time to devote to a search, I was obliged to forego that gratification. I however hope to see you next week when I shall again be in New York.

I have long taken a deep interest in the relations of our countries, and have made to the Minister of Foreign Affairs of Mexico, through a countryman residing there, and to friends in England, communications touching the design which some of my slaveholding and insatiable countrymen cherish of wresting from her the noble and beautiful province of Texas, an event most deeply to be deprecated, whether we regard the peace and welfare of two contiguous and friendly nations, or the cause of universal liberty. I will not now expatiate upon general topics. I trust the time will come when I can converse with you at large upon the interesting points in which this question more than any existing one abounds. My object is to impart some particular facts which have come to my knowledge during a recent visit to Philadelphia.

The Hon. Hutchins G. Burton, formerly a representative in Congress from the State of North Carolina, and more recently Governor of that State, has made a purchase of 40,000 acres in Texas. Week before last he was in Philadelphia, and declared to a near relative (to whom he proposed to give 4,000 acres, and a dozen slaves if he would remove thither) that the reason of his making said purchase, was that Texas was soon to be annexed to the United States, that President Jackson had declared to him at the city of Washington on the occasion of his calling upon him in his journey to Philadelphia, that "we *must have it,* that if 10,000 men would not do 100,000 should, and that it was his intention to make Burton the first Governor of the new territory." My informant likewise stated that Jackson had made a similar declaration to other persons, whose names I have, belonging to Virginia and North Carolina, at two several times.

I am aware, as doubtless you are, that the seizure of a portion of your country by the Executive Authority of mine, would be a gross and palpable violation of our constitution; but when I consider that a person is invested with that authority, who has never hesitated to trample on the constitution and laws, whenever they stood in the way of any favorite object, I am constrained to say that your Government and nation may place no confidence in any protection, which our own institutions may seem to promise to their rights and interests.

There is an impatient and almost irrepressible desire in the inhabitants of the South and Southwest to lay hold on Texas. Emigrants have pushed in under your mild and hospitable laws, with a view to facilitate a conquest, or negotiation (nearly the same thing) and to be enemies in the midst of you. If President Jackson should say the word, 20,000 volunteers from the slave States would be mustered on the frontiers of Texas in six weeks. The terror which the discussion of the subject of slavery, now existing to so great an extent in our country, inspires throughout the slave States, tends to inflame the desire of the South to seize *your lands.* After witnessing the utter disregard, which they have manifested for the laws of their own country and the lives of their countrymen, can you suppose that in pursuit of the same objects and flying from the same supposed dangers, they will pay any respect to the laws of nations, or show more tenderness for the lives of *your* countrymen? Be assured they will not. They want Texas for a market of slaves, and for cheap portions for their sons and daughters; and rely upon it, Sir, that as soon as they can venture upon a violent aggression, they will attempt it. I regret to believe this, but long observation and considerable attention to the history of our Union have convinced me that it is true, and my love of Justice and Liberty impel me to say it.

Make any use you please of this letter, if by so doing you can further the objects, which we have in common—the preservation of the integrity of the Mexican Republic, and the prevention of the introduction by "the sons of liberty" of slavery into a country now free, free so far as laws can make it so. I have the Honor to be

Very respectfully your ob't serv't.
D. L. CHILD.

The Abolitionists Encourage Anti-Slavery Efforts Among Children

ટ≫

The following letters from Henry C. Wright to Garrison and the "Petitions for Minors" indicate the interest shown by Abolitionists in sponsoring anti-slavery efforts by children. Henry Wright (1797–1870) is described by Louis Filler, the historian, as "the radical of radicals: a creator of radicalisms and the originator of many of Garrison's formulas." He was hatmaker turned minister who was ordained in 1823. Although a native of Sharon, Connecticut, he lived in West Newbury, Massachusetts, until 1833. He joined the New England Anti-Slavery Society in May 1835, and met Garrison for the first time in November of the same year.

Wright's letter was printed in the Liberator *on February 25, 1837, while "Petitions for Minors" appeared in the* Liberator *on July 14, 1837.*

BEGIN WITH THE CHILDREN

DEAR GARRISON,

It has long been a settled truth with me, that if we would regenerate and save this world, we must direct our efforts to children. We must bring God's truth to bear on mind in its infancy and childhood, before it becomes moulded and fashioned to sin. Would you overthrow Intemperance, War or Slavery? Begin with children and train their minds to habits of just feeling and acting, and you may hope for great success. But, once let the mind become inbued with the *martial spirit*—which is the same as the spirit of slaveholding, a spirit which leads man to domineer over his brother, to crush him and despoil him—and according to the counsel of God, that mind will not depart from this diabolical spirit. For, if a child will not depart from it when you train him up in the way he *should* go, he, of course, will not depart from it, if you train him up in the way he should *not* go. The following is the substance of an *Anti-Slavery Lecture,* delivered to an assembly of Children, with their parents, in this city, a few days since:

"Children, when God made man, how much lower than the angels did he make him?" "A little lower." *"Over what did God give man dominion?"* "Over the beasts of the field, the fowls of the air, and the fish of the sea." *"What is meant by having dominion over any thing?"* "To own it, and to do with it as you please." *"What did God give us a right to use as we please?"* 'All the beasts and creeping things, and all the earth." *"Where did God put all these things—the beasts, birds, fish, and all inanimate things?"* "Under the feet of man." *"What does that mean?"* "That they are to be entirely subject to our will." *"Why do not dumb beasts resist when man attempts to subject them to his will?"* "Because God made them to be subject to man."

"To whom did God give the right to exercise dominion over man? To Angels?" "No, sir." *"Why not? The Angels are superior to men."* "Because the Angels would not know how to govern us, and we should not like to be governed by them." *"The Angels know more than we do. Why should they not rule over us?"* "God would not let

them have dominion over us, because he knew they would be liable to hurt us, and bring us into trouble." *"Don't you think the Angels would like to have dominion over us, if God would let them?"* "No sir—because *they are too good,"* said a little girl. *"Did God give the beasts a right to rule over us?"* "No, sir, he gave us dominion over them." *"If God would not give the Angels dominion over us, did he give us dominion over each other?"* "No, sir; God never gave man a right to rule over man." *"Who then has dominion over man?"* "God." *"Whom ought we to obey?"* "God." *"To whose will ought we to be entirely subject?"* "To God's will." *"Suppose some* man *tries to set up his own authority over you, and to make you subject to his will—what ought you to do?"* "We ought to tell him that God is our ruler, and that no man has a right to exercise dominion over us." *"If you won't obey God, and be subject to his authority, what will God do with you?"* "He will punish us all in hell forever." *"Whose will ought you to wish to have done in this world?"* "God's will. We should pray to God, 'Thy kingdom come, thy will be done on earth as it is in heaven.' " *"What are those called who are brought under the dominion of their fellow men?"* "Slaves." *"Should not slaves pray that their master's will may be done?"* "No, sir." *"Ought you to pray that the President's or Governor's will might be done on earth?"* "No, sir—never." *"Some wicked people pray that* General Jackson's *will might be done. Some pray that the will of the* people *might be done. Whose will did you say you ought to pray might be done?"* "God's will—and no body's else." *"Do you suppose any* christian *would ever wish to have dominion over a fellow being?"* "No, sir—because if he is a christian, he will want everybody to be in subjection to God, and not to himself." *"True, dear children; God never gave to one man dominion over another. He never made us to be subject to the will of any man. But God made us all to obey him, and be in subjection to him, and to no one else. We must yield our- selves entirely up to God, to let him do with us as he pleases. When men attempt to get dominion over us, as slaveholders do, and as* wicked *rulers do, they impiously invade the rights of God, and try to put God out of the way so that he shall not rule over us. What then is slavery?"* "It is when one man usurps dominion over another." *"Who are slaveholders?"* "All those wicked people who desire to have dominion over man, and make him subject to *their* will instead of *God's* will."

Such, dear brother, is in substance, a part of a lecture to more than hundred children in New York. They all seemed to feel that God, and God *alone, has a right of dominion over man.* I believe this is God's eternal truth. God reserved to himself the sole and exclusive right of dominion over man. He has never given up this right to any other being. God is the Ruler. To his sceptre we should bow, and to none other. But, dear Garrison, what a scene this earth presents! One continued, bloody struggle of man to gain dominion over his brother—to hurl God from the throne, and trample his brother beneath his feet! God gave to man dominion, *absolute* dominion, over all inferior creation. It would seem that this would satisfy the largest ambition. But no. Man is not content with that. He would ride over his brother, and trample him beneath his feet. Every man, who *desires* to obtain dominion over man, has the slaveholding spirit, and he would become a slave-holder in *fact,* if he had the power. All *human* governments that ever *did* or *do* exist, are, in the main, only efforts of man to acquire dominion over man. The very spirit of slaveholding pervades every government on the globe. Our government, though it embody some of the truest and noblest sentiments of divine liberty, is yet a *slaveholding* government.

Sir, the time must come when man must take his hand off from his brother—his feet from his neck. Man must give up his usurped dominion over man; and the empire of God over man be fully and eternally established and recognized. *"Thy Kingdom come."* God's kingdom will come, and man's dominion eternally cease. Every yoke, imposed by man on his brother, must be broken; and God's kingdom come, and God's throne be established in every heart. God speed the day. Then shall War and Slavery retire to that bottomless pit whence they came, and all shall shout—*"The Lord reigns; let the earth rejoice."*

H. C. WRIGHT,
Children's A. S. Agent

NEW YORK, Jan. 24, 1837.

———

PETITIONS FOR MINORS

The Boston Juvenile Anti-Slavery Society has procured to be printed a large number of the following forms of petitions for minors. Members of that society are now engaged in circulating them for signatures in this city, and we hope that measures will be taken to circulate them in every town in the State. Abolitionists should aid and encourage their children in this good work. The petitions are designed for both boys and girls. Copies can be had at the Anti-Slavery Office, 25 Cornhill.

I.

To the Senate and House of Representatives of the United States.

The undersigned, minors, of ———— in the State of ———— respectfully pray your honorable body immediately to abolish slavery and the slave trade in the District of Columbia, and in all other territories where you have power to exercise "exclusive legislation."

II.

To the Senate and House of Representatives of the United States.

The undersigned, minors, of ———— in the State of ———— respectfully pray your honorable body so to "regulate commerce among the several States," as to stop all trade in men, women and children.

Gerrit Smith Defends the Right of Abolitionists to Discuss Slavery

ào

> On October 21, 1835, about 600 delegates met in Utica, New York, to form a state anti-slavery society. The meeting was attacked by a mob and a riot ensued. Gerrit Smith (1797–1874), who was present at the meeting but who until then had been a member of the American Colonization Society and had refused to joint the American Anti-Slavery Society despite his opposition to slavery, invited the members of the convention to move to Peterboro, his place of residence about thirty miles away, and there to continue their meeting. A large number

accepted his invitation and assembled the next day in the Presbyterian church of Peterboro. There Smith delivered the address, part of which is reprinted here. The text is from Samuel J. May's Some Recollections of the Anti-Slavery Conflict, *Boston, 1869, pp. 400–403.*

Speech of Gerrit Smith

On returning home from Utica last night, my mind was so much excited with the horrid scenes of the day, and the frightful encroachments made on the right of free discussion, that I could not sleep, and at three o'clock I left my bed and drafted this resolution:

> *Resolved,* That the right of free discussion, given to us by God, and asserted and guarded by the laws of our country, is a right so vital to man's freedom and dignity and usefulness, that we can never be guilty of its surrender, without consenting to exchange that freedom for slavery, and that dignity and usefulness for debasement and worthlessness.

I love our free and happy government, but not because it confers any new rights upon us. Our rights spring from a nobler source than human constitutions and governments—from the favor of Almighty God.

We are not indebted to the Constitution of the United States, or of this State, for the right of free discussion. We are thankful that they have hedged it about with so noble a defence. We are thankful, I say, that they have neither restrained nor abridged it; but we owe them no thanks for our possession of rights which God gave us. And the proof that he gave them is in the fact that he requires us to exercise them.

When, then, this right of free discussion is invaded, this home-bred right, which is yours, and is mine, and belongs to every member of the human family, it is an invasion of something which was not obtained by human concession, something as old as our own being, a part of the original man, a component portion of our own identity, something which we cannot be deprived of without dismemberment, something which we never can deprive ourselves of without ceasing to be MEN.

This right, so sacred and essential, is now sought to be trammelled, and is in fact virtually denied . . . Men in denying this right are not only guilty of violating the Constitution, and destroying the blessings bought by the blood and toil of our fathers, but guilty of making war with God himself. I want to see this right placed on this true, this infinitely high ground, as a DIVINE right. I want to see men defend it and exercise it with that belief. I want to see men determined to maintain, to their extremest boundaries, all the rights which God has given them for their enjoyment, their dignity, and their usefulness.

We are even now threatened with legislative restrictions on this right. Let us tell our legislators, in advance, that we cannot bear any. The man who attempts to interpose such restrictions does a grievous wrong to God and man, which we cannot bear. Submit to this, and we are no longer what God made us to be,—MEN. Laws to gag men's mouths, to seal up their lips, to freeze up the warm gushings of the heart, are laws which the free spirit cannot brook; they are laws contrary alike to the nature of man and the commands of God; laws destructive of human happiness and the divine constitution; and before God and man they are null and void. They defeat the very purposes for which God made man, and throw him mindless, helpless, and worthless at the feet of the oppressor.

And for what purpose are we called to throw down our pens, and seal up our lips, and sacrifice our influence over our fellow-men by the use of free discussion? If it were for an object of benevolence that we are called to renounce that freedom of speech with which God made us, there would be some color of fitness in the demand; but such a sacrifice the cause of truth and mercy never calls us to make. That cause requires the exertion, not the suppression, of our noblest powers. But here we are called on to degrade and unman ourselves, and to withhold from our fellow-men that influence which we ought to exercise for their good. And for what? I will tell you for what. That the oppressed may lie more passive at the feet of the oppressor; that one sixth of our American people may never know their rights; that two and a half millions of our countrymen, crushed in the cruel folds of slavery, may remain in all their misery and despair, without pity and without hope.

For such a purpose, so wicked, so inexpressibly mean, the Southern slaveholder calls on us to lie down like whipped and trembling spaniels at this feet. Our reply is this: Our republican spirits cannot submit to such conditions. God did not make us, Jesus did not redeem us, for such vile and sinful uses.

I knew before that slavery would not survive free discussion. But the demands recently put forth by the South for our surrender of the right of discussion, and the avowed reasons of that demand, involve a full concession of this fact, that free discussion is incompatible with slavery. The South, by her own showing, admits that slavery cannot live unless the North is tongue-tied. Now you, and I, and all these Abolitionists, have two objections to this: One is, we desire and purpose to employ all our influence lawfully and kindly and temperately to deliver our Southern brethren from bondage, and never to give rest to our lips or our pens till it is accomplished. The other objection is that we are not willing to be slaves ourselves. The enormous and insolent demands put forth by the South show us that the question is now, not only whether the blacks shall continue to be slaves, but whether our necks shall come under the yoke. While we are trying to break it off from others, we are called to see to it that it is not fastened on our own necks also.

It is said: "The South will not molest our liberty if we will not molest their slavery; they do not wish to restrict us if we will cease to speak of their peculiar institution." Our liberty is not our *ex gratia* privilege, conceded to us by the South, and which we are to have more or less, as they please to allow. No, sir! The liberty which the South proffers us, to speak and write and print, if we do not touch that subject, is a liberty we do not ask, a liberty which we do not accept, but which we scornfully reject.

It is not to be disguised, sir, that war has broken out between the South and the North, not easily to be terminated. Political and commercial men, for their own purposes, are industriously striving to restore peace; but the peace which they may accomplish will be superficial and hollow. True and permanent peace can only be restored by removing the cause of the war—that is, *slavery*. It can never be established on any other terms. The sword now drawn will not be sheathed until that deep and damning stain is washed out from our nation. It is idle, criminal, to speak of peace on any other terms.

Whom shall we muster on our side in this great battle between liberty and slavery? The many never will muster in such a cause, until they first see unequivocal signs of its triumph. We don't want the many, but the truehearted, who are not skilled in the weapons of carnal warfare. We don't want the politicians, who, to secure the votes of the South, care not if slavery is perpetual. We don't want the merchant, who, to secure the custom of the South, is willing to applaud slavery, and leave his countrymen, and their children, and their children's children to the tender mercies of slavery forever.

We want only one class of men for this warfare. Be that class ever so small, we want only those who will stand on the rock of Christian principle. We want men who can defend the right of free discussion on the ground that God gave it. We want men who will act with unyielding honesty and firmness. We have room for all such, but no room for the time-serving and selfish.

Francis Jackson Defends Freedom of Speech

ह✦

> *On October 21, 1835, a Boston mob forced the adjournment of the annual meeting of the Boston Female Anti-Slavery Society and almost hanged Garrison. Francis Jackson (1789– 1861), who had been active in municipal affairs in Boston, thereupon invited the society to hold its next meeting at his home. The meeting was held there on November 19. As Oliver Johnson writes in his biography of Garrison, "those present were not sure that the house would not be sacked or burned." There were no untoward incidents, however. The Massachusetts Anti-Slavery Society then asked Samuel J. May, its corresponding secretary, to express its thanks to Jackson for the use of his home. Jackson's reply is a beautifully worded defense of freedom of speech. For years there-*

after he served as president of the Massachusetts Anti-Slavery Society.

The following letters, by May and Jackson, were printed in a volume entitled Right and Wrong in Boston. Report of the Boston Female Anti-Slavery Society; with a Concise Statement of Events, Previous and Subsequent to the Annual Meeting of 1835. *Published by the Society, Boston, 1836, pp. 96–99.*

BOSTON, Nov. 21, 1835.

FRANCIS JACKSON, ESQ.

DEAR SIR—Yesterday, at a meeting of the Board of Managers of the Massachusetts Anti-Slavery Society, I was directed by a unanimous vote, to express to you the high sense, which the Board entertains of your generosity and noble independence, in proffering as you did, unsolicited, the use and protection of your dwelling house, to the Boston Female Anti-Slavery Society, when they had just been expelled by lawless violence from a public hall. The duty thus assigned me, sir, it is far more delightful to undertake, than it will be easy for me to perform in a suitable manner. If any thing should awaken our gratitude and high admiration, it is the conduct of a man, who steps forth and takes a decided stand in resistance to the multitude, when they are rioting in the way of evil countenanced and encouraged by the rich and influential, faintly resisted by the rulers of the people, and scarcely reproved, even by the guardians of the public morals. Such a man, like a rock fallen into a rapid stream, may turn the whole current of popular thought and feeling—preserve the ancient landmarks, and avert devastation and ruin.

The outrages recently committed in various places, but especially in this city, will be an epoch, not merely in the history of the anti-slavery cause, but of our country. They have revealed, so that the blind may see, the alarming state of our guilty land. If this disclosure does not arouse the people to re-assert and vindicate their rights, then are they already *slaves in spirit*—and are fitted to become themselves the abject subjects of some despot, who will ere long rise and make his will their law. The citizens of Boston have presumed to do, what the Constitution of the United States peremptorily forbids even Congress to attempt. *They have "abridged the freedom of speech." They have trampled upon "the right of the people peaceably to assemble."*

The apathy of our city government, and the tone of our newspapers (with two or three honorable exceptions) are indeed ominous of evil; But I cannot yet despair of Boston, or our country. Other minds I know were affected as your's was, by the late exhibition of the spirit of anarchy in our midst; and I trust many more, whom I do not know, have been likewise moved. I will not believe that there are not yet many left, in this birth-place of the American revolution, who understand on what is based the security of our civil and religious privileges, and who duly appreciate the importance of maintaining principle and law, and justice and order.

I doubt not, sir, that your noble example will quicken others to manifest openly their attachment to what is dearer to *true freemen,* than houses and lands, and all earthly riches and honors.

I am, sir, with gratitude
and sincere respect, yours,
SAMUEL J. MAY,
Cor. Sec. Mass. Anti-Slavery Society

BOSTON, Nov. 25, 1835.

DEAR SIR—I have the honor to acknowledge the receipt of your highly esteemed letter of the 21st inst., written in behalf of the managers of the Massachusetts Anti-Slavery Society; and expressing in very flattering terms, their approbation of my conduct in granting to the ladies of the Anti-Slavery Society, the use of my dwelling house, for their annual meeting.

That meeting was, to all present, a most interesting and impressive one. It will ever be treasured by me, among the highly pleasing recollections of my life, that it was my good fortune to extend to those respectable ladies the protection of my roof, after they had been reviled, insulted, and driven from their own hall by a mob.

But in tendering them the use of my dwelling house, sir, I not only had in view their accommodation, but also, according to my humble measure, to recover and perpetuate the right of free discussion, which has been shamefully trampled on. A great principle has been assailed; one which lies at the very foundation of our republican institutions.

If a large majority of this community choose to turn a deaf ear to the wrongs, which are inflicted upon their countrymen in other portions of the land—if they are content to turn away from the sight of oppression, and "pass by on the other side"—so it must be.

But when they undertake in any way to impair or annul my right to speak, write, and publish upon any subject, and more especially upon enormities, which are the common concern of every lover of his country and his kind—so it must not be—so it shall not be, if I for one can prevent it. Upon this great right let us hold on at all hazards. And should we, in its exercise, be driven from public halls to private dwellings, one house at least shall be consecrated to its preservation. And if, in defence of this sacred privilege, which man did not give me, and shall not (if I can help it) take from me, this roof and these walls shall be leveled to the earth. Let them fall if they must; they cannot crumble in a better cause. They will appear of very little value to me, after their owner shall have been whipt into silence.

Mobs and gag laws, and the other contrivances by which fraud or force would stifle enquiry, will not long work well in this community. They betray the essential rottenness of the cause, they are meant to strengthen. These outrages are doing their work with the reflecting.

Happily, one point seems already to be gaining universal assent, that slavery cannot long survive free discussion. Hence the efforts of the friends and apologists of slavery to break down this right. And hence the immense stake, which the enemies of slavery hold, in behalf of freedom and mankind, in its preservation. The contest is therefore substantially between liberty and slavery.

As slavery cannot exist with free discussion—so neither can liberty breathe without it. Losing this, we, too, shall not be freemen indeed, but little, if at all, superior to the millions we now seek to emancipate.

With the highest respect,
Your friend,
FRANCIS JACKSON

REV. S. J. MAY, *Cor. Sec. Mass. A. S. S.*

Leaders of the American Anti-Slavery Society Reply to an Attack by President Andrew Jackson

ॐ

This letter was prominently featured by the Abolitionist press at the time of its issuance in December, 1835, and was later reprinted in the appendix to a volume by William Jay, entitled A View of the Action of the Federal Government, in Behalf of Slavery, *published by the American Anti-Slavery Society in 1839.*

To the PRESIDENT OF THE UNITED STATES:

SIR—In your message to Congress of the 7th instant, are the following passages: "I must also invite your attention to the painful excitement produced in the South, by attempts to circulate through the mails, inflammatory appeals, *addressed to the passions of the slaves,* in prints and in various sorts of publications, *calculated to stimulate them to insurrection, and produce all the horrors of a servile war.* There is, doubtless, no respectable portion of our countrymen who can be so far misled as to feel any other sentiment than that of indignant regret, at conduct so destructive of the harmony and peace of the country, and *so repugnant to the principles of our national compact, and to the dictates of humanity and religion."* You remark, that it is fortunate that the people of the North have "given so strong and impressive a tone to the sentiments entertained against the proceedings of the misguided persons who have engaged in these *unconstitutional and wicked attempts."* And you proceed to suggest to Congress "the propriety of passing such a law as will prohibit, under severe penalties, the circulation in the southern States, through the mails, of incendiary publications, *intended to instigate the slaves to insurrection."*

A servile insurrection, as experience has shown, involves the slaughter of the whites, without respect to sex or age. Hence, sir, the purport of the information you have communicated to Congress and to the world, is, that there are American citizens who, in violation of the dictates of humanity and religion, have engaged in unconstitutional and wicked attempts to circulate, through the mails, inflammatory appeals addressed to the passions of the slaves, and which appeals, as is implied in the object of your proposed law, are *intended* to stimulate the slaves to indiscriminate massacre. Recent events irresistibly confine the application of your remarks to the officers and

"*Resolved,* That the President, in relation to the public revenue, has assumed upon himself authority and power not conferred by the Constitution and laws, but in derogation of both."

On the 5th of the ensuing month, you transmitted to that body your "solemn protest" against their decision. Instructed by your example, we now, sir, in behalf of the Society of which we are the constituted organs, and in behalf of all who are associated with it, present to you this, our "solemn protest," against your grievous and unfounded accusations.

Should it be supposed, that in thus addressing you, we are wanting in the respect due to your exalted station, we offer, in our vindication, your own acknowledgment to the Senate: "Subject only to the restraints of truth and justice, the free people of the United States have the undoubted right as individuals, or collectively, orally, or in writing, at such times and in such language and form as they may think proper, to discuss his (the President's) official conduct, and to express and promulgate their opinions concerning it."

In the exercise of this "undoubted right," we protest against the judgment you have pronounced against the abolitionists.

First. Because, in rendering that judgment officially, you assumed a power not belonging to your office.

You complained that the resolution censuring your conduct, "though adopted by the Senate in its legislative capacity, is, in its effects and in its characteristics, essentially *judicial.*" And thus, sir, although the charges of which we complain were made by you in your executive capacity, they are, equally with the resolution, essentially *judicial.* The Senate adjudged that your conduct was unconstitutional. You pass the same judgment on our efforts. Nay, sir, you go farther than the Senate. That body forebore to impeach your motives—but you have assumed the prerogatives, not only of a court of law, but of conscience—and pronounce our efforts to be *wicked* as well as unconstitutional.

Secondly. We protest against the *publicity* you have given to your accusations.

You felt it to be a grievance, that the charge against you was "spread upon the Journal of the Senate, published to the nation and to the world—made part of our enduring archives, and incorporated in the history of the age. The punishment of removal from office, and future disqualification, does not follow the decision; but the *moral influence* of a solemn declaration by a majority of the Senate, that the accused is guilty of the offence charged upon him, has been as effectually secured as if the like declaration had been made upon an impeachment expressed in the same terms."

And is it nothing, sir, that we are officially charged by the President of the United States, with wicked and unconstitutional efforts, and with harboring the most execrable intentions; and, this too, in a document spread upon the Journals of both Houses of Congress, published to the nation and to the world, made part of our enduring archives, and incorporated in the history of the age? It is true, that although you have given judgment against us, you cannot award execution. We are not, indeed, subjected to the penalty of murder; but need we ask you, sir, what must be the *moral influence* of your declaration, that we have intended its perpetration?

Thirdly. We protest against your condemnation of us *unheard.*

What, sir, was your complaint against the Senate? "Without notice, *unheard,* and untried, I find myself charged, on the records of the Senate, and in a form unknown in our country, with the high crime of violating the laws and Constitution of my country. No notice of the charge was given to the accused, and no opportunity afforded him to respond to the accusation—to meet his accusers face to face—to cross-examine the witnesses—to procure counteracting testimony, or to be heard in his defence."

Had you, sir, done to others, as it thus seems you would that others should do to you, no occasion would have been given for this protest. You most truly assert, in relation to the conduct of the Senate, "It is the policy of our benign system of jurisprudence, to secure in all criminal proceedings, and even in the most trivial litigations, a fair, unprejudiced, and impartial trial." And by what authority, sir, do you except such of your fellow-citizens as are known as abolitionists, from the benefit of this benign system? When has a fair, unprejudiced, and impartial trial been accorded to those who dare to maintain that all

men are equally entitled to life, liberty, and the pursuit of happiness?
What was the trial, sir, which preceded the judgment you have
rendered against them?

Fourthly. We protest against the *vagueness* of your charges.

We cannot more forcibly describe the injustice you have done us
than by adopting your own indignant remonstrance, against what
you deemed similar injustice on the part of the Senate: "Some of the
first principles of natural right and enlightened jurisprudence, have
been violated in the very form of the resolution. It carefully abstains
from averring in *which* of the late proceedings the President has assumed upon himself authority and power not conferred by the Constitution and laws. Why was not the certainty of the offence, the
nature and cause of the accusation, set out in the manner required in
the Constitution, before even the humblest individual, for the smallest
crime, can be exposed to condemnation? Such a specification was due
to the accused, that he might direct his defence to the real points of
attack. A more striking illustration of the soundness and necessity
of the rules which forbid *vague and indefinite generalities,* and require
a reasonable certainty in all judicial allegations, and a more glaring
instance of the violation of these rules, has seldom been exhibited."

It has been reserved for you, sir, to exhibit a still more striking
illustration of the importance of these rules, and a still more glaring
instance of their violation. You have accused an indefinite number
of your fellow-citizens, without designation of name or residence, of
making unconstitutional and wicked efforts, and of harboring intentions which could be entertained only by the most depraved and
abandoned of mankind; and yet you carefully abstain from averring
which article of the Constitution they have transgressed; you omit
stating when, where, and by whom these wicked attempts were made;
you give no specification of the inflammatory appeals which you
assert have been addressed to the passions of the slaves. You well
know that the *"moral influence"* of your charges will affect thousands
of your countrymen, many of them your political friends—some of
them heretofore honored with your confidence—most, if not all of
them, of irreproachable characters; and yet, by the very vagueness
of your charges, you incapacitate each one of this multitude from
proving his innocence.

Fifthly. We protest against your charges, because they are *untrue*.
Surely, sir, the burthen of proof rests upon you. If you possess evi-

dence against us, we are by your own showing, entitled to "an opportunity to cross-examine witnesses, to procure counteracting testimony, and to be heard in [*our*] defence." You complained that you had been denied such an opportunity. It was not to have been expected, then, that you would make the conduct of the Senate the model of your own. Conscious of the wrong done to you, and protesting against it, you found yourself compelled to enter on your defence. You have placed us in similar circumstances, and we proceed to follow your example:

The substance of your various allegations may be embodied in the charge, that *we have attempted to circulate, through the mails, appeals addressed to the passions of the slaves, calculated to stimulate them to insurrection, and with the intention of producing a servile war.*

It is deserving of notice, that the *attempt* to circulate our papers, is alone charged upon us. It is not pretended that we have put our appeals into the hands of a single slave, or that, in any instance, our endeavors to excite a servile war have been crowned with success. And in what way was our most execrable attempts made? By secret agents, traversing the slave country in disguise, stealing by night into the hut of the slave, and there reading to him our inflammatory appeals? You, sir, answer this question by declaring, that we attempted the mighty mischief by circulating our appeals "THROUGH THE MAILS!" And are the southern slaves, sir, accustomed to receive periodicals by mail? Of the thousands of publications mailed from the Anti-Slavery office for the South, did you ever hear, sir, of one solitary paper being addressed to a slave? Would you know to whom they were directed, consult the southern newspapers, and you will find them complaining that they were sent to public officers, clergymen, and other influential citizens. Thus it seems we are incendiaries, who place the torch in the hands of him whose dwellings we would fire! We are conspiring to excite a servile war, and announce our design to the masters, and commit to their care and disposal the very instruments by which we expect to effect our purpose! It has been said that thirty or forty of our papers were received at the South, directed to free people of color. We cannot deny the assertion, because these papers may have been mailed by others, for the sinister purpose of charging the act upon us. We are, however, ready to make our several affidavits, that not one paper, with our knowledge, or by our authority, has ever been sent to any such person in a slave State. The free people of color at the South can exert no influence in behalf of the enslaved; and we have no disposition to excite odium against them, by making them the recipients of our publications.

Your proposal that a law should be passed, punishing the circulation, through the mails, of papers *intended to excite the slaves to insurrection,* necessarily implies that such papers are now circulated; and you expressly and positively assert, that we have attempted to circulate appeals addressed to the passions of the slaves, and *calculated to produce all the horrors of a servile war.* We trust, sir, your proposed law, so portentous to the freedom of the press, will not be enacted, till you have furnished Congress with stronger evidence of its necessity than unsupported assertions. We hope you will lay before that body, for its information, the papers to which you refer. This is the more necessary, as the various public journals and meetings which have denounced us for entertaining insurrectionary and murderous designs, have in no instance been able to quote from our publications, a single exhortation to the slaves to break their fetters, or the expression of a solitary wish for a servile war.

How far our writings are *"calculated"* to produce insurrection, is a question which will be variously decided according to the latitude in which it is discussed. When we recollect that the humble schoolbook, the tale of fiction, and the costly annual have been placed under the ban of southern editors for trivial allusions to slavery—and that a southern divine has warned his fellow-citizens of the danger of permitting slaves to be present at the celebration of our national festival, where they might listen to the Declaration of Independence, and to eulogiums on liberty—we have little hope that our disquisitions on human rights will be generally deemed safe and innocent, where those rights are habitually violated. Certain writings of one of your predecessors, President Jefferson, would undoubtedly be regarded, in some places, so insurrectionary as to expose to popular violence whoever should presume to circulate them.

As therefore, sir, there is no common standard by which the criminality of opinions respecting slavery can be tested, we acknowledge the foresight which prompted you to recommend, that the "severe penalties" of your proposed law should be awarded, not according to the character of the publication, but the *intention* of the writer. Still, sir, we apprehend that no trivial difficulties will be experienced in the application of your law. The writer may be anonymous, or beyond the reach of prosecution, while the porter who deposits the papers in the post-office, and the mail carrier who transports them, having no evil intentions, cannot be visited with the "severe penalties"; and thus will your law fail in securing to the South that entire exemption from all discussion on the subject of slavery, which it so vehemently desires. The success of the attempt already made to establish a censorship of the press, is not such as to invite farther encroachment on the rights of the people to publish their sentiments.

In your protest, you remarked to the Senate: "The whole Executive power being vested in the President, who is *responsible* for its exercise, it is a necessary consequence that he should have a right to employ agents of his *own choice,* to aid him in the performance of his duties, and to *discharge* them when he is no longer *willing* to be RESPONSIBLE for their acts. He is equally bound to take care that the laws be faithfully executed, whether they impose duties on the highest officer of State, or the *lowest subordinates* in any of the departments."

It may not be uninteresting to you, sir, to be informed in what manner your "Subordinate" in New York, who, on your "responsibility," is exercising the functions of Censor of the American press, discharges the arduous duties of this untried, and until now, unheard of office. We beg leave to assure you, that his task is executed with a simplicity of principle, and celebrity of despatch, unknown to any Censor of the press in France or Austria. Your subordinate decides upon the incendiary character of the publications committed to the post-office, by a glance at the wrappers or bags in which they are contained. No packages sent to be mailed from our office, and directed to a slave State, can escape the vigilance of this inspector of canvass and brown paper. Even your own protest, sir, if in an anti-slavery envelope, would be arrested on its progress to the South, as "inflammatory, incendiary, and insurrectionary in the highest degree."

No veto, however, is *as yet* imposed on the circulation of publications from any printing-office but our own. Hence, when we desire to send "appeals" to the South, all that is necessary is, to insert them in some newspaper that espouses our principles, pay for as many thousand copies as we think proper, and order them to be mailed according to our instructions.

Such, sir, is the worthless protection purchased for the South, by the most unblushing and dangerous usurpation of which any public officer has been guilty since the organization of our Federal Government. Were the Senate, in reference to your acknowledged responsibility for the conduct of your subordinates, to resolve "that the President, in relation to the suppression of certain papers in the New York Post Office, has assumed upon himself authority and power not conferred by the Constitution and laws, but in derogation of both"; instead of protesting against the charge, you would be compelled to acknowledge its truth, and you would plead the necessity of the case in your vindication. The weight to be attached to such a plea, may be learned from the absurdity and inefficacy of the New York Censorship. Be assured, sir, your proposed law to punish the *intentions* of an author, will, in its practical operations, prove equally impotent.

And now, sir, permit us respectfully to suggest to you, the propriety of ascertaining the *real* designs of abolitionists, before your apprehensions of them lead you to sanction any more trifling with the LIBERTY OF THE PRESS. You assume it as a fact, that abolitionists are miscreants, who are laboring to effect the massacre of their southern brethren. Are you aware of the extent of the reproach which such an assumption casts upon the character of your countrymen? In August last, the number of Anti-slavery Societies known to us was 263; we have *now* the names of more than 350 societies, and accessions are daily made to the multitude who embrace our principles. And you can think it possible, sir, that these citizens are deliberately plotting murder, and furnishing us with funds to send publications to the South "intended to instigate the slaves to insurrection"? Is there any thing in the character and manners of the free States, to warrant the imputation on their citizens of such enormous wickedness? Have you ever heard, sir, of whole communities in these States subjecting obnoxious individuals to a mock trial, and then, in contempt of law, humanity, and religion, deliberately murdering them? You have seen, in the public journals, great rewards offered for the perpetration of horrible crimes. We appeal to your candor, and ask, were these rewards offered by abolitionists, or by men whose charges against abolitionists you have condescended to sanction and disseminate?

And what, sir, is the character of those whom you have in your message held up to the execration of the civilized world? Their enemies being judges, they are *religious* fanatics. And what are the haunts of these plotters of murder? The pulpit, the bench, the bar, the professor's chair, the hall of legislation, the meeting for prayer, the temple of the Most High. But strange and monstrous as is this conspiracy, still you believe in its existence, and call on Congress to counteract it. Be persuaded, sir, the moral sense of the community is abundantly sufficient to render this conspiracy utterly impotent the moment its machinations are exposed. Only PROVE the assertions and insinuations in your message, and you dissolve in an instant every Anti-slavery Society in our land. Think not, sir, that we shall interpose any obstacle to an inquiry into our conduct. We invite, nay, sir, we entreat the appointment by Congress of a Committee of Investigation to visit the Anti-slavery Office in New York. They shall be put in possession of copies of all the publications that have been issued from our press. Our whole correspondence shall be submitted to their inspection; our accounts of receipts and expenditures shall be spread before them, and we ourselves will cheerfully answer under oath whatever interrogatories they may put to us relating to the charges you have advanced.

Should such a committee be denied, and should the law you propose, stigmatizing us as felons, be passed without inquiry into the truth of your accusation, and without allowing us a hearing, then shall we make the language of your protest our own, and declare that, "If such proceedings shall be approved and sustained by an intelligent people, then will the great contest with arbitrary power which had established in statutes, in bills of rights, in sacred charters, and in constitutions of government, the right of every citizen to a notice before trial, to a hearing before condemnation, and to an impartial tribunal for deciding on the charge, have been made in VAIN."

Before we conclude, permit us, sir, to offer you the following assurances.

Our principles, our objects, and our measures, are wholly uncontaminated by considerations of party policy. Whatever may be our respective opinions as citizens, of men and measures, as abolitionists we have expressed no political preferences, and are pursuing no party ends. From neither of the gentlemen nominated to succeed you, have we any thing to hope or fear; and to neither of them do we intend as abolitionists, to afford any aid or influence. This declaration will, it is hoped, satisfy the partizans of the rival candidates, that it is not necessary for them to assail our rights by way of convincing the South that they do not possess our favor.

We have addressed you, sir, on this occasion, with republican plainness, and Christian sincerity; but with no desire to derogate from the respect that is due to you, or wantonly to give you pain. To repel your charges, and to disabuse the public, was a duty we owed to ourselves, to our children, and above all to the great and holy cause in which we are engaged. That cause we believe is approved by our Maker; and while we retain this belief, it is our intention, trusting to His direction and protection, to persevere in our endeavors to impress upon the minds and hearts of our countrymen, the sinfulness of claiming property in human beings, and the duty and wisdom of immediately relinquishing it.

When convinced that our endeavors are wrong, we shall abandon them; but such conviction must be produced by other arguments than vituperation, popular violence, or penal enactments.

> ARTHUR TAPPAN,
> WILLIAM JAY,
> JOHN RANKIN,
> ABRAHAM L. COX,
> JOSHUA LEAVITT,
> SIMEON S. JOSELYN,
> LEWIS TAPPAN,
> THEODORE S. WRIGHT,
> SAMUEL E. CORNISH,
> ELIZUR WRIGHT, JR.
> *Executive Committee*

NEW YORK, Dec. 26, 1835.

Abolition As the Cause of All Humanity

ॐ

Dr. Charles Follen was born in Germany in 1796. After teaching at the University of Jena and at the University of Basle, where he was professor of civil law, he was forced to flee Europe because of his liberal views and came to this country in 1824. He became a teacher of German in Harvard College in 1825, and was appointed professor of German literature in 1830. In the same year he became a naturalized citizen. The publication of the Liberator *struck a responsive chord in Follen, and soon after the formation of the New England Anti-Slavery Society he joined that organization and was elected one of its vice-presidents. As a result, he lost his position at Harvard. He next served as pastor of a Unitarian church in New York, but lost that position too, after two years, because of his anti-slavery preaching. Soon after being appointed pastor of a congregation of liberal Christians in East Lexington, he lost his life in the fire of the ill-fated steamer* Lexington, *on January 13, 1840.*

The following address, of which a part is here reprinted, was delivered on January 20, 1836, before the Massachusetts Anti-Slavery Society. It was included in the appendix to The Life of Charles Follen, *by E. L. Follen, Boston, 1844.*

SPEECH BEFORE THE ANTI-SLAVERY SOCIETY
───

At the Annual Meeting of the Massachusetts Anti-slavery Society, January 20th, 1836, Rev. Professor Follen offered the following resolution:

Resolved, that we consider the Anti-slavery cause as the cause of philanthropy, with regard to which all human beings; white men and colored men, citizens and foreigners, men and women, have the same duties and the same rights.

Philanthropy means the love of man; and the love of man is the true and only foundation of the Anti-slavery cause. Our whole creed is summed up in this single position, that the slave is a man, created by God in his own image, and, therefore, by divine right, a freeman. The slave is a man, and we are men; this is the only needful and all-sufficient title, from which every Anti-slavery society, and every Abolitionist, derive their duties and their rights. Every human being, whether colored or white, foreigner or citizen, man or woman, is, in virtue of a common nature, a rightful and responsible defender of the natural rights of all. These are the sentiments of every Abolitionist: these the principles of the Declaration of Independence, which was intended to make this whole nation one great Anti-slavery Society. . . .

And now, Mr. President, I come to the last topic of my resolution. I maintain, that, with regard to the anti-slavery cause, *men* and *women* have the same duties and the same rights. The ground I take on this point is very plain. I wish to spare you, I wish to spare myself, the worthless and disgusting task of replying, in detail, to all the coarse attacks and flattering sophisms by which men have endeavoured to entice or to drive women from this and from many other spheres of moral action. "Go home and spin!" is the well-meaning advice of the domestic tyrant of the old school. "Conquer by personal charms and fashionable attractions!" is the brilliant career marked out for her by the idols and the idolaters of fashion. "Never step out of the bounds of decorum and the *customary* ways of doing good," is the sage advice of maternal caution. "Rule by obedience, by submission sway!" is the golden saying of the moralist poet, sanctioning female servitude, and pointing out a resort and compensation in female cunning. What with the fear of the insolent remarks about women, in which those of the dominant sex, whose bravery is the generous offspring of conscious impunity, are particularly apt to indulge, and with the still stronger fear of being thought unfeminine—it is, indeed, a proof of uncommon moral courage, or of an overpowering sense of religious duty and sympathy with the oppressed, that a woman is induced to embrace the unpopular, unfashionable, obnoxious principles of the Abolitionists. Popular opinion, the habits of society, are all calculated to lead women to consider the place, the privileges, and the duties, which etiquette has assigned to them as their peculiar portion, as more important than those which nature has given them in common with men. Men have at all times been inclined to allow to women peculiar privileges, while withholding from them essential rights. In the progress of civilization and Christianity, one right after another has been conceded, one occupation after another has been placed within the reach of women. Still are we far from a practical acknowledgment of the simple truth, that the rational and moral nature of man is the foundation of all rights and duties, and that women as well as men are rational and moral beings. It is on this account that I look upon the formation of Ladies' anti-slavery societies as an event of the highest interest, not only for its direct beneficial bearing on the cause of emancipation, but still more as an indication of the moral growth of society. Women begin to feel, that the place which men have marked out for them is but a small part of what society owes to them, and what they themselves owe to society, to the whole human family, and to that Power to whom each and all are indebted and accountable for the use of the powers intrusted to them. It is, indeed, a consoling thought, that such is the providential adaptation of all things, that the toil and the sufferings of the slave, however unprofitable to himself, and however hopeless, are not wholly thrown away and vain—that the master who has deprived him of the fruits of his industry, of every motive and opportunity for exercising his highest faculties, has not been able to prevent his exercising, unconsciously, a moral and spiritual influence all over the world, breaking down every unnatural restraint, and calling forth the simplest and deepest of all human emotions, the feeling of a man for his fellow-man, and bringing out the strongest intellectual and moral powers to his rescue. It is, indeed, natural, that the cry of misery, the call for help, that is now spreading far and wide, and penetrating the inmost recesses of society, should thrill, with peculiar power, through the heart of woman. For it is woman, injured, insulted woman, that exhibits the most baneful and hateful influences of slavery. But I cannot speak of what the free woman ought and must feel for her enslaved sister—because I am overwhelmed by the thought of what we men, we, who have mothers, and wives, and daughters, should not only feel, but do, and dare, and sacrifice, to drain the marshes whose exhalations infect the moral atmosphere of society.

The remarks I have made in support of my resolution may be summed up in a few words. The only object of the anti-slavery societies is, to restore the slave to his natural rights. To promote this object, all human beings, white men and colored men, citizens and foreigners, men and women, have the same moral calling, simply because, in virtue of a common rational and moral nature, all human beings are in duty bound, and divinely authorized, to defend their own and each other's *natural rights.*

Our rights, our duties, with regard to the oppressed, require and authorize the use of all lawful and moral means, to accomplish the great object of deliverance. As members of this Union, we are debarred all direct political influence with regard to the legal existence of slavery in other States. But slavery in the District of Columbia and in the Territories, as well as the internal slave-trade, are evils within the reach of our Federal Legislature, and, consequently, within the control and responsibility of every citizen of the Union.

The guilt of the existence of slavery within the bounds of the Federal legislation, rests upon every citizen who is not exerting himself to the utmost, by free discussion and petitions to Congress, that this cruel and disgraceful inconsistency may be removed. But the sphere of moral action is not confined within the limits of our political rights. The North is connected with the South by numerous relations, which may be made so many channels of influence on the minds and consciences of the slave-holders. There are family connexions, commercial relations, political and religious interests, by which individuals of different States are brought in contact, and a continual intercourse is thus kept up between the free North and the slave-holding South. With all these means of private intercourse within our reach, we require no alteration in the Constitution, we demand no especial aid from Congress or from any State Legislature, to induce the slave-holders, by moral motives and by considerations of enlightened self-interest, to rid themselves of this great evil. We require of government nothing but to be protected in the exercise of one undoubted constitutional right, a right which, as Gerrit Smith justly observes, has a deeper foundation than the Constitution which solemnly secures it, being grounded on the nature of man and the sovereign decree of his Creator. Let us dismiss all controversy concerning the exciting question, whether, or how far the Constitution sanctions slavery; but let us assert and defend the freedom of communication by speaking, writing, and printing, which is the first requisite of the freeman, and the last hope of the slave. Slavery and free discussion, Sir, it is well known, cannot live together. They will quarrel until one of them quits the neighbourhood.

We claim freedom of communication with the slave-holder of the South, as well as with the advocates of slavery, and those who think themselves justified in their neutrality at the North. We contend with a national prejudice; we aim at a national reform. Every individual, who is free from the long-cherished and deep-rooted prejudice, which prevents the white men of the North, as well as those of the South, from looking upon the colored man, as a man, and a brother, is in duty bound to become a fellow-laborer in this work of reform. For this reason, our societies are founded, not on the exclusive principle of election, but on the broad, philanthropic ground of free admission; we elect no one, but cordially receive every one who may elect himself. Our audiences do not consist of select companies; but as the Report which you have accepted, eloquently sets forth, in humble imitation of Jesus and the Apostles, we address all who have ears to hear and will hear.

We are told, we must not agitate this subject—let it alone, and it will remedy itself. This is not the course of Providence. Such reformations are never accomplished without human means. God will not indulge us in our indolence, and do the work without our instrumentality.

The Declaration of Independence, so far as those in bonds are concerned, is a dead letter; and we must not rest from our labors until it is raised from the dead.

A Negro Abolitionist Condemns Discrimination

ॐ

Reverend Theodore S. Wright was a Negro minister in New York City who was an active Abolitionist. This address was delivered before the New York Anti-Slavery Society on Sep-

tember 20, 1837. *It was published in the* Liberator *when first delivered and was included in Carter G.* Woodson's volume, Negro Orators and Their Orations, *Washington, D. C., 1925, pp. 92–95.*

PREJUDICE AGAINST THE COLORED MAN

By Theodore S. Wright

Mr. President, with much feeling do I rise to address the society on this resolution, and I should hardly have been induced to have done it had I not been requested. I confess I am personally interested in this resolution. But were it not for the fact that none can feel the lash but those who have it upon them, that none know where the chain galls but those who wear it, I would not address you.

This is a serious business, sir. The prejudice which exists against the colored man, the free man is like the atmosphere, everywhere felt by him. It is true that in these United States and in this State, there are men, like myself, colored with the skin like my own, who are not subjected to the lash, who are not liable to have their wives and their infants torn from them; from whose hand the Bible is not taken. It is true that we may walk abroad; we may enjoy our domestic comforts, our families; retire to the closet; visit the sanctuary, and may be permitted to urge on our children and our neighbors in well doing. But sir, still we are slaves—everywhere we feel the chain galling us. It is by that prejudice which the resolution condemns, the spirit of slavery, the law which has been enacted here, by a corrupt public sentiment, through the influence of slavery which treats moral agents different from the rule of God, which treats them irrespective of their morals or intellectual cultivation. This spirit is withering all our hopes, and ofttimes causes the colored parent as he looks upon his child, to wish he had never been born. Often is the heart of the colored mother, as she presses her child to her bosom, filled with sorrow to think that, by reason of this prejudice, it is cut off from all hopes of usefulness in this land. Sir, this prejudice is wicked.

If the nation and church understood this matter, I would not speak a word about that killing influence that destroys the colored man's reputation. This influence cuts us off from everything; it follows us up from childhood to manhood; it excludes us from all stations of profit, usefulness and honor; takes away from us all motive for pressing forward in enterprises, useful and important to the world and to ourselves.

In the first place, it cuts us off from the advantages of the mechanic arts almost entirely. A colored man can hardly learn a trade, and if he does it is difficult for him to find any one who will employ him to work at the trade, in any part of the State. In most of our large cities there are associations of mechanics who legislate out of their society colored men. And in many cases where our young men have learned trades, they have had to come to low employments for want of encouragement in those trades.

It must be a matter of rejoicing to know that in this vicinity colored fathers and mothers have the privileges of education. It must be a matter of rejoicing that in this vicinity colored parents can have their children trained up in schools—at present, we find the colleges barred against them.

I will say nothing about the inconvenience which I have experienced myself, and which every man of color experiences, though made in the image of God. I will say nothing about the inconvenience of traveling; how are we frowned upon and despised. No matter how we may demean ourselves, we find embarrassments everywhere.

But sir, this prejudice goes farther. It debars men from heaven. While sir, slavery cuts off the colored portion of the community from religious privileges, men are made infidels. What, they demand, is your Christianity? How do you regard your brethren? How do you treat them at the Lord's table? Where is your consistency in talking about the heathen, traversing the ocean to circulate the Bible everywhere, while you frown upon them at the door? These things meet us and weigh down our spirits.

And, sir, the constitution of society, molded by this prejudice, destroys souls. I have known extensively, that in revivals which have been blessed and enjoyed in this part of the country, the colored population were overlooked. I recollect an instance. The Lord God was pouring out His Spirit. He was entering every house, and sinners were converted. I asked, Where is the colored man? Where is my brother? Where is my sister? Who is feeling for him or her? Who is weeping for them? Who is endeavoring to pull them out of the fire? No reply was made. I was asked to go round with one of the elders and visit them. We went and they humbled themselves. The Church commenced efficient efforts, and God blessed them as soon as they began to act for these people as though they had souls.

And sir, the manner in which our churches are regulated destroys souls. Whilst the church is thrown open to everybody, and one says come, come in and share the blessings of the sanctuary, this is the gate of heaven—he says to the colored man, *be careful where you take your stand.* I know an efficient church in this State, where a respectable colored man went to the house of God, and was going to take a seat in the gallery, and one of the officers contended with him, and said, "You cannot go there, sir."

In one place the people had come together to the house of the Lord. The sermon was preached—the emblems were about to be administered—and all at once the person who managed the church thought the value of the pews would be diminished if the colored people sat in them. They objected to their sitting there, and the colored people left and went into the gallery, and that, too, when they were thinking of handling the memorials of the broken body and shed blood of the Savior! And, sir, this prejudice follows the colored man everywhere, and depresses his spirits.

Thanks be to God, there is a buoyant principle which elevates the poor down-trodden colored man above all this—it is that there is society which regards man according to his worth; it is the fact, that when he looks up to Heaven he knows that God treats him like a moral agent, irrespective of caste or the circumstances in which he may be placed. Amid the embarrassments which he has to meet, and the scorn and contempt that is heaped upon him, he is cheered by the hope that he will be disenthralled, and soon, like a bird set forth from its cage, wing his flight to Jesus, where he can be happy, and look down with pity on the man who despises the poor slave for being what God made him, and who despises him because he is identified with the poor slave. Blessed be God for the principles of the Gospel. Were it not for these, and for the fact that a better day is dawning, I would not wish to live. Blessed be God for the antislavery movement. Blessed be God that there is a war waging with slavery, that the granite rock is about to be rolled from its base. But as long as the colored man is to be looked upon as an inferior caste, so long will they disregard his cries, his groans, his shrieks.

I rejoice, sir, in this Society; and I deem the day when I joined this Society as one of the proudest days of my life. And I know I can die better, in more peace to-day, to know there are men who will plead the cause of my children.

Let me, through you, sir, request this delegation to take hold of this subject. This will silence the slaveholder, when he says where is your love for the slave? Where is your love for the colored man who is crushed at your feet? Talking to us about emancipating our slaves when you are enslaving them by your feelings, and doing more violence to them by your prejudice, than we are to our slaves by our treatment. They call on us to evince our love for the slave, by treating man as man, the colored man as a man, according to his worth.

Elijah P. Lovejoy Defends His Right to Free Speech

ɕ❧

On November 7, 1837, Elijah P. Lovejoy (1802–1837), born in Maine and trained for the ministry at Princeton, who had been forced to leave St. Louis, Missouri, where he had edited the Observer, *a weekly newspaper, was slain by a mob in Alton, Illinois, as he sought to defend his fourth press from being destroyed. The following address was delivered by him at a public meeting in Alton, several days before his death. It is reprinted from the* Memoir of the Rev. Elijah P. Lovejoy; Who Was Murdered in Defence of the Liberty of the Press, at Alton, Illinois, Nov. 7, 1837, *by Joseph C. and Owen Lovejoy, New York, 1838, pp. 278–281.*

Mr. Chairman—it is not true, as has been charged upon me, that I hold in contempt the feelings and sentiments of this community, in reference to the question which is now agitating it. I respect and appreciate the feelings and opinions of my fellow-citizens, and it is one of the most painful and unpleasant duties of my life, that I am called upon to act in opposition to them. If you suppose, sir, that I have published sentiments contrary to those generally held in this community, because I delighted in differing from them, or in occasioning a disturbance, you have entirely misapprehended me. But, sir, while I value the good opinion of my fellow-citizens, as highly as any one, I may be permitted to say, that I am governed by higher considerations than either the favour or the fear of man. I am impelled to the course I have taken, because I fear God. As I shall answer it to my God in the great day, I dare not abandon my sentiments, or cease in all proper ways to propagate them.

I, Mr. Chairman, have not desired, or asked any *compromise*. I have asked for nothing but to be protected in my rights as a citizen— rights which God has given me, and which are guaranteed to me by the constitution of my country. Have I, sir, been guilty of any infraction of the laws? Whose good name have I injured? When and where have I published any thing injurious to the reputation of Alton? Have I not, on the other hand, laboured, in common, with the rest of my fellow-citizens, to promote the reputation and interests of this city? What, sir, I ask, has been my offence? Put your finger upon it—define it—and I stand ready to answer for it. If I have committed any crime, you can easily convict me. You have public sentiment in your favour. You have your juries, and you have your attorney [looking at the Attorney-General] and I have *no doubt* you can *convict* me. But if I have been guilty of no violation of law, why am I hunted up and down continually like a partridge upon the mountains? Why am I threatened with the *tar-barrel*? Why am I waylaid every day, and from night to night, and my life in jeopardy every hour?

You have, sir, made up, as the lawyers say, a false issue; there are not two parties between whom there can be a *compromise*. I plant myself, sir, down on my unquestionable *rights*, and the question to be decided is, whether I shall be protected in the exercise, and enjoyment of those rights—*that is the question, sir*—whether my property shall be protected, whether I shall be suffered to go home to my family at night without being assailed, and threatened with tar and feathers, and assassination; whether my afflicted wife, whose life has been in jeopardy, from continued alarm and excitement, shall night after night be driven from a sick bed into the garret to save her life from the brickbats and violence of the mobs; *that sir, is the question.* [Here, much affected and overcome by his feelings, he burst into tears. Many, not excepting even his enemies, wept—several sobbed aloud, and the sympathies of the whole meeting were deeply excited. He continued.] Forgive me, sir, that I have thus betrayed my weakness. It was the allusion to my family that overcame my feelings. Not, sir, I assure you, from any fears on my part. I have no personal fears. Not that I feel able to contest the matter with the whole community, I know perfectly well I am not. I know, sir, that you can tar and feather me, hang me up, or put me into the Mississippi, without the least difficulty. But what then? Where shall I go? I have been made to feel that if I am not safe at Alton, I shall not be safe any where. I recently visited St. Charles to bring home my family, and was torn from their frantic embrace by a mob. I have been beset night and day at Alton. And now if I leave here and go elsewhere, violence may overtake me in my retreat, and I have no more claim upon the protection of any other community than I have upon this; and I have concluded, after consultation with my friends, and earnestly seeking counsel of God, to *remain at Alton,* and here to insist on protection in the exercise of my rights. If the civil authorities refuse to protect me, I must look to God; and if I die, I have determined to make my grave in Alton.

The Murder of Lovejoy, As Seen by Wendell Phillips

ઠ๛

Wendell Phillips (1811–1884), Boston-bred and Harvard-educated, delivered this address on December 8, 1837, at a meeting in Boston's Faneuil Hall called to protest the murder of Lovejoy. He had several months earlier joined the Aboli-

*tionist movement and had spoken at anti-slavery meetings
but this was his first address before so large an assembly.
William Ellery Channing, the Boston clergyman, was one of
those responsible for calling the meeting. He had already
spoken when James T. Austin, Attorney General of the Commonwealth, arose and delivered a diatribe against the Abolitionists, castigated Dr. Channing, and emphasized that Lovejoy
had "died as a fool dieth." It was in reply to this address that
Phillips, who had not expected to participate, rose and spoke.
The text of the address is reprinted from* Speeches, Lectures,
and Letters, *by Wendell Phillips, Boston and New York, 1884,
pp. 2–10.*

MR. CHAIRMAN—We have met for the freest discussion of
these resolutions, and the events which gave rise to them. [Cries of
"Question," "Hear him," "Go on," "No gagging," etc.] I hope I shall
be permitted to express my surprise at the sentiments of the last
speaker—suprise not only at such sentiments from such a man, but at
the applause they have received within these walls. A comparison has
been drawn between the events of the Revolution and the tragedy at
Alton. We have heard it asserted here, in Faneuil Hall, that Great
Britain had a right to tax the Colonies, and we have heard the mob at
Alton, the drunken murderers of Lovejoy, compared to those patriot
fathers who threw the tea overboard! [Great applause.] Fellow-
citizens, is this Faneuil Hall doctrine? ["No, no!"] The mob at Alton
were met to wrest from a citizen his just rights—met to resist the
laws. We have been told that our fathers did the same; and the
glorious mantle of Revolutionary precedent has been thrown over the
mobs of our day. To make out their title to such defence, the gentleman says that the British Parliament had a right to tax these Colonies.
It is manifest that, without this, his parallel falls to the ground; for
Lovejoy had stationed himself within constitutional bulwarks. He
was not only defending the freedom of the press, but he was under his
own roof, in arms with the sanction of the civil authority. The men
who assailed him went against and over the laws. The mob, as the
gentleman terms it—mob, forsooth! Certainly we sons of the tea-
spillers are a marvellously patient generation—the "orderly mob"
which assembled in the Old South to destroy the tea were met to

resist, not the laws, but illegal exactions. Shame on the American who calls the tea-tax and stamp-act laws! Our fathers resisted, not the King's prerogative, but the King's usurpation. To find any other account, you must read our Revolutionary history upside down. Our State archives are loaded with arguments of John Adams to prove the taxes laid by the British Parliament unconstitutional—beyond its power. It was not till this was made out that the men of New England rushed to arms. The arguments of the Council Chamber and the House of Representatives preceded and sanctioned the contest. To draw the conduct of our ancestors into a precedent for mobs, for a right to resist laws we ourselves have enacted, is an insult to their memory. The difference between the excitements of those days and our own, which the gentleman in kindness to the latter has overlooked, is simply this: the men of that day went for the right, as secured by the laws. They were the people rising to sustain the laws and constitution of the Province. The rioters of our day go for their own wills, right or wrong. Sir, when I heard the gentleman lay down principles which place the murderers of Alton side by side with Otis and Hancock, with Quincy and Adams, I thought those pictured lips [pointing to the portraits in the Hall] would have broken into voice to rebuke the recreant American—the slanderer of the dead. [Great applause and counterapplause.] The gentleman said that he should sink into insignificance if he dared to gainsay the principles of these resolutions. Sir, for the sentiments he has uttered, on soil consecrated by the prayers of Puritans and the blood of patriots, the earth should have yawned and swallowed him up.

[Applause and hisses, with cries of "Take that back." The uproar became so great that for a long time no one could be heard. At length G. Bond, Esq., and Hon. W. Sturgis came to Mr. Phillips's side at the front of the platform. They were met with cries of "Phillips or nobody." "Make him take back 'recreant,' " "He sha'n't go on till he takes it back." When it was understood they meant to sustain, not to interrupt, Mr. Phillips, Mr. Sturgis was listened to, and said: "I did not come here to take any part in this discussion, nor do I intend to; but I do entreat you, fellow-citizens, by everything you hold sacred—I conjure you by every association connected with this Hall, consecrated by our fathers to freedom of discussion—that you listen to every man who addresses you in decorous manner." Mr. Phillips resumed.]

Fellow-citizens, I cannot take back my words. Surely the Attorney-General, so long and well known here, needs not the aid of your hisses against one so young as I am—my voice never before heard within these walls!

Another ground has been taken to excuse the mob, and throw doubt and discredit on the conduct of Lovejoy and his associates. Allusion has been made to what lawyers understand very well—the "conflict of laws." We are told that nothing but the Mississippi River rolls between St. Louis and Alton; and the conflict of laws somehow or other gives the citizens of the former a right to find fault with the defender of the press for publishing his opinions so near their limits. Will the gentleman venture that argument before lawyers? How the laws of the two States could be said to come into conflict in such circumstances I question whether any lawyer in this audience can explain or understand. No matter whether the line that divides one sovereign State from another be an imaginary one or ocean-wide, the moment you cross it the State you leave is blotted out of existence, so far as you are concerned. The Czar might as well claim to control the deliberations of Faneuil Hall, as the laws of Missouri demand reverence, or the shadow of obedience, from an inhabitant of Illinois.

I must find some fault with the statement which has been made of the events at Alton. It has been asked why Lovejoy and his friends did not appeal to the executive—trust their defence to the police of the city. It has been hinted that, from hasty and ill-judged excitement, the men within the building provoked a quarrel, and that he fell in the course of it, one mob resisting another. Recollect, Sir, that they did act with the approbation and sanction of the Mayor. In strict truth, there was no executive to appeal to for protection. The Mayor acknowledged that he could not protect them. They asked him if it was lawful for them to defend themselves. He told them it was, and sanctioned their assembling in arms to do so. They were not, then, a mob; they were not merely citizens defending their own property; they were in some sense the *posse comitatus*, adopted for the occasion into the police of the city, acting under the order of the magistrate. It was civil authority resisting lawless violence. Where, then, was the imprudence? Is the doctrine to be sustained here, that it is *imprudent* for men to aid magistrates in executing the laws?

Men are continually asking each other, Had Lovejoy a right to resist? Sir, I protest against the question, instead of answering it.

Lovejoy did not resist, in the sense they mean. He did not throw himself back on the natural right of self-defence. He did not cry anarchy and let slip the dogs of civil war, careless of the horrors which would follow.

Sir, as I understand this affair, it was not an individual protecting his property; it was not one body of armed men resisting another, and making the streets of a peaceful city run blood with their contentions. It did not bring back the scenes in some old Italian cities, where family met family, and faction met faction, and mutually trampled the laws under foot. No; the men in that house were regularly *enrolled*, under the sanction of the Mayor. There being no militia in Alton, about seventy men were enrolled with the approbation of the Mayor. These relieved each other every other night. About thirty men were in arms on the night of the sixth, when the press was landed. The next evening, it was not thought necessary to summon more than half that number; among these was Lovejoy. It was, therefore, you perceive, Sir, the police of the city resisting rioters—civil government breasting itself to the shock of lawless men.

Here is no question about the right of self-defence. It is in fact simply this: Has the civil magistrate a right to put down a riot?

Some persons seem to imagine that anarchy existed at Alton from the commencement of these disputes. Not at all. "No one of us," says an eyewitness and a comrade of Lovejoy, "has taken up arms during these disturbances but at the command of the Mayor." Anarchy did not settle down on that devoted city till Lovejoy breathed his last. Till then the law, represented in his person, sustained itself against its foes. When he fell, civil authority was trampled under foot. He had "planted himself on his constitutional rights—appealed to the laws—claimed the protection of the civil authority—taken refuge under the broad shield of the Constitution. When through that he was pierced and fell, he fell but one sufferer in a common catastrophe." He took refuge under the banner of liberty—amid its folds; and when he fell, its glorious stars and stripes, the emblem of free institutions, around which cluster so many heart-stirring memories, were blotted out in the martyr's blood.

It has been stated, perhaps inadvertently, that Lovejoy or his comrades fired first. This is denied by those who have the best means of knowing. Guns were first fired by the mob. After being twice fired on, those within the building consulted together and deliberately returned the fire. But suppose they did fire first. They had a right so to do; not only the right which every citizen has to defend himself; but the further right which every civil officer has to resist violence. Even if Lovejoy fired the first gun, it would not lessen his claim to our sympathy, or destroy his title to be considered a martyr in defence of a free press. The question now is, Did he act within the Constitution and the laws? The men who fell in State Street on the 5th of March, 1770, did more than Lovejoy is charged with. They were the first assailants. Upon some slight quarrel they pelted the troops with every missile within reach. Did this bate one jot of the eulogy with which Hancock and Warren hallowed their memory, hailing them as the first martyrs in the cause of American liberty?

If, Sir, I had adopted what are called Peace principles, I might lament the circumstances of this case. But all you who believe, as I do, in the right and duty of magistrates to execute the laws, join with me and brand as base hypocrisy the conduct of those who assemble year after year on the 4th of July, to fight over the battles of the Revolution, and yet "Damn with faint praise," or load with obloquy, the memory of this man, who shed his blood in defence of life, liberty, property, and the freedom of the press!

Throughout that terrible night I find nothing to regret but this, that within the limits of our country, civil authority should have been so prostrated as to oblige a citizen to arm in his own defence, and to arm in vain. The gentleman says Lovejoy was presumptuous and imprudent—he "died as the fool dieth." And a reverend clergyman of the city tells us that no citizen has a right to publish opinions disagreeable to the community. If any mob follows such publication, on *him* rests its guilt! He must wait, forsooth, till the people come up to it and agree with him! This libel on liberty goes on to say that the want of right to speak as we think is an evil inseparable from republican institutions! If this be so, what are they worth? Welcome the despotism of the Sultan, where one knows what he may publish and what he may not, rather than the tyranny of this many-headed monster, the mob, where we know not what we may do or say, till some fellow-citizen has tried it, and paid for the lesson with his life. This clerical absurdity chooses as a check for the abuses of the press, not the *law*, but the dread of a mob. By so doing, it deprives not only the individual and the minority of their rights, but the majority also, since the expression of *their* opinion may sometimes provoke disturbance from the minority. A few men may make a mob as well as many. The majority, then, have no right, as Christian men, to utter their sentiments, if by any possibility it may lead to a mob! Shades of Hugh Peters and John Cotton, save us from such pulpits!

Imprudent to defend the liberty of the press! Why? Because the defence was unsuccessful? Does success gild crime into patriotism, and the want of it change heroic self-devotion to imprudence? Was Hampden imprudent when he drew the sword and threw away the scabbard? Yet he, judged by that single hour, was unsuccessful. After a short exile, the race he hated sat again upon the throne.

Imagine yourself present when the first news of Bunker Hill battle reached a New England town. The tale would have run thus: "The patriots are routed—the redcoats victorious—Warren lies dead upon the field." With what scorn would that *Tory* have been received, who should have charged Warren with *imprudence*! Who should have said that, bred a physician, he was "out of place" in that battle, and "died as the *fool dieth*"! [Great applause.] How would the intimation have been received, that Warren and his associates should have waited a better time? But if success be indeed the only criterion of prudence, *Respice finem*—wait till the end.

Presumptuous to assert the freedom of the press on American ground! Is the assertion of such freedom before the age? So much before the age as to leave one no right to make it because it displeases the community? Who invents this libel on his country? It is this very thing which entitles Lovejoy to greater praise. The disputed right which provoked the Revolution—taxation without representation—is far beneath that for which he died. [Here there was a strong and general expression of disapprobation.] One word, gentlemen. As much as *thought* is better than money, so much is the cause in which Lovejoy died nobler than a mere question of taxes. James Otis thundered in this Hall when the King did but touch his *pocket*. Imagine, if you can, his indignant eloquence, had England offered to put a gag upon his lips. [Great applause.]

The question that stirred the Revolution touched our civil interests. *This* concerns us not only as citizens, but as immortal beings. Wrapped up in its fate, saved or lost with it, are not only the voice of the statesman, but the instructions of the pulpit, and the progress of our faith.

The clergy "marvellously out of place" where free speech is battled for—liberty of speech on national sins? Does the gentleman remember that freedom to preach was first gained, dragging in its train freedom to print? I thank the clergy here present, as I reverence their predecessors, who did not so far forget their country in their immediate profession as to deem it duty to separate themselves from the struggle of '76—the Mayhews and Coopers, who remembered they were citizens before they were clergymen.

Mr. Chairman, from the bottom of my heart I thank that brave little band at Alton for resisting. We must remember that Lovejoy had fled from city to city—suffered the destruction of three presses patiently. At length he took counsel with friends, men of character, of tried integrity, of wide views, of Christian principle. They thought the crisis had come: it was full time to assert the laws. They saw around them, not a community like our own, of fixed habits, of character moulded and settled, but one "in the gristle, not yet hardened into the bone of manhood." The people there, children of our older States, seem to have forgotten the blood-tried principles of their fathers the moment they lost sight of our New England hills. Something was to be done to show them the priceless value of the freedom of the press, to bring back and set right their wandering and confused ideas. He and his advisers looked out on a community, staggering like a drunken man, indifferent to their rights and confused in their feelings. Deaf to argument, haply they might be stunned into sobriety. They saw that of which we cannot judge, the *necessity* of resistance. Insulted law called for it. Public opinion, fast hastening on the downward course, must be arrested.

Does not the event show they judged rightly? Absorbed in a thousand trifles, how has the nation all at once come to a stand? Men begin, as in 1776 and 1640, to discuss principles, to weigh characters, to find out where they are. Haply we may awake before we are borne over the precipice.

I am glad, Sir, to see this crowded house. It is good for us to be here. When Liberty is in danger, Faneuil Hall has the right, it is her duty, to strike the key-note for these United States. I am glad, for one reason, that remarks such as those to which I have alluded have been uttered here. The passage of these resolutions, in spite of this opposition, let by the Attorney-General of the Commonwealth, will show more clearly, more decisively, the deep indignation with which Boston regards this outrage.

An Abolitionist Study of West India Emancipation

ह‍‍

In 1837, the American Anti-Slavery Society sent James A.
Thome and J. Horace Kimball to the West Indies to study the
results of the emancipation of the slaves which had taken
place there in August 1834. The result of their study was a
volume they wrote, entitled Emancipation in the West Indies.
A Six Months' Tour in Antigua, Barbadoes, and Jamaica, in
the Year 1837, published in New York, in 1838, by the American Anti-Slavery Society. The following is the introduction
to the book.

INTRODUCTION

It is hardly possible that the success of British West India
Emancipation should be more conclusively proved, than it has been
by the absence among us of the exultation which awaited its failure.
So many thousands of the citizens of the United States, without
counting slaveholders, would not have suffered their prophesyings to
be falsified, if they could have found whereof to manufacture fulfilment. But it is remarkable that, even since the first of August, 1834,
the evils of West India emancipation on the lips of the advocates of
slavery, or, as the most of them nicely prefer to be termed, the
opponents of abolition, have remained in the future tense. The bad
reports of the newspapers, spiritless as they have been compared with
the predictions, have been traceable, on the slightest inspection, not
to emancipation, but to the illegal continuance of slavery, under the
cover of its legal substitute. Not the slightest reference to the rash
act, whereby the thirty thousand slaves of Antigua were immediately
"turned loose," now mingles with the croaking which strives to defend
our republican slavery against argument and common sense.

The Executive Committee of the American Anti-Slavery Society,
deemed it important that the silence which the pro-slavery press of

the United States has seemed so desirous to maintain in regard to what is strangely enough termed the "great experiment of freedom," should be thoroughly broken up by a publication of facts and testimony collected on the spot. To this end, REV. JAMES A. THOME, and JOSEPH H. KIMBALL, ESQ., were deputed to the West Indies to make the proper investigations. Of their qualifications for the task, the subsequent pages will furnish the best evidence: it is proper, however, to remark, that Mr. Thome is thoroughly acquainted with our own system of slavery, being a native and still a resident of Kentucky, and the son of a slaveholder (happily no longer so), and that Mr. Kimball is well known as the able editor of the *Herald of Freedom*, published at Concord, New Hampshire.

They sailed from New York, the last of November, 1836, and returned early in June, 1837. They improved a short stay at the Danish island of St. Thomas, to give a description of slavery as it exists there, which, as it appeared for the most part in the anti-slavery papers, and as it is not directly connected with the great question at issue, has not been inserted in the present volume. Hastily touching at some of the other British islands, they made Antigua, Barbadoes, and Jamaica, successively the objects of their deliberate and laborious study—as fairly presenting the three grand phases of the "experiment"—Antigua, exemplifying immediate unrestricted abolition; Barbadoes, the best working of the apprenticeship, and Jamaica the worst. Nine weeks were spent in Antigua, and the remainder of their time was divided between the other two islands.

The reception of the delegates was in the highest degree favorable to the promotion of their object, and their work will show how well they have used the extraordinary facilities afforded them. The committee have, in some instances, restored testimonials which their modesty led them to suppress, showing in what estimation they themselves, as well as the object of their mission, were held by some of the most distinguished persons in the islands which they visited.

So wide was the field before them, and so rich and various the fruit to be gathered, that they were tempted to go far beyond the strength supplied by the failing health they carried with them. Most nobly did they postpone every personal consideration to the interests of the cause, and the reader will, we think, agree with us, that they have achieved a result which undiminished energies could not have been expected to exceed—a result sufficient, if any thing could be, to justify the sacrifice it cost them. We regret to add that the labors and exposures of Mr. Kimball, so far prevented his recovery from the disease[1] which obliged him to resort to a milder climate, or perhaps we should say aggravated it, that he has been compelled to leave to his colleague, aided by a friend, nearly the whole burden of preparing for the press—which, together with the great labor of condensing from the immense amount of collected materials, accounts for the delay of the publication. As neither Mr. Thome nor Mr. Kimball were here while the work was in the press, it is not improbable that trivial errors have occurred, especially in the names of individuals.

It will be perceived that the delegates rest nothing of importance on their own unattested observation. At every point they are fortified by the statements of a multitude of responsible persons in the islands, whose names, when not forbidden, they have taken the liberty to use in behalf of humanity. Many of these statements were given in the handwriting of the parties, and are in the possession of the Executive Committee. Most of these island authorities are as unchallengeable on the score of previous leaning towards abolitionism, as Mr. McDuffie or Mr. Calhoun would be two years hence, if slavery were to be abolished throughout the United States to-morrow.

Among the points established in this work, beyond the power of dispute or cavil, are the following:

1. The act of IMMEDIATE EMANCIPATION in Antigua, was not attended with any disorder whatever.

2. That the emancipated slaves have readily, faithfully, and efficiently worked for wages from the first.

3. That wherever there has been any disturbance in the working of the apprenticeship, it has been invariably by the fault of the masters, or of the officers charged with the execution of the "Abolition Act."

4. That the prejudice of caste is fast disappearing in the emancipated islands.

5. That the apprenticeship was not sought for by the planters as a *preparation for freedom.*

---

[1] We learn that Mr. Kimball closed his mortal career at Pembroke, N. H. April 12th, in the 25th year of his age. Very few men in the Anti-Slavery cause have been more distinguished, than this lamented brother, for the zeal, discretion and ability with which he has advocated the cause of the oppressed. "Peace to the memory of a man of worth!"

6. That no such preparation was needed.

7. That the planters who have fairly made the "experiment," now greatly prefer the new system to the old.

8. That the emancipated people are perceptibly rising in the scale of civilization, morals, and religion.

From these established facts, reason cannot fail to make its inferences in favor of the two and a half millions of slaves in our republic. We present the work to our countrymen who yet hold slaves, with the utmost confidence that its perusal will not leave in their minds a doubt, either of the duty or perfect safety of *immediate emancipation*, however it may fail to persuade their hearts—which God grant it may not!

By order of the Executive Committee of the American Anti-Slavery Society.

NEW YORK, April 28th, 1838.

Angelina Grimké Presents the Essence of Abolition

ৈ

Angelina E. Grimké (1805–1879) and her sister Sarah (1792–1873) were members of a prominent South Carolina slaveholding family. Their father was a justice of the South Carolina Supreme Court. They became Quakers as the result of a visit to Philadelphia, renounced slavery, left the South for good and in 1835 joined the anti-slavery movement. In 1838, Angelina married Theodore Weld, the prominent anti-slavery leader.

Catharine E. Beecher (1800–1874), the daughter of Reverend Lyman Beecher of Boston, had published a small book in 1837 entitled An Essay on Slavery and Abolitionism, with reference to the Duty of American Females, *which condemned Abolitionist interference with Southern slavery as*

*unjustified and criticized female participation in public dis-
cussions. The book was addressed to Angelina Grimké. She
replied in a series of thirteen letters which were published in
the* Liberator. *These were then published as a pamphlet in
1838, under the title of* "Letters to Catharine E. Beecher, in
Reply to an Essay on Slavery and Abolitionism, Addressed to
A. E. Grimké." *Revised by the author, Boston, Isaac Knapp,
1838.*

LETTER I. FUNDAMENTAL PRINCIPLE OF ABOLITIONISTS

BROOKLINE, MASS. 6 *month,* 12*th,* 1837

MY DEAR FRIEND: Thy book has appeared just at a time,
when, from the nature of my engagements, it will be impossible for
me to give it that attention which so weighty a subject demands.
Incessantly occupied in prosecuting a mission, the responsibilities of
which task all my powers, I can reply to it only by desultory letters,
thrown from my pen as I travel from place to place. I prefer this
mode to that of taking as long a time to answer it, as thou didst to
determine upon the best method by which to counteract the effect of
my testimony at the north—which, as the preface of thy book informs
me, was thy main design.

Thou thinkest I have not been "sufficiently informed in regard to
the feelings and opinions of Christian females at the North" on the
subject of slavery; for that in fact they hold the same *principles* with
Abolitionists, although they condemn their measures. Wilt thou permit me to receive their principles from thy pen? Thus instructed,
however misinformed I may heretofore have been, I can hardly fail of
attaining to accurate knowledge. Let us examine them, to see how far
they correspond with the principles held by Abolitionists.

The great fundamental principle of Abolitionists is, that man cannot rightfully hold his fellow man as property. Therefore, we affirm,
that *every slaveholder is a man-stealer.* We do so, for the following
reasons: to steal a man is to rob him of himself. It matters not
whether this be done in Guinea, or Carolina; a man is a *man*, and *as*
a man he has *inalienable* rights, among which is the right to personal
liberty. Now if every man has an *inalienable* right to personal liberty,
it follows, that he cannot rightfully be reduced to slavery. But I find
in these United States, 2,250,000 men, women and children, robbed

of that to which they have an *inalienable* right. How comes this to pass? Where millions are plundered, are there no *plunderers*? If, then, the slaves have been robbed of their liberty, *who* has robbed them? Not the man who stole their forefathers from Africa, but he who now holds them in bondage; no matter *how* they came into his possession, whether he inherited them, or bought them, or seized them at their birth on his own plantation. The only difference I can see between the original man-stealer, who caught the African in his native country, and the American slaveholder, is, that the former committed *one* act of robbery, while the other perpetrates the same crime *continually*. Slaveholding is the perpetrating of acts, all of the same kind, in a *series*, the first of which is technically called man-stealing. The *first* act robbed the man of himself; and the same state of mind that prompted *that act, keeps up the series,* having *taken* his all from him: it *keeps* his all from him, not only *refusing* to *restore*, but still robbing him of all he gets, and as fast as he gets it. Slaveholding, then, is the *constant or habitual perpetration of the act of man-stealing*. To *make* a slave is *man-stealing—the* ACT *itself*—to *hold* him such is man-stealing—the *habit*, the *permanent* state, made up of *individual* acts. In other words—to *begin* to hold a slave is man-stealing—to *keep on* holding him is merely a *repetition* of the first act—a doing of the same identical thing *all the time*. A series of the same acts continued for a length of time is a *habit*—a permanent state. And the *first* of this series of the *same* acts that make up this *habit* or state is just like all the rest.

If every slave has a right to freedom, then surely the man who withholds that right from him to-day is a man-stealer, though he may not be the first person who has robbed him of it. Hence we find that Wesley says, "Men-*buyers* are *exactly on a level with* men-*stealers*." And again—"Much less is it possible that any child of man should ever be *born a slave*." Hear also Jonathan Edwards—"To hold a man in a state of slavery, is to be *every day guilty* of robbing him of his liberty, or of *man-stealing*." And Grotius says—"Those are men-stealers who abduct, *keep,* sell or buy *slaves* or freemen."

If thou meanest merely that *acts* of that *same nature*, but differently located in a series, are designated by different terms, thus pointing out their different *relative positions*, then thy argument concedes what we affirm—the identity in the *nature* of the acts, and thus it dwindles to a mere philological criticism, or rather a mere play upon words.

These are Abolition sentiments on the subject of slaveholding; and although our principles are universally held by our opposers at the North, yet I am told on the 44th page of thy book, that "the word man-stealer has one peculiar signification, and is no more synonymous with slaveholder than it is with sheep-stealer." I must acknowledge, thou hast only confirmed my opinion of the difference which I had believed to exist between Abolitionists and their opponents. As well might Saul have declared, that he held similar views with Stephen, when he stood by and kept the raiment of those who slew him.

I know that a broad line of distinction is drawn between our principles and our measures, by those who are anxious to "avoid the appearance of evil"—very desirous of retaining the fair character of enemies to slavery. Now, our *measures* are simply the carrying out of our *principles*; and we find, that just in proportion as individuals embrace our principles, in spirit and in truth, they cease to cavil at our measures. Gerrit Smith is a striking illustration of this. Who cavilled more at Anti-Slavery *measures*, and who more ready now to acknowledge his former blindness? Real Abolitionists know full well, that the slave never has been, and never can be, a whit the better for mere abstractions, floating in the *head* of any man; and they also know, that *principles, fixed in the heart,* are things of another sort. The former have never done any good in the world, because they possess no vitality, and therefore cannot bring forth *the fruits* of holy, untiring effort; but the latter live in the lives of their possessors, and breathe in their words. And I am free to express my belief, that *all* who really and heartily approve our *principles*, will also approve our *measures*; and that, too, just as certainly as a good tree will bring forth good fruit.

But there is another peculiarity in the views of Abolitionists. We hold that the North is guilty of the crime of slaveholding—we assert that it is a *national* sin: on the contrary, in thy book, I find the following acknowledgment: "*Most* persons in the non-slaveholding States, have considered the matter of southern slavery as one in which they were no more called to interfere, than in the abolition of the press-gang system in England, or the tithe-system in Ireland." Now I cannot see how the same principles can produce such entirely different opinions. "Can a good tree bring forth corrupt fruit?" This I deny, and cannot admit what thou art anxious to prove, viz. that

"Public opinion may have been *wrong* on this point, and yet *right* on all those great *principles* of rectitude and justice relating to slavery." If Abolition principles are generally adopted at the North, how comes it to pass, that there is no abolition action here, except what is put forth by a few despised fanatics, as they are called? Is there any living faith without works? Can the sap circulate vigorously, and yet neither blossoms put forth nor fruit appear?

Again, I am told on the 7th page, that all Northern Christians believe it is a sin to hold a man in slavery for *"mere purposes of gain"*; as if this was the *whole* abolition principle on this subject. I can assure thee that Abolitionists do not stop here. Our principle is, that *no circumstances can ever justify* a man in holding his fellow man as *property*; it matters not what *motive* he may give for such a monstrous violation of the laws of God. The claim to him as *property* is an annihilation of his right to himself, which is the foundation upon which all his other rights are built. It is high-handed robbery of Jehovah; for He has declared, "All souls are *mine*." For myself, I believe there are hundreds of thousands at the South, who do *not* hold their slaves, by any means, as much "for purposes of gain," as they do from *the lust of power*: this is the passion that reigns triumphant there, and those who do not know this, have much yet to learn. Where, then, is the similarity in our views?

I forbear for the present, and subscribe myself,

Thine, but not in the bonds of gospel Abolitionism,

A. E. GRIMKÉ.

An Abolitionist Editor Condemns Racial Discrimination

ह•

The author of this essay, Nathaniel Peabody Rogers (1794–1846), was a New Hampshire lawyer, Abolitionist, poet and editor. In 1838, he became editor of the Herald of Freedom,

an anti-slavery newspaper that had been established by the
New Hampshire Anti-Slavery Society in 1835. His later views
on nonresistance and no-government brought him into conflict
with the New Hampshire Anti-Slavery Society and a severing
of his connection with the newspaper as well as with Garrison.
A volume of his writings was published in Concord, in 1847,
by John R. French, and was entitled A Collection from the
Newspaper Writings of Nathaniel Peabody Rogers. The following essay was included, pp. 44–47.

COLOR-PHOBIA
[From the *Herald of Freedom* of November 10, 1838.]

Our people have got it. They have got it in the blue,
collapse stage. Many of them have got it so bad, they can't get well.
They will die of it. It will be a mercy, if the nation does not. What a
dignified, philosophic malady! Dread of complexion. They don't know
they have got it—or think, rather, they took it the natural way. But
they were inoculated. It was injected into their veins and *incided*
into their systems, by old Doctor Slavery, the great doctor that the
famous Dr. Wayland studied with. There is a kind of varioloid type,
called *colonization.* They generally go together, or all that have one
are more apt to catch the other. Inoculate for one (no matter which),
and they will have both, before they get over it. The remedy and the
preventive, if taken early, is a kine-pock sort of matter, by the name
of *anti-slavery.* It is a safe preventive and a certain cure. None that
have it, genuine, ever catch slavery or colonization or the color-
phobia. You can't inoculate either into them. It somehow changes
and redeems the constitution, so that it is unsusceptible of them. An
abolitionist can sleep safely all night in a close room, where there
has been a colonization meeting the day before. He might sleep with
R. R. Gurley and old Dr. Proudfit, three in a bed, and not catch it.
The remedy was discovered by Dr. William Lloyd Jenner-Garrison.

This color-phobia is making terrible havoc among our communities. Anti-slavery *drives it out*, and after a while cures it. But it
is a base, low, vulgar ailment. It is meaner, in fact, than the itch. It is
worse to get rid of than the "seven years' itch." It is fouler than Old
Testament leprosy. It seems to set the dragon into a man, and make
him treat poor, dark-skinned folks like a tiger. It goes hardest with

dark-complect white people. They have it longer and harder than light-skinned people. It makes them sing out "Nigger—nigger," sometimes in their sleep. Sometimes they make a noise like this, "Darkey—darkey—darkey." Sometimes, "Wully—wully—wully." They will turn up their noses, when they see colored people, especially if they are of a pretty rank, savory habit of person, themselves. They are generally apt to turn up their noses, as though there was some "bad smell" in the neighborhood, when they have it bad, and are naturally pretty odoriferous. It is a tasty disorder—a beautiful ailment; very genteel, and apt to go in "first families." We should like to have Hogarth take a sketch of a community that had it—of ours, for instance, when the St. Vitus' fit was on. We have read somewhere of a painter, who made so droll a picture, that he died a-laughing at the sight of it. Hogarth might not laugh at this picture. It would be a sight to cry at, rather than laugh, especially if he could see the poor objects of our frenzy, when the fit is on—which indeed is all the time, for it is an unintermittent. Our attitude would be most ridiculous and ludicrous, if it were not too mortifying and humiliating and cruel. Our Hogarth would be apt to die of something else than laughter, at sight of his sketch.

The courtly malady is the secret of all our anti-abolition, and all our mobocracy. It shuts up all the consecrated meeting-houses—and all the *temples of justice*, the court-houses, against the friends of negro liberty. It is all alive with fidgets about *desecrating the Sabbath* with anti-slavery lectures. It thinks anti-slavery pew-owners can't go into them, or use their pulpit, when it is empty, without leave of the minister whom they employ to preach in it. It will forcibly shut people out of their own houses and off their own land—not with the respectful violence of enemies and trespassers, but the contemptuous unceremoniousness of the plantation overseer—mingled moreover with the slavish irascibility of the poor negro, when he holds down his fellow-slave for a flogging. It sneers at human rights through the *free* press. It handed John B. Mahan over to the alligators of Kentucky. It shot Elijah P. Lovejoy at Alton. It dragged away the free school, at Canaan. It set Pennsylvania Hall a-fire. It broke Miss Crandall's school windows, and threw filth into her well. It stormed the female prayer meeting in Boston, with a "property and standing" forlorn hope. It passed the popish resolution at Littleton, in Grafton county. It shut up the meeting-house at Meredith Bridge, against minister and all—and the homely court-house there, and howled like bedlam around the little, remote district school-house, and broke the windows at night. It excludes consideration and prayer in regard to the forlorn and christian-made heathenism of the American colored man, from county conferences and clerical associations. It broods over the mousings of the New York Observer, and gives *keenness* to the edge and point of its New Hampshire name-sake. It votes anti-slavery lectures out of the New Hampshire state house, and gives it *public hearing* on petitions, in a seven by nine committee room. It answers the most insulting mandate of southern governors, calling for violations of the state constitution and bill of rights, by legislative report and resolves that the paramount rights of slavery are safe enough in New Hampshire, without these violations. It sneers and scowls at woman's speaking *in company*, unless to simper, when she is flattered by a fool of the masculine or neuter gender. It won't sign an anti-slavery petition, for fear it will put back emancipation half a century. It votes in favor of communing with slaveholders, and throwing the pulpit wide open to men-stealers, to keep peace in the churches, and prevent disunion. It will stifle and strangle sympathy for the slave and "remembrance of those in bonds," to prevent disturbance of religious revivals. It will sell the American slave to buy Bibles, or hire negro-hating and negro-buying missionaries for foreign heathen of all quarters but christian-wasted Africa. It prefers *American* lecturers on slavery, to having that foreign emissary, George Thompson, come over here, to interfere with American rights and prejudices. It abhors "church action" and "meddling with politics." In short, it abhors slavery in the abstract—wishes it might be done away, but denies the right of any body or any thing to devise its overthrow, but slavery itself and slave-holders. It prays for the poor slave, that he might be elevated, while it stands both feet on his breast to keep him down. It prays God might open a way in his own time for the deliverance of the slave, while it stands, with arms akimbo, right across the way he has already opened. Time would fail us to tell of its extent and depth in this free country, or the deeds it has done. Anti-slavery must cure it, or it must die out like the incurable drunkards.

An Abolitionist Protests Against the Participation of Women in the American Anti-Slavery Society

२०

> *One of the primary causes of the division within Abolitionist ranks in 1840 was the question of the place of women within the anti-slavery movement. Garrison and his followers favored complete integration of women in all facets of the society's work. In 1839, a large number of members, many of whom were outstanding leaders, issued a public statement opposing such participation. The statement was published in the* Liberator *on May 31, 1839, with notes and comments by Garrison. The statement, with Garrison's comments, follows.*

PROTEST

We the undersigned, members and delegates of the American Anti-Slavery Society, as a duty, and therefore a right, hereby protest against the principle, assumed by a majority of persons representing said Society at its present meeting, that women have the right of originating, debating, and voting on questions which come before said Society, and are eligible to its various offices:—and we protest against the assumption of said principle for the following, among other reasons, viz:

1. Because it is contrary to the expectation, design, and spirit of the Constitution of said Society, as clearly indicated by the proceedings of the framers of that instrument, at the commencement, in the progress, and at the completion of the work.[1]

---

[1] The attentive reader can hardly fail to be struck with the resemblance which this "reason" bears to a very common argument of slaveholders against the construction which abolitionists put upon the Declaration of Independence, the national and state Constitutions, and the Bills of Rights. These documents (excepting some of the State Constitutions) make no distinction of color, or rank, but recognize the inalienable rights of *all* men. But, say the slaveholders, they were not intended to include negroes, and therefore "it is contrary to the expectation, design, and spirit" of these instruments to insist that colored people

2. Because it is at variance with the construction of said instrument, as made known by the constant usage of the Society from its first to its present meeting.

3. Because it is repugnant to the wishes, the wisdom, or the moral sense of many of the early and present members of said Society, and devoted friends to the cause for which that Society was organized.

4. Because, though assumed by a majority of persons representing said Society in its present meeting, we believe it to be wide from the expression of the general sense of the abolitionists of this country of either sex, and, if not objected to in this formal manner, might seem to be the unqualified and unlimited sanction of the friends of the slave and the asserters of his rights.

5. Because it is rather the expression of local and sectarian feelings, of recent origin, than of those broad sentiments which existed among the friends of our great enterprise at its beginning, and which led to the framing of the Society on a foundation where all sects might stand and wield the potent weapon of our warfare against the oppression of our brethren.

6. Because in conformity with these broad sentiments, and in opposition to local and party peculiarity, the American Society, at its first meeting, so far from contemplating the principle which is now for the first time assumed by the aforesaid majority, recommended the organization of distinct societies of the female sex.[2]

7. Because, how much and how conscientiously soever we might differ in respect to the abstract question of the rights of women and the propriety of their action in large deliberative bodies, yet waiving entirely any expression here of sentiment on this subject, we are persuaded that the principle which is, at this meeting, for the first time,

---

should be admitted to the rights, privileges, and immunities of citizens on terms of equality with the whites! There is no reason to suppose that the framers of the Constitution of Massachusetts intended by that instrument to free the slaves. Was the decision of the Supreme Court, whereby liberty was proclaimed to all the inhabitants of Massachusetts, therefore null and void on that account? Nay, verily. Much is made of the fact that women were not signers of the Declaration of Sentiments, and that they have not heretofore been enrolled at our annual meetings. But this argument proves too much. There were no minors nor Jews in the Convention at Philadelphia in 1833. Does it therefore follow that all such persons are disqualified from being members of the American Anti-Slavery Society? We trow not.

[2] So also it recommended the formation of Young Men's and Juvenile Societies. Are all minors therefore excluded from the privileges of membership?

assumed as aforesaid, is well fitted to bring *unnecessary* reproach and embarrassment to the cause of the enslaved, inasmuch as that principle is at variance with the general usage and sentiment of this and all other nations, under whatever form of government, and of every age: and while we thus speak, we also declare, that if the assumption of the aforesaid principle was, in our belief, demanded by the great law of right, and by a Divine constitution, necessary to rescue this nation from the great crime and curse of slavery, we would not hesitate to assume it in defiance of universal custom and sentiment, but would do so by openly and manfully changing either the Constitution of our Society, or our organization itself.

In offering this Protest, we refrain from expressing any opinion respecting the propriety of those, whose right to the contemplated membership was contested, voting on the question of said right, as was done in the present case, preferring to leave such proceeding to the obvious conclusion of common sense.[3]

New Jersey

Wm R Weeks, Newark, Thomas P Hunt, do. Andrew M. Torbut, Paterson.

Connecticut

F A Perkins, Norwich, Geo Hall, Northfield, H G Ludlow, N Haven, C P Brush, do. Amos G Beman, do. A C Luca, do. James Quinnard, Norwalk, Randolph Lindsley, Meriden, Julius Pratt, do. Lewis Beers, Jr., Stratford, W L Wilson, Middletown.

New York City

G Ratrie Parburt, A Libolt, La Roy Sunderland, James G Birney, Roe Lockwood, W S Dorr, Joshua Bishop, Patrick Reason, Charles W Denison, Hiram Barney, M R Berry, S W Benedict, John Jay, Thos L Jinnings, Robert Aikman, Jr., James Hildreth, Wm W Patton, Lyman W Gilbert, Edward A Lambert, N E Johnson, Albert O Wilcox, Lewis Tappan, Thomas Downing, John W Sleight, Robert Laird, Duncan Dunbar, Hezekiah D Sharpe, Alfred Smith, Asa Parker,

---

[3] It should be remembered that several women voted in the negative on this question—i.e. *voted* that they *ought not to vote!*

James Wallin, Darius E Jones, Arthur C Cox, Samuel D Burchard, Henry H Loomis, Geo D Little, Aug. J Gillett, Anthony Lane, Wm D Cooledge, Geo H Williams, T McNamee, Edward Corning, Henry C Bowen, Geo M Tracy, O W Norton, Edwin Wilcox, Robert R Kellogg, Charles Kellogg, Samuel Leeds, Jr., George Storrs, Sumner Davidson, Elisha W Chester, F W Graves.

Massachusetts

J E Fuller, Boston, A A Phelps, do. Geo Russell, do. Alanson St. Clair, do. Geo Allen, Shrewsbury, D W Alvord, Greenfield, Joseph Hurlbut, Curtisville, O Scott, Lowell, Samuel Osgood, Springfield, Phineas Crandall, Fall River, J A Canfield, Andover, T E Turner, do. James Birney, Jr., do. Sewall Harding, Medway, Daniel Wise, Quincy, Geo H Smith, Salem, C T Torrey, do. D Butler, Dorchester, Timothy Merritt, Lynn, Geo Goodyear, Ashburnham, Israel Trask, Beverly.

New York

Abm Requa, Poughkeepsie, Hiram H Kellogg, Clinton, Amos Savage, Utica, Edward C Pritchett, do. E W True, Pittsford, Stephen Stanley, Auburn, L C Lockwood, N Windson, J R Wilson, Coldenham, W E Whiting, Brooklyn, Nath Colver, Greenwich, Fayette Shipherd, Troy, John Low, Dutchess Co.

Vermont

E D Barber, Middlebury, J W Hale, Brandon.

Maine

Ebenezer Dole, Hallowell, Eben Dole, Jr., do. Ichabod Codding, do. C C Cone, Brunswick.

New Hampshire

Jared Perkins, Nashua, Silas Curtis, do. W H Brewster, Derry.

Michigan

Warren Isham, Detroit.

Pennsylvania

Chas W Gardner, Philadelphia, Henry Grew, do. Samuel D Hastings, do. Geo M Alsop, do.

Illinois

Geo W Gale, Galesburg.

Rhode Island

Hiram Brooks, Providence, John Waugh, do.

Theodore Weld on American Slavery

ॐ

> *Theodore Weld (1803–1895) produced one of the most important books in anti-slavery literature when he wrote* American Slavery As It Is: Testimony of a Thousand Witnesses. *The volume was published by the American Anti-Slavery Society in New York in 1839. Wendell Phillips called it "that encyclopaedia of facts and storehouse of arguments." Characteristic of Weld's modesty was the fact that the title page carried no name. The following selection constitutes the introduction to the volume.*

INTRODUCTION

Reader, your are empannelled as a juror to try a plain case and bring in an honest verdict. The question at issue is not one of law, but of fact—"What is the actual condition of the slaves in the United States?" A plainer case never went to a jury. Look at it. TWENTY-SEVEN HUNDRED THOUSAND PERSONS in this country, men, women, and children, are in SLAVERY. Is slavery, as a condition for human beings, good, bad, or indifferent? We submit the question without argument. You have common sense, and conscience, and a human heart—pronounce upon it. You have a wife, or a husband, a child, a father, a mother, a brother or a sister—make the case your own, make it theirs, and bring in your verdict. The case of Human Rights against Slavery has been adjudicated in the court of conscience times innumerable. The same verdict has always been rendered—"Guilty"; the same sentence has always been pronounced, "Let it be accursed"; and human nature, with her million echoes, has rung it round the world in every language under heaven, "Let it be accursed. Let it be accursed." His heart is false to human nature, who will not say "Amen." There is not a man on earth who does not believe that slavery is a curse. Human beings may be inconsistent, but human *nature* is true to herself. She has uttered her testimony against slavery with a shriek ever since the monster was begotten; and till it perishes amidst the execrations of the universe, she will traverse the world on its track, dealing her bolts upon its head, and dashing against it her condemning brand. We repeat it, every man knows that slavery is a curse. Whoever denies this, his lips libel his heart. Try him; clank the chains in his ears, and tell him they are for *him*; give him an hour to prepare his wife and children for a life of slavery; bid him make haste and get ready their necks for the yoke, and their wrists for the coffle chains, then look at his pale lips and trembling knees, and you have *nature's* testimony against slavery.

Two millions seven hundred thousand persons in these States are in this condition. They were made slaves and are held such by force, and by being put in fear, and this for no crime! Reader, what have you to say of such treatment? Is it right, just, benevolent? Suppose I should seize you, rob you of your liberty, drive you into the field, and make you work without pay as long as you live, would that be justice and kindness, or monstrous injustice and cruelty? Now, every body knows that the slaveholders do these things to the slaves every day, and yet it is stoutly affirmed that they treat them well and kindly, and that their tender regard for their slaves restrains the masters from inflicting cruelties upon them. We shall go into no metaphysics to show the absurdity of this pretence. The man who *robs* you every day, is, forsooth, quite too tenderhearted ever to cuff or kick you! True, he can snatch your money, but he does it gently lest he should hurt you. He can empty your pockets without qualms, but if your *stomach* is empty, it cuts him to the quick. He can make you work a life time without pay, but loves you too well to let you go hungry. He fleeces you of your *rights* with a relish, but is shocked if you work bareheaded in summer, or in winter without warm stockings. He can make you go without your *liberty,* but never without a shirt. He can crush, in you, all hope of bettering your condition, by vowing that you shall die his slave, but though he can coolly torture your feelings, he is too compassionate to lacerate your back—he can break your heart, but he is very tender of your skin. He can strip you of all protection and thus expose you to all outrages, but if you are exposed to the *weather,* half clad and half sheltered, how yearn his tender bowels! What! Slaveholders talk of treating men well, and yet not only rob them of all they get, and as fast as they get it, but rob them of *themselves,* also; their very hands and feet, all their muscles, and limbs, and senses, their bodies and minds, their time and liberty and earnings, their free speech and rights of conscience, their right to acquire knowledge, and property, and reputation; and yet they, who plunder them of all these, would fain make us believe that their soft hearts ooze out so lovingly toward their slaves that they always keep them well housed and well clad, never push them too hard in the field, never make their dear backs smart, nor let their dear stomachs get empty.

But there is no end to these absurdities. Are slaveholders dunces, or do they take all the rest of the world to be, that they think to bandage our eyes with such thin gauzes? Protesting their kind regard for those whom they hourly plunder of all they have and all they get! What! when they have seized their victims, and annihilated all their *rights,* still claim to be the special guardians of their *happiness!* Plunderers of their liberty, yet the careful suppliers of their wants? Robbers of their earnings, yet watchful sentinels round their interests, and kind providers for their comfort? Filching all their time, yet granting generous donations for rest and sleep? Stealing the use of their muscles, yet thoughtful of their ease? Putting them under *drivers,* yet careful that they are not hard-pushed? Too humane forsooth to stint the stomachs of their slaves, yet force their *minds* to starve, and brandish over them pains and penalties, if they dare to reach forth for the smallest crumb of knowledge, even a letter of the alphabet!

It is no marvel that slaveholders are always talking of their *kind treatment* of their slaves. The only marvel is, that men of sense can be gulled by such professions. Despots always insist that they are merciful. The greatest tyrants that ever dripped with blood have assumed the titles of "most gracious," "most clement," "most merciful," &c., and have ordered their crouching vassals to accost them thus. When did not vice lay claim to those virtues which are the opposites of its habitual crimes? The guilty, according to their own showing, are always innocent, and cowards brave, and drunkards sober, and harlots chaste, and pickpockets honest to a fault. Every body understands this. When a man's tongue grows thick, and he begins to hiccough and walk cross-legged, we expect him, as a matter of course, to protest that he is not drunk; so when a man is always singing the praises of his own honesty, we instinctively watch his movements and look out for our pocket-books. Whoever is simple enough to be hoaxed by such professions, should never be trusted in the streets without somebody to take care of him. Human nature works out in slaveholders just as it does in other men, and in American slaveholders just as in English, French, Turkish, Algerine, Roman and Grecian. The Spartans boasted of their kindness to their slaves, while they whipped them to death by thousands at the altars of their gods. The Romans lauded their own mild treatment of their bondmen, while they branded their names on their flesh with hot irons, and when old, threw them into their fish ponds, or like Cato "the Just," starved them to death. It is the boast of the Turks that they treat their slaves as though they were their children, yet their common name for them is "dogs," and for the merest trifles, their feet are bastinadoed to a jelly, or their heads clipped off with the scimetar. The Portuguese pride themselves on their gentle bearing toward their slaves, yet the streets of Rio Janeiro are filled with naked men and women yoked in pairs to carts and wagons, and whipped by drivers like beasts of burden.

Slaveholders, the world over, have sung the praises of their tender mercies towards their slaves. Even the wretches that plied the African slave trade, tried to rebut Clarkson's proofs of their cruelties, by speeches, affidavits, and published pamphlets, setting forth the accommodations of the "middle passage," and their kind attentions to the comfort of those whom they had stolen from their homes, and kept stowed away under hatches, during a voyage of four thousand miles. So, according to the testimony of the autocrat of the Russias, he exercises great clemency towards the Poles, though he exiles them by thousands to the snows of Siberia, and tramples them down by millions, at home. Who discredits the atrocities perpetrated by Ovando in Hispaniola, Pizarro in Peru, and Cortez in Mexico—because they filled the ears of the Spanish Court with protestations of their benignant rule? While they were yoking the enslaved natives like beasts to the draught, working them to death by thousands in their mines, hunting them with bloodhounds, torturing them on racks, and broiling them on beds of coals, their representations to the mother country teemed with eulogies of their parental sway! The bloody atrocities of Philip II., in the expulsion of his Moorish subjects, are matters of imperishable history. Who disbelieves or doubts them? And yet his courtiers magnified his virtues and chanted his clemency and his mercy, while the wail of a million victims, smitten down by a tempest of fire and slaughter let loose at his bidding, rose above the *Te Deums* that thundered from all Spain's cathedrals. When Louis XIV. revoked the edict of Nantz, and proclaimed two millions of his subjects free plunder for persecution—when from the English channel to the Pyrennees the mangled bodies of the Protestants were dragged on reeking hurdles by a shouting populace, he claimed to be "the father of his people," and wrote himself "His most *Christian* Majesty."

But we will not anticipate topics, the full discussion of which more naturally follows than precedes the inquiry into the actual condition and treatment of slaves in the United States.

As slaveholders and their apologists are volunteer witnesses in their own cause, and are flooding the world with testimony that their slaves are kindly treated; that they are well fed, well clothed, well housed, well lodged, moderately worked, and bountifully provided with all things needful for their comfort, we propose—first, to disprove their assertions by the testimony of a multitude of impartial witnesses, and then to put slaveholders themselves through a course of cross-questioning which shall draw their condemnation out of their own mouths. We will prove that the slaves in the United States are treated with barbarous inhumanity; that they are overworked, underfed, wretchedly clad and lodged, and have insufficient sleep; that they are often made to wear round their necks iron collars armed with prongs, to drag heavy chains and weights at their feet while working in the field, and to wear yokes, and bells, and iron horns; that they are often kept confined in the stocks day and night for weeks together, made to wear gags in their mouths for hours or days, have some of their front teeth torn out or broken off, that they may be easily detected when they run away; that they are frequently flogged with terrible severity, have red pepper rubbed into their lacerated flesh, and hot brine, spirits of turpentine, &c., poured over the gashes to increase the torture; that they are often stripped naked, their backs and limbs cut with knives, bruised and mangled by scores and hundreds of blows with the paddle, and terribly torn by the claws of cats, drawn over them by their tormentors; that they are often hunted with blood hounds and shot down like beasts, or torn in pieces by dogs; that they are often suspended by the arms and whipped and beaten till they faint, and when revived by restoratives, beaten again till they faint, and sometimes till they die; that their ears are often cut off, their eyes knocked out, their bones broken, their flesh branded with red hot irons; that they are maimed, mutilated and burned to death over slow fires. All these things, and more, and worse, we shall *prove*. Reader, we know whereof we affirm, we have weighed it well; *more and worse* WE WILL PROVE. Mark these words, and read on; we will establish all these facts by the testimony of scores and hundreds of eye witnesses, by the testimony of *slaveholders* in all parts of the slave states, by slaveholding members of Congress and of state legislatures, by ambassadors to foreign courts, by judges, by doctors of divinity, and clergymen of all denominations, by merchants, mechanies [*sic*], lawyers and physicians, by presidents and professors in colleges and *professional* seminaries, by planters, overseers and drivers. We shall show, not merely that such deeds are committed, but that they are frequent; not done in corners, but before the sun; not in one of the slave states, but in all of them; not perpetrated by brutal overseers and drivers merely, but by magistrates, by legislators, by professors of religion, by preachers of the gospel, by governors of states, by "gentlemen of property and standing," and by delicate females moving in the "highest circles of society." We know, full well, the outcry that will be made by multitudes, at these declarations; the multiform cavils, the flat denials, the charges of "exaggeration" and "falsehood" so often bandied, the sneers of affected contempt at the credulity that can believe such things, and the rage and imprecations against those who give them currency. We know, too, the threadbare sophistries by which slaveholders and their apologists seek to evade such testimony. If they admit that such deeds are committed, they tell us that they are exceedingly rare, and therefore furnish no grounds for judging of the general treatment of slaves; that occasionally a brutal wretch in the *free* states barbarously butchers his wife, but that no one thinks of inferring from that, the general treatment of wives at the North and West.

They tell us, also, that the slaveholders of the South are proverbially hospitable, kind, and generous, and it is incredible that they can perpetrate such enormities upon human beings; further, that it is absurd to suppose that they would thus injure their own property, that self interest would prompt them to treat their slaves with kindness, as none but fools and madmen wantonly destroy their own property; further, that Northern visitors at the South come back testifying to the kind treatment of the slaves, and that the slaves themselves corroborate such representations. All these pleas, and scores of others, are bruited in every corner of the free States; and who that hath eyes to see, has not sickened at the blindness that saw not, at the palsy of heart that felt not, or at the cowardice and sycophancy that dared not expose such shallow fallacies? We are not to be turned from our purpose by such vapid babblings. In their appropriate places, we propose to consider these objections and various others, and to show their emptiness and folly.

The foregoing declarations touching the inflictions upon slaves, are not hap-hazard assertions, nor the exaggerations of fiction conjured up to carry a point; nor are they the rhapsodies of enthusiasm, nor crude conclusions, jumped at by hasty and imperfect investigation, nor the aimless outpourings either of sympathy or poetry; but they are proclamations of deliberate, well-weighed convictions, produced by accumulations of proof, by affirmations and affidavits, by written testimonies and statements of a cloud of witnesses who speak what they know and testify what they have seen, and all these impregnably fortified by proofs innumerable, in the relation of the slaveholder to his slave, the nature of arbitrary power, and the nature and history of man.

Of witnesses whose testimony is embodied in the following pages, a majority are slaveholders, many of the remainder have been slaveholders, but now reside in free States.

Another class whose testimony will be given, consists of those who have furnished the results of their own observation during periods of residence and travel in the slave States.

We will first present the reader with a few *Personal Narratives* furnished by individuals, natives of slave states and others, embodying, in the main, the results of their own observation in the midst of slavery—facts and scenes of which they were eye-witnesses.

In the next place, to give the reader as clear and definite a view of the actual condition of slaves as possible, we propose to make specific points; to pass in review the various particulars in the slave's condition, simply presenting sufficient testimony under each head to settle the question in every candid mind. The examination will be conducted by stating distinct propositions, and in the following order of topics.

1. *The Food of the Slaves, the Kinds, Quality and Quantity, also, the Number and Time of Meals Each Day,* &c
2. *Their Hours of Labor and Rest*
3. *Their Clothing*
4. *Their Dwellings*
5. *Their Privations and Inflictions*
6. *In conclusion,* a variety of *Objections and Arguments* will be considered which are used by the advocates of slavery to set aside the force of testimony, and to show that the slaves are kindly treated.

Between the larger divisions of the work, brief personal narratives will be inserted, containing a mass of facts and testimony, both general and specific.

James G. Birney Frees His Slaves and Writes Against Slavery

ð

> *James G. Birney (1792–1857) was one of a small number of men and women who, though born in the South, enrolled themselves in the anti-slavery movement. Born in Kentucky*

of slaveholding parents, he later moved to Alabama, where, as a lawyer, he entered politics and was a member of the State legislature. He met Theodore Weld as early as 1832, in Huntsville, Alabama, where he had been living, and was deeply influenced by him. After moving to Kentucky, he freed his slaves and organized the Kentucky Society for the Gradual Relief of the State from Slavery. After being forced to leave Danville, Kentucky, where he sought to establish an antislavery newspaper, he moved to Cincinnati, Ohio, where he published a newspaper, The Philanthropist, *for a short while. He was later appointed secretary of the American Anti-Slavery Society, which he served until the division of 1840. An anti-Garrisonian and political Abolitionist, he was presidential candidate of the Liberty Party in 1840 and 1844.*

The following affidavit, in which he freed the slaves inherited at the death of his father, is dated September 3, 1839 and appeared in the Liberator *on October 4, 1839.*

The selection entitled "American Slavery," is from a pamphlet by Birney, entitled "The American Churches, the Bulwarks of American Slavery," *published in England in 1840, and republished in this country in 1842. The second American edition, which was an enlarged edition, was reprinted in 1885, in Concord, New Hampshire, by Parker Pillsbury. The selection presented here is from that edition, pp. 7–11, 48.*

Know all Men by these Presents,
That I, JAMES G. BIRNEY, *late of Kentucky, but now having my residence in the city of New York,*

Believing that slaveholding is inconsistent with natural justice, with the precepts and spirit of the christian religion, and with the Declaration of American Independence, and wishing to testify in favor of them all, do hereby emancipate, and forever set free, the following named slaves, which have come into my possession, as one of the heirs of my father, the late JAMES BIRNEY, *of Jefferson county, Kentucky,* they being all the slaves held by the said JAMES BIRNEY, deceased at the time of his death.

Their names and description are as follows:

DAVY MYERS, about sixty-five years old, black, slender, five feet seven or eight inches high.

ESTHER, his wife, about sixty years old, yellowish, common size.

NELSON MYERS, son of Davy and Esther, about thirty-two years old, black, light made, about five feet six inches high.

CHARLES MYERS, also son of Davy and Esther, next in age to Nelson, black, about five feet seven or eight inches high.

MARIA MYERS, daughter of Davy and Esther, next in age to Charles, black, tall; and her five children, Martha, a girl about thirteen years, now living with *C. M. Polk, in Illinois*—Judy, eleven years old, now living with *Lev. Lindsey, Esq., in Princeton, Kentucky,* and to remain with him, by an agreement of my late father, until she arrives at the age of twenty years. Rosa, a girl of about eight years— James, a boy of four years—and Daniel, an infant.

LOUISA MYERS, also daughter of Davy and Esther, next in age to Maria, black, light made, well looking.

DAVY MYERS, Junior, a son of Davy and Esther, next in age to Louisa, black, tall, light made.

ESTHER, a daughter of Davy and Esther, and wife of *TOM DEER* (hereafter to be mentioned), next in age to Davy, tall, yellowish; also her two children—Polly, about three years old, and Anna, an infant.

JACKSON MYERS, a son of Davy and Esther, next in age to Esther, common height, yellowish.

FREDERICK MYERS, a son of Davy and Esther, next in age to Jackson, about seventeen years old, yellowish.

MICHAEL MYERS, also son of Davy and Esther, next in age to Frederick—supposed to be sixteen years old on the first day of next January, black, light made. By contract heretofore made, he is to remain in the service of the *Hon. John J. Marshall,* to be instructed in agricultural pursuits, until the 1st day of January, 1845, when, it is supposed, he will be twenty-one years old.

TOM DEER, about twenty-six years old, heavy made, black, the husband of the younger Esther.

BILLY CLARKE, about fifty years old, mulatto, now in Lexington.

KEZIAH, a woman about fifty years old, yellowish, now at *Wm. Hughes' in Danville.*

In testimony of the above, I have hereunto set my name and affixed my seal, this third day of September, in the year of our Lord, one thousand eight hundred and thirty-nine.

JAMES G. BIRNEY, *Seal.*

Witnesses

ANNA R. MARSHALL   CHAS. E. MARSHALL
A. BAYLESS   W. L. BRECKINRIDGE

AMERICAN SLAVERY

The extent to which most of the churches in America are involved in the guilt of supporting the slave system is known to but few in this country.[1] So far from being even suspected by the great mass of the religious community here, it would not be believed but on the most indisputable evidence. Evidence of this character it is proposed now to present—applying to the Methodist Episcopal, the Baptist, the Presbyterian, and the Protestant Episcopal churches. It is done with a single view to make the British Christian public acquainted with the real state of the case—in order that it may in the most intelligent and effective manner exert the influence it possesses with the American churches to persuade them to purify themselves from a sin that has greatly debased them, and that threatens in the end wholly to destroy them.

The following *memoranda* will assist English readers in more readily apprehending the force and scope of the evidence.

I. Of the twenty-six American states, thirteen are slave states. Of the latter, Maryland, Virginia, Kentucky, Missouri, and Tennessee (in part), are slave-*selling* states; the states south of them are slave-*buying* and slave-*consuming sates.*

II. Between the slave-selling and slave-buying states the slave-trade is carried on extensively and systematically. The slave-trader, on completing his purchases for a single adventure, brings the gang together at a convenient point; confines the men in double rows to a large chain running between the rows, by means of smaller lateral chains tightly riveted around the wrists of the slaves, and connected with the principal chain. They are in this way driven along the high-

[1] England—where this pamphlet was first published.

ways (the small boys, the women, and girls following), without any release from their chains till they arrive at the ultimate place of sale. Here they occupy barracoons, till they are disposed of, one by one, or in lots, to those who will give most for them.

III. Ministers and office-bearers, and members of churches are slave-holders—buying and selling slaves (not as the regular slave-trader), but as their convenience or interest may from time to time require. As a general rule, the itinerant preachers in the Methodist church are not permitted to hold slaves—but there are frequent exceptions to the rule, especially of late.

IV. There are in the United States, about 2,487,113 slaves, and 386,069 *free people of color*. Of the slaves, 80,000 are members of the Methodist church; 80,000 of the Baptist; and about 40,000 of the other churches. These church members have no exemption from being sold by their owners as other slaves are. Instances are not rare of slaveholding members of churches selling slaves who are members of the same church with themselves. And members of churches have followed the business of slave-auctioneers.

V. In most of the slave states the master is not permitted formally to emancipate, unless the emancipated person be removed from the state (which makes the formal act unnecessary), or, unless by a special act of the legislature. If, however, he disregard the law, and permit the slave to go at liberty and "do" for himself, the law—on the theory that every slave ought to have a master to *see to him*—directs him to be sold for the benefit of the state. Instances of this, however, must be very rare. The people are better than their laws—for the writer, during a residence of more than thirty years in the slave states, never knew an instance of such a sale, nor has he ever heard of one that was fully proved to have taken place.

VI. There is no law in any of the slave states forbidding the slave-holder to remove his slaves to a free state; nor against his giving the slaves themselves a "pass" for that purpose. The laws of some of the *free* states present obstructions to the settlement of colored persons within their limits—but these obstructions are not insurmountable, and if the validity of the laws should be tried in the tribunals, it would be found they are unconstitutional.

VII. In the slave states a slave cannot be a witness in any case, civil or criminal, in which a white is a party. Neither can a free colored person, except in Louisiana, Ohio, Indiana, and Illinois (free states), make colored persons incompetent as witnesses in any case in which a white is a party. In Ohio, a white person can prove his own ("book") account, not exceeding a certain sum, by his own oath or affirmation. A colored person cannot, as against a white. In Ohio the laws regard all who are mulattoes, or above the grade of mulattoes, as *white*.

VIII. There is no law in the slave states forbidding the several church authorities making slaveholding an offence, for which those guilty of it might be excluded from membership.

The Society of Friends exists in the slave states—it excludes slave-holders.

The United Brethren exist as a church in Maryland and Virginia, slave states. Their Annual Conference for these two states (in which are thirty preachers) met in February [1840]. The following is an extract from its minutes:

> No charge is preferred against any [preachers] except Franklin Echard and Moses Michael.
>
> It appeared in evidence that Moses Michael was the owner of a female slave, which is contrary to the discipline of our church. Conference therefore resolved, that unless brother Michael manumit or set free such slave in six months, he no longer be considered a member of our church.

IX. When ecclesiastical councils excuse themselves from acting for the removal of slavery from their respective communions by saying, they cannot *legislate* for the abolition of slavery; that slavery is a *civil* or *political* institution; that it "belongs to Caesar," and not to the church to put an end to it—they shun the point at issue. To the church member who is a debauchee, a drunkard, a seducer, a murderer, they find no difficulty in saying, "We cannot indeed proceed against your person, or your property—*this* belongs to Caesar, to the *tribunals* of the country, to the *legislature;* but we can suspend or wholly cut you off from the communion of the church, with a view to your repentance and its purification." If a white member should by force or intimidation, day after day, deprive another white member of his property, the authorities of the churches would expel him from their body, should he refuse to made restitution or reparation, although it could not be *enforced* except through the tribunals, over which they have no control. There is, then, nothing to prevent these authorities from saying to the slaveholder, "Cease being a slaveholder and remain in the church, or continue a slaveholder and go out of it. You have your choice."

X. The slave states make it penal to teach the slaves to read. So also some of them to teach the *free colored people* to read. Thus a free colored parent may suffer the penalty for teaching his own children to read even the Scriptures. None of the slaveholding churches, or religious bodies, so far as is known, have, at any time, remonstrated with the legislatures against this iniquitous legislation, or petitioned for its repeal or modification. Nor have they reproved or questioned such of their members, as, being also members of the legislatures, sanctioned such legislation by their votes.

XI. There is no systematic instruction of the slave-members of churches, either orally or in any other way.

XII. Uniting with a church makes no change in the condition of slaves *at home.* They are thrown back just as before, among their old associates, and subjected to their corrupting influences.

XIII. But little pains are taken to secure their attendance at public worship on Sundays.

XIV. The "house-servants" are rarely present at family worship; the "field-hands," never.

XV. It is only one here and there who seems to have any intelligent views of the nature of Christianity, or of a future life.

XVI. In the Methodist, Baptist, Presbyterian, and Episcopal churches, the colored people, during service, sit in a particular part of the house, now generally known as the *negro pew.* They are not permitted to sit in any other, nor to hire or purchase pews as other people, nor would they be permitted to sit, even if invited, in the pews of white persons. This applies to all colored persons, whether *members* or not, and even to *licensed ministers* of their respective connections. The "negro pew" is almost as rigidly kept up in the free states as in the slave.

XVII. In some of the older slave states, as Virginia and South Carolina, churches, in their *corporate* character, hold slaves, who are generally hired out for the support of the minister. The following is taken from the Charleston *Courier* of February 12th, 1835:

Field Negroes, by Thomas Gadsden.

On Tuesday, the 17th instant, will be sold, at the north of the Exchange, at ten o'clock, a prime gang of ten NEGROES, accustomed to the culture of cotton and provisions, belonging to the INDEPENDENT CHURCH, in *Christ's Church Parish* . . . Feb. 6.

XVIII. Nor are instances wanting in which negroes are *bequeathed* for the benefit of the Indians. . . .

Postscript

We would have the reader bear in mind, that the foregoing presents but one side of the anti-slavery cause in the several churches whose proceedings have been considered; and that in them all, there are abolitionists earnestly laboring to purify them from the defilements of slavery; and that they have strong encouragement to proceed, not only in view of what they have already effected toward that end, but in the steady increase of their numbers, and in other omens of success.

We wish him also to bear in mind, that the churches which have been brought before him are not the only American churches which are guilty in giving their countenance and support to slavery. Of others we have said nothing, simply because, to examine their cases, would be to make this work too long for the object we have in view—and because enough has been said to show substantially the state of the slavery question in America, so far as the CHURCH in that country is connected with it.

Lastly—we take pleasure in assuring him that there are considerable portions of the Methodist, Baptist, and Presbyterian churches, as well as the entire of some of the smaller religious bodies in America, that maintain a commendable testimony against slavery and its abominations.

A Negro Abolitionist Protests against Jim Crow Railroads in Massachusetts

ह>

> *Charles Lenox Remond (1810–1873) was described by Carter G. Woodson, the great Negro historian, as "the ablest representative of the Negro race" prior to the appearance of Frederick Douglass. He was an active Abolitionist, was employed as an agent of the American Anti-Slavery Society for many years, and in 1840 he attended the London World Anti-Slavery Conference. He remained abroad for two years, lecturing in Great Britain and Ireland with great effectiveness. Soon after his return to Massachusetts, he was confronted with segregation on one of the railroads of that state and became involved in the campaign then being carried on by the Abolitionists to abolish the practice. In February 1842, he testified before a legislative committee of the Massachusetts House of Representatives that was then holding hearings on the issue. Segregation was finally abolished in April 1843. For a history of the entire affair, see this author's "Jim Crow Railroads in Massachusetts," American Quarterly, Volume VIII (Spring 1956), pp. 61–75.*
>
> *The following address by Remond appeared in the* Liberator *on February 25, 1842.*

THE RIGHTS OF COLORED CITIZENS IN TRAVELING
By Charles Lenox Remond

Before the legislative committee in the House of Representatives, respecting the rights of colored citizens in traveling, &c:

Mr. Chairman, and Gentlemen of the Committee: In rising at this time, and on this occasion, being the first person of color who has ever addressed either of the bodies assembling in this building, I should, perhaps, in the first place, observe that, in consequence of the many misconstructions of the principles and measures of which I am the humble advocate, I may in like manner be subject to similar misconceptions from the moment I open my lips in behalf of the prayer of the petitioners for whom I appear, and therefore feel I have the right at least to ask, at the hands of this intelligent Committee, an impartial hearing; and that whatever prejudices they may have imbibed, be eradicated from their minds, if such exist. I have, however, too much confidence in their intelligence, and too much faith in their determination to do their duty as the representatives of this Commonwealth, to presume they can be actuated by partial motives. Trusting, as I do, that the day is not distant, when, on all questions touching the rights of the citizens of this State, men shall be considered great only as they are good—and not that it shall be told, and painfully experienced, that, in this country, this State, aye, this city, the Athens of America, the rights, privileges and immunities of its citizens are measured by complexion, or any other physical peculiarity or conformation, especially such as over which no man has any control. Complexion can in no sense be construed into crime, much less be rightfully made the criterion of rights. Should the people of color, through a revolution of Providence, become a majority, to the last I would oppose it upon the same principle; for, in either case, it would be equally reprehensible and unjustifiable—alike to be condemned and repudiated. It is JUSTICE I stand here to claim, and not FAVOR for either complexion.

And now, sir, I shall endeavor to confine my remarks to the same subject which has occupied the attention of the Committee thus far, and to stand upon the same principle which has been so ably and so eloquently maintained and established by my esteemed friend, Mr. Phillips.

Our right to citizenship in this State has been acknowledged and secured by the allowance of the elective franchise and consequent taxation; and I know of no good reason, if admitted in this instance, why it should be denied in any other.

With reference to the wrongs inflicted and injuries received on railroads, by persons of color, I need not say they do not end with the termination of the route, but, in effect, tend to discourage, disparage and depress this class of citizens. All hope of reward for upright conduct is cut off. Vice is them becomes a virtue. No distinction is made by the community in which we live. The most vicious is treated as well as the most respectable, both in public and private.

But it is said we all look alike. If this is true, it is not true that we all behave alike. There is a marked difference; and we claim a recognition of this difference.

In the present state of things, they find God's provisions interfered with in such a way, by these and kindred regulations, that virtue may not claim her divinely appointed rewards. Color is made to obscure the brightest endowments, to degrade the fairest character, and to check the highest and most praiseworthy aspirations. If the colored man is vicious, it makes but little difference; if besotted, it matters not; if vulgar, it is quite as well; and he finds himself as well treated, and received as readily into society, of those of an opposite character. Nay, the higher our aspirations, the loftier our purposes and pursuits, does this iniquitous principle of prejudice fasten upon us, and especial pains are taken to irritate, obstruct and injure. No reward of merit, no remuneration for services, no equivalent is rendered the deserving. And I submit, whether this unkind and unchristian policy is not well calculated to make every man disregardful of his conduct, and every woman unmindful of her reputation.

The grievances of which we complain, be assured, sir, are not imaginary, but real—not local, but universal—not occasional, but continual, every day matter of fact things—and have become, to the disgrace of our common country, matter of history.

Mr. Chairman, the treatment to which colored Americans are exposed in their own country finds a counterpart in no other; and I am free to declare that, in the course of nineteen months' traveling in England, Ireland, and Scotland, I was received, treated and recognized, in public and private society, without any regard to my complexion. From the moment I left the American packet ship in Liverpool, up to the moment I came in contact with it again, I was never reminded of my complexion; and all that know anything of my usage in the American ship, will testify that it was unfit for a brute, and none but one could inflict it. But how unlike that afforded in the British steamer *Columbia!* Owing to my limited resources, I took a steerage passage. On the first day out, the second officer came to inquire after my health; and finding me the only passenger in that part part of the ship, ordered the steward to give me a berth in the second cabin; and from that hour until my stepping on shore at Boston, every politeness was shown me by the officers, and every kindness and attention by the stewards; and I feel under deep and lasting obligations to them, individually and collectively.

In no instance was I insulted or treated in any way distinct or dissimilar from other passengers or travelers, either in coaches, railroads, steampackets, or hotels; and if the feeling was entertained, in no case did I discover its existence.

I may with propriety here relate an accident, illustrative of the subject now under consideration. I took a passage ticket at the steampacket office in Glasgow, for Dublin; and on going into the cabin to retire, I found the berth I had engaged occupied by an Irish gentleman and merchant. I enquired if he had not mistaken the number of his berth. He thought not. On comparing tickets, we saw that the clerk had given two tickets of the same number; and it appeared I had received mine first. The gentleman at once offered to vacate the berth, against which I remonstrated, and took my berth in an opposite stateroom. Here, sir, we discover treatment just, impartial, reasonable; and we ask nothing beside.

There is a marked difference between social and civil rights. It has been well and justly remarked, by my friend Mr. Phillips, that we all claim the privilege of selecting our society and associations; but, in civil rights, one man has not the prerogative to define rights of another. For instance, sir, in public conveyances, for the rich man to usurp the privileges to himself, to the injury of the poor man, would be submitted to in no well regulated society. And such is the position suffered by persons of color. On my arrival home from England, I went to the railway station, to go to Salem, being anxious to see my parents and sisters as soon as possible—asked for a ticket—paid 50 cents for it, and was pointed to the American designation car. Having previously received information of the regulations, I took my seat peaceably, believing it better to suffer wrong than do wrong. I felt then, as I felt on many occasions prior to leaving home, unwilling to descend so low as to bandy words with the superintendents, or contest my rights with conductors, or any others in the capacity of servants of any stage or steamboat company, or railroad corporation; although I never, by any means, gave evidence that, by my submission, I intended to sanction usages which would derogate from uncivilized, much less long and loud professing and high pretending America.

Bear with me while I relate an additional occurrence. On the morning after my return home, I was obliged to go to Boston again, and on going to the Salem station I met two friends, who enquired if I had any objection to their taking seats with me. I answered, I should be

most happy. They took their seats accordingly, and soon afterwards
one of them remarked to me—"Charles, I don't know if they will
allow us to ride with you." It was some time before I could understand what they meant, and, on doing so, I laughed—feeling it to be
a climax to every absurdity I had heard attributed to Americans. To
say nothing of the wrong done those friends, and the insult and indignity offered me by the appearance of the conductor, who ordered
the friends from the car in a somewhat harsh manner—they immediately left the carriage.

On returning to Salem some few evenings afterwards, Mr. Chase,
the superintendent on this road, made himself known to me by re-
calling bygone days and scenes, and then enquired if I was not glad
to get home after so long an absence in Europe. I told him I was glad
to see my parents and family again, and this was the only object I
could have, unless he thought I should be glad to take a hermit's life
in the great pasture; inasmuch as I never felt to loathe my American
name so much as since my arrival. He wished to know my reasons
for the remark. I immediately gave them, and wished to know of him,
if, in the event of his having a brother with red hair, he should find
himself separated while traveling because of this difference, he should
deem it just. He could make no reply. I then wished to know if the
principle was not the same; and if so, there was an insult implied by
his question.

In conclusion, I challenged him as the instrument inflicting the
manifold injuries upon all not colored like himself to the presentation
of an instance in any other Christian or unchristian country, tolerat-
ing usages at once so disgraceful, unjust and inhuman. What if some
few of the West or East India planters and merchants should visit our
liberty-loving country, with their colored wives—how would he manage? Or, if R. M. Johnson, the gentleman who has been elevated to
the second office in the gift of the people, should be traveling from
Boston to Salem, if he was prepared to separate him from his wife
or daughters. [Involuntary burst of applause, instantly restrained.]

Sir, it happens to be my lot to have a sister a few shades lighter
than myself; and who knows, if this state of things is encouraged,
whether I may not on some future occasion be mobbed in Washington
Street, on the supposition of walking with a white young lady! [Sup-
pressed indications of sympathy and applause.]

Gentlemen of the Committee, these distinctions react in all their wickedness—to say nothing of their concocted and systematized odiousness and absurdity—upon those who instituted them; and particularly so upon those who are illiberal and mean enough to practise them.

Mr. Chairman, if colored people have abused any rights granted them, or failed to exhibit due appreciation of favors bestowed, or shrunk from dangers or responsibility, let it be made to appear. Or if our country contains a population to compare with them in loyalty and patriotism, circumstances duly considered, I have it yet to learn. The history of our country must ever testify in their behalf. In view of these and many additional considerations, I unhestitatingly assert their claim, on the naked principle of merit, to every advantage set forth in the Constitution of this Commonwealth.

Finally, Mr. Chairman, there is in this and other States a large and growing colored population, whose residence in your midst has not been from choice (let this be understood and reflected upon), but by the force of circumstances over which they never had control. Upon the heads of their oppressors and calumniators be the censure and responsibility. If to ask at your hands redress for injuries, and protection in our rights and immunities, as citizens, is reasonable, and dictated alike by justice, humanity and religion, you will not reject, I trust, the prayer of your petitioners.

Before sitting down, I owe it to myself to remark, that I was not appraised of the wish of my friends to appear here until passing through Boston, a day or two since; and having been occupied with other matters, I have had no opportunity for preparation on this occasion. I feel much obliged to the Committee for their kind, patient, and attentive hearing. [Applause.]

An Abolitionist View of the American Church and Slavery

ℰ⮞

Stephen S. Foster (1809–1881) was a New Hampshire-born Dartmouth College graduate who studied for awhile at the Union Theological Seminary but abandoned the ministry in favor of a reformer's career. He became an anti-slavery lecturer in 1830. He was a nonresistant whose picturesque language involved him in more riots than was perhaps true of most other Abolitionists. One of his favorite declarations, usually in a church, was that the Methodist Episcopal Church —because of its support of slavery—was worse than any brothel in New York City. The action usually started immediately thereafter. The following selections are from his book, The Brotherhood of Thieves: or, A True Picture of the American Church and Clergy: A Letter to Nathaniel Barney of Nantucket, *Boston, Anti-Slavery Office, 1844, 72 pp.*

LETTER

ESTEEMED FRIEND:

In the early part of last autumn, I received a letter from you, requesting me to prepare an article for the press, in vindication of the strong language of denunciation of the American church and clergy, which I employed at the late Anti-Slavery Convention on your island, and which was the occasion of the disgraceful mob, which disturbed and broke up that meeting. In my answer, I gave you assurance of prompt compliance with your request; but, for reasons satisfactory to myself, I have failed to fulfil my promise, up to the present time. The novelty of the occasion has now passed away; the deep and malignant passions which were stirred in the bosoms of no inconsiderable portion of your people, have, doubtless, subsided; but the important *facts* connected with it are yet fresh in the memories of all; and, as the occasion was one of general, not local, interest, and the spirit which was there exhibited was a fair specimen of the gen-

eral temper and feeling of our country towards the advocates of equal
rights and impartial justice, I trust it will not be deemed amiss in me
to make it a subject of public notice, even at this late period.

But in the remarks which I propose to make, it will be no part of
my object to vindicate myself in the opinion of the public, against
the foul aspersions of those whose guilty quiet my preaching may have
disturbed. Indeed, to tell the truth, I place a very low estimate on the
good opinions of my countrymen—quite as low, I think, as they do on
mine, if I may judge from their very great anxiety to have me speak
well of them, which I *positively* never can, so long as their national
capital is a human flesh-mart, and their chief magistrate is a slave-
breeder. The most that I can do is to pledge myself never to mob
them, nay, that I will not even be *displeased* with them, for speaking
ill of me, while their character remains what it now is. My opponents,
among whom rank most of the church and clergy of the country,
have disturbed a majority of the meetings which I have attended,
within the last nine months, by drunken, murderous mobs, and, in
several instances, they have inflicted severe injury upon my person;
but I value this violence and outrage as proof of their deep conviction of the truth and power of what I say. I deem the *reproach* of such
men sufficient praise. And I here tender them my thanks for the high
compliment they have so often paid to my opinions, in the extreme
measures to which they have resorted to *compel* me to speak in their
praise. But so long as their character remains such that I can bestow
no commendations, I shall ask none in return.

Nor is it my intention, in this letter, to weaken, by explanations,
the force of my testimony against the popular religion of our country,
for the purpose of allaying the bloody spirit of persecution which has
of late characterized the opposition to my course. True, my life is in
danger, especially whenever I attempt to utter my sentiments in
houses dedicated to what is called the worship of God; but He who
has opened to my view other worlds, in which to reap the rewards
and honors of a life of toil and suffering in the cause of truth and
human freedom, in this, has taught me to "be not afraid of them that
kill the body, and after that have no more that they can do." Hence
I have no pacificatory explanations to offer, no coward disclaimers to
make. But I shall aim to present to the comprehension of the humblest individual, into whose hands this letter may chance to fall, a clear
and comprehensive view of the intrinsic moral character of that class

of our countrymen who claim our respect and veneration, as ministers and followers of the Prince of Peace. I am charged with having done them great injustice in my public lectures, on that and various other occasions. Many of these, who make this charge, doubtless, honestly think so. To correct their error—to reflect on their minds the light which God has kindly shed on mine—to break the spell in which they are now held by the sorcery of a designing priesthood, and prove that priesthood to be a "Brotherhood of Thieves" and the "Bulwark of American Slavery"—is all that I shall aim to do.

But I ought, perhaps, in justice to those who know nothing of my religious sentiments, except from the misrepresentations of my enemies, to say, that I have no feelings of personal hostility towards any portion of the church or clergy of our country. As children of the same Father, they are endeared to me by the holiest of all ties; and I am as ready to suffer, if need be, in defence of their rights, as in defence of the rights of the Southern slave. My objections to them are purely conscientious. I am a firm believer in the Christian religion, and in Jesus, as a divine being, who is to be our final Judge. I was born and nurtured in the bosom of the church, and for twelve years was among its most active members. At the age of twenty-two, I left the allurements of an active business life, on which I had just entered with fair prospects, and, for seven successive years, cloistered myself within the walls of our literary institutions, in "a course of study preparatory to the ministry." The only object I had in view in changing my pursuits, at this advanced period of life, was to render myself more useful to the world, by extending the principles of Christianity, as taught and lived out by their great Author. In renouncing the priesthood and an organized church, and laboring for their overthrow, my object is still the same. I entered them on the supposition that they were, what from a child I had been taught to regard them, the enclosures of Christ's ministers and flock, and his chosen instrumentalities for extending his kingdom on the earth. I have left them from an unresistible conviction, in spite of my early prejudices, that they are a "hold of every foul spirit," and the devices of men to gain influence and power. And, in rebuking their adherents as I do, my only object is to awaken them, if possible, to a sense of their guilt and moral degradation, and bring them to repentance, and a knowledge of the true God, of whom most of them are now lamentably ignorant, as their lives clearly prove.

The remarks which I made at your Convention were of a most grave and startling character. They strike at the very foundation of all our popular ecclesiastical institutions, and exhibit them to the world as the apologists and supporters of the most atrocious system of oppression and wrong, beneath which humanity has ever groaned. They reflect on the church the deepest possible odium, by disclosing to public view the chains and handcuffs, the whips and branding-irons, the rifles and bloodhounds, with which her ministers and deacons bind the limbs and lacerate the flesh of innocent men and defenceless women. They cast upon the clergy the same dark shade which Jesus threw over the ministers of his day, when he tore away the veil beneath which they had successfully concealed their diabolical schemes of personal aggrandizement and power, and denounced them before all the people, as a "den of thieves," as "fools and blind," "whited sepulchres," "blind guides, which strain at a gnat, and swallow a camel," "hypocrites, who devour widows' houses, and for a pretence make long prayers," "liars," "adulterers," "serpents," "a generation of vipers," who could not "escape the damnation of hell." But, appalling and ominous as they were, I am not aware that I gave the parties accused, or their mobocratic friends, any just cause of complaint. They were all spoken in public, in a free meeting, where all who dissented from me were not only invited, but warmly urged, to reply. I was an entire stranger among you, with nothing but the naked truth and a few sympathizing friends to sustain me, while the whole weight of popular sentiment was in their favor. Was the controversy unequal on their part? Were they afraid to meet me with the same honorable weapons which I had chosen? Conscious innocence seldom consents to tarnish its character by a dishonorable defence. Had my charges been unfounded, a refutation of them, under the circumstances, would have been most easy and triumphant. My opponents, had they been innocent, could have acquitted themselves honorably, and overwhelmed their accuser in deep disgrace, without the necessity of resorting to those arguments which appeal only to one's fears of personal harm, and which are certain to react upon their authors, when the threatened danger subsides.

But if all that I have alleged against them be true, it was obviously my right, nay, my imperative duty, to make the disclosures which I did, even though it might be, as you well know it was, at the peril of my life, and the lives of my associates.

In exposing the deep and fathomless abominations of those *pious* thieves, who gain their livelihood by preaching sermons and stealing babies, I am not at liberty to yield to any intimidations, however imposing the source from which they come. The right of speech— the liberty to utter our own convictions *freely,* at all times and in all places, at discretion, unawed by fear, unembarrassed by force—is the gift of God to every member of the family of man, and should be preserved inviolate; and for one, I can consent to surrender it to no power on earth, but with the loss of life itself. Let not the petty tyrants of our land, in church or state, think to escape the censures which their crimes deserve, by hedging themselves about with the frightful penalties of human law, or the more frightful violence of a drunken and murderous mob. There live the men who are not afraid to die, even though called to meet their fate within the gloomy walls of a dismal prison, with no kind hand to wipe the cold death-sweat from their sinking brow; and they scorn a fetter on *limb* or *spirit.* They know their rights, and know how to defend them, or to obtain more than an equivalent for their loss, in the rewards of a martyr to the right. While life remains, they will speak, and speak *freely,* though it be in "A Voice from the Jail"; nor will they treat the crimes and vices of slave-breeding priests, and their consecrated abettors of the North, with less severity than they do the crimes and vices of other marauders on their neighbors' property and rights. Nor should the friends of freedom be alarmed at the consequences of this faithful dealing with "spiritual wickedness in high places." The mobs which it creates are but the violent contortions of the patient, as the deep gashes of the operator's knife severs the infected limb from his sickly and emaciated body.

The fact, that my charges against the religious sects of our country were met with violence and outrage, instead of sound arguments and invalidating testimony, is strong presumptive evidence of their truth. The innocent never find occasion to resort to this disgraceful mode of defence. If our clergy and church were the ministers and church of Christ, would their reputation be defended by drunken and murderous mobs? Are brickbats and rotten eggs the weapons of truth and Christianity? Did Jesus say to his disciples, "Blessed are ye when the *mob* shall speak well of you, and shall defend you"? The church, slavery, and the mob, are a queer trinity! And yet that they are a trinity—that they all "agree in one"—cannot be denied. Every assault

which we have made on the bloody slave system, as I shall hereafter
show, has been promptly met and repelled by the church, which is
herself the claimant of several hundred thousand slaves; and whenever we have attempted to expose the guilt and hypocrisy of the
church, the *mob* has uniformly been first and foremost in her defence.
But I rest not on presumptive evidence, however strong and conclusive, to sustain my allegations against the American church and
clergy. The proof of their identity with slavery, and their consequent
deep and unparalleled criminality, is positive and overwhelming, and
is fully adequate to sustain the gravest charges, and to justify the most
denunciatory language that has ever fallen from the lips of their most
inveterate opponents.

I said at your meeting, among other things, that the American
church and clergy, as a body, were thieves, adulterers, man-stealers,
pirates, and murderers; that the Methodist Episcopal church was
more corrupt and profligate than any house of ill-fame in the city of
New York; that the Southern ministers of that body were desirous
of perpetuating slavery for the purpose of supplying themselves with
concubines from among its hapless victims; and that many of our
clergymen were guilty of enormities that would disgrace an Algerine
pirate!! These sentiments called forth a burst of holy indignation from
the *pious* and *dutiful* advocates of the church and clergy, which overwhelmed the meeting with repeated showers of stones and rotten
eggs, and eventually compelled me to leave your island, to prevent
the shedding of human blood . . .

This violence and outrage on the part of the church were, no doubt,
committed to the glory of God and the honor of religion, although
the connection between rotten eggs and holiness of heart is not very
obvious. It is, I suppose, one of the mysteries of religion which lay-
men cannot understand without the aid of the clergy; and I therefore
suggest that the pulpit make it a subject of Sunday discourse. But are
not the charges here alleged against the clergy strictly and literally
true? I maintain that they are true to the very letter; that the clergy
and their adherents are literally, and beyond all controversy, a
"brotherhood of thieves"; and, in support of this opinion, I submit
the following considerations:

You will agree with me, I think, that slaveholding involves the
commission of all the crimes specified in my first charge, viz., theft,
adultery, man-stealing, piracy, and murder. But should you have any

doubts on this subject, they will be easily removed by analyzing this atrocious outrage on the laws of God, and the rights and happiness of man, and examining separately the elements of which it is composed . . .

By this brief analysis of slavery, we stamp upon the forehead of the slaveholder, with a brand deeper than that which marks the victim of his wrongs, the infamy of theft, adultery, manstealing, piracy, and murder. We demonstrate, beyond the possibility of doubt, that he who enslaves another—that is, robs him of his right to himself, to his own hands, and head, and feet, and transforms him from a free moral agent into a mere *brute,* to obey, not the commands of God, but his claimant—is guilty of every one of these atrocious crimes. And in doing this, we have only demonstrated what, to every reflecting mind, is self-evident. Every man, if he would but make the case of the slave his own, would feel in his inmost soul the truth and justice of this charge. But these are the crimes which I have alleged against the American church and clergy. Hence, to sustain my charge against them, it only remains for me to show that they are slaveholders. That they are slaveholders—party to a conspiracy against the liberty of more than two millions of our countrymen, and, as such, are guilty of the crimes of which they stand accused—I affirm, and will now proceed to prove . . .

It is a common but mistaken opinion, that, to constitute one a slaveholder, he must be the claimant of slaves. That title belongs alike to the slave-claimant, and all those who, by their countenance or otherwise, lend their influence to support the slave system. If I aid or countenance another in stealing, I am a thief, though he receive all the booty . . . Hence all who, through their political or ecclesiastical connections, aid or countenance the master in his work of death, are slaveholders, and, as such, are stained with all the moral turpitude which attaches to the man who, by their sanction, wields the bloody lash over the heads of his trembling victims, and buries it deep in their quivering flesh. Nay, the human *hounds* which guard the plantation, ever eager to bark on the track of the flying fugitive, are objects of deeper indignation and abhorrence than even its lordly proprietor.

How stands this matter, then, in regard to the American church and clergy? Is it true of them that they are either claimants of slaves or *watch-dogs* of the plantation? Such, I regret to say, is the shameful and humiliating fact. It is undeniably true, that, with comparatively few exceptions, they occupy one of these two positions in relation to the "peculiar institution." Thousands of the ministers, and tens of thousands of the members of the different sects, are actually claimants of slaves. They buy and sell, mortgage and lease, their own "brethren in the Lord," not unfrequently breaking up families, and scattering their bleeding fragments over all the land, never to be gathered again till the archangel's trump shall wake their slumbering ashes into life. . . .

> With great respect and affection,
> Your sincere friend,
> S. S. FOSTER.

CANTERBURY, N. H., July, 1843.

Can Abolitionists Vote or Take Office Under the United States Constitution?

ह•

> *This was the title of a pamphlet published in 1845 in defense of the newly adopted policy of the American Anti-Slavery Society of not voting or taking office under the Constitution and of striving for a policy of Northern secession from the Union. This policy was embodied in the Abolitionist slogan, "No union with slaveholders." The pamphlet was published in New York by the American Anti-Slavery Society and included an introduction by Wendell Phillips. The selection that follows is the introduction.*

INTRODUCTION

The American Anti-Slavery Society, at its Annual Meeting in May, 1844, adopted the following Resolution:

Resolved, That secession from the present United States government is the duty of every abolitionist; since no one can take office, or throw a vote for another to hold office, under the United States Constitution, without violating his anti-slavery principles, and rendering himself an abettor of the slaveholder in his sin.

The passage of this Resolution has caused two charges to be brought against the Society: *First,* that it is a no-government body, and that the whole doctrine of non-resistance is endorsed by this vote; and *secondly,* that the Society transcended its proper sphere and constitutional powers by taking such a step.

The logic which infers that because a man thinks the Federal Government bad, he must necessarily think *all* government so, has at least, the merit and the charm of novelty. There is a spice of arrogance just perceptible, in the conclusion that the Constitution of these United States is so perfect, that one who dislikes it could never be satisfied with any form of government whatever!

Were O'Connell and his fellow Catholics non-resistants, because for two hundred years they submitted to exclusion from the House of Lords and the House of Commons, rather than qualify themselves for a seat by an oath abjuring the Pope? Were the *nonjuring* Bishops of England non-resistants, when they went down to the grave without taking their seats in the House of Lords, rather than take an oath denying the Stuarts and to support the House of Hanover? Both might have purchased power at the price of one annual falsehood. There are some in this country who do not seem to think that price at all unreasonable. It were a rare compliment indeed to the non-resistants, if every exhibition of rigid principle on the part of an individual is to make the world suspect him of leaning towards their faith.

The Society is not opposed to government, but only to *this* Government based upon and acting for slavery.

With regard to the second charge, of exceeding its proper limits and trespassing on the rights of the minority, it is enough to say, that the object of the American Anti-Slavery Society is the "entire abolition of slavery in the United States." Of course it is its duty to find out all the sources of pro-slavery influence in the land. It is its right, it is its duty to try every institution in the land, no matter how venerable, or sacred, by the touch-stone of anti-slavery principle; and if it finds any one false, to proclaim that fact to the world, with more or less of energy, according to its importance in society. It has tried the Constitution, and pronounced it unsound.

No member's conscience need be injured—The qualification for membership remains the same, "the belief that slave-holding is a heinous crime." No new test has been set up—but the majority of the Society, for the time being, faithful to its duty of trying every institution by the light of the present day—of uttering its opinion on every passing event that touches the slave's welfare, has seen it to be duty to sound forth its warning.

No Union with Slaveholders

No one who did not vote for the Resolution is responsible for it. No one is asked to quit our platform. We, the majority, only ask him to extend to our opinions the same toleration that we extend to him, and agreeing to differ on this point, work together where we can. We proscribe no man for difference of opinion.

It is said, that having refused in 1840, to say that a man *ought to vote,* on the ground that such a resolution would be tyrannical and intolerant, the Society is manifestly inconsistent now in taking upon itself to say that no abolitionist *can* consistently vote. But the inconsistency is only apparent and not real.

There may be a thousand reasons why a particular individual ought not to do an act, though the act be innocent in itself. It would be tyranny therefore in a society which can properly take notice of but one subject, slavery, to promulgate the doctrine that all its members ought to do any particular act, as for instance, to vote, to give money, to lecture, to petition, or the like. The particular circumstances and opinions of each one must regulate his actions. All we have a right to ask is, that he do for the slave's cause as much as he does for any other of equal importance. But when an act is wrong, it is no intolerance to say to the whole world that it ought *not to be done.* After the abolitionist has granted that slavery is wrong, we have the right to judge him by his own principles, and arraign him for inconsistency that, so believing, he helps the slaveholder by his oath.

The following pages have been hastily thrown together in explanation of the vote above recited. They make no pretension to a full argument of the topic. I hope that in a short time I shall get leisure sufficient to present to our opponents, unless some one does it for me, a full statement of the reasons which have led us to this step.

I am aware that we non-voters are rather singular. But history, from the earliest Christians downwards, is full of instances of men who refused all connection with government, and all the influence which office could bestow, rather than deny their principles, or aid in doing wrong. Yet I never heard them called either idiots or over-scrupulous. Sir Thomas More need never have mounted the scaffold, had he only consented to take the oath of supremacy. He had only to tell a lie with solemnity, as we are asked to do, and he might not only have saved his life, but, as the trimmers of his day would have told him, doubled his influence. Pitt resigned his place as Prime Minister of England, rather than break faith with the Catholics of Ireland. Should I not resign a petty ballot rather than break faith with the slave? But I was specially glad to find a distinct recognition of the principle upon which we have acted, applied to a different point, in the life of that Patriarch of the Anti-Slavery enterprise, Granville Sharpe. It is in a late number of the *Edinburgh Review*. While an underclerk in the War Office, he sympathized with our fathers in their struggle for independence. "Orders reached his office to ship munitions of war to the revolted colonies. If his hand had entered the account of such a cargo, it would have contracted in his eyes the stain of innocent blood. To avoid this pollution, he resigned his place and his means of subsistence at a period of life when he could no longer hope to find any other lucrative employment." As the thoughtful clerk of the War Office takes his hat down from the peg where it has used to hang for twenty years, methinks I hear one of our opponents cry out, "Friend Sharpe, you are absurdly scrupulous." "You may innocently aid Government in doing wrong," adds another. While the Liberty Party yelps at his heels, "My dear sir, you are quite losing your influence!" And indeed it is melancholy to reflect how, from that moment the mighty underclerk of the War Office (!) dwindled into the mere Granville Sharpe of history! The man of whom Mansfield and Hargrave were content to learn law, and Wilberforce, philanthropy.

One friend proposes to vote for men who shall be pledged not to take office unless the oath of the Constitution is dispensed with, and who shall then go on to perform in their offices only such duties as we, their constituents, approve. He cites, in support of his view, the election of O'Connell to the House of Commons, in 1828, I believe, just one year before the "Oath of Supremacy," which was the objectionable one to the Catholics, was dispensed with. Now, if we stood in the same circumstances as the Catholics did in 1828, the example would be in point. When the public mind is thoroughly revolutionized, and ready for the change, when the billow has reached its height and begins to crest into foam, then such a measure may bring matters to a crisis. But let us first go through, in patience, as O'Connell did, our twenty years of agitation. Waiving all other objections, this plan seems to me mere playing at politics, and an entire waste of effort. It loses our high position as moral reformers; it subjects us to all that malignant opposition and suspicion of motives which attend the array of parties; and while thus closing up our access to the national conscience, it wastes in fruitless caucussing and party tactics, the time and the effort which should have been directed to efficient agitation.

The history of our Union is lesson enough, for every candid mind, of the fatal effects of every, the least, compromise with evil. The experience of the fifty years passed under it, shows us the slaves trebling in numbers—slaveholders monopolizing the offices and dictating the policy of the Government—prostituting the strength and influence of the Nation to the support of slavery here and elsewhere—trampling on the rights of the free States, and making the courts of the country their tools. To continue this disastrous alliance longer is madness. The trial of fifty years only proves that it is impossible for free and slave States to unite on any terms, without all becoming partners in the guilt and responsible for the sin of slavery. Why prolong the experiment? Let every honest man join in the outcry of the American Anti-Slavery Society,

NO UNION WITH SLAVEHOLDERS
WENDELL PHILLIPS.

BOSTON, Jan. 15, 1845.

A Former Slave Issues an Anti-Slavery Newspaper

ह∾

Frederick Douglass (1817–1895), escaped slave, Abolitionist, newspaper editor and writer, launched his newspaper, The North Star, with Martin R. Delany as co-editor in 1847. The first number appeared on December 3. The following is an editorial from that number.

To Our Oppressed Countrymen

We solemnly dedicate the *North Star* to the cause of our long oppressed and plundered fellow countrymen. May God bless the offering to your good! It shall fearlessly assert your rights, faithfully proclaim your wrongs, and earnestly demand for you instant and even-handed justice. Giving no quarter to slavery at the South, it will hold no truce with oppressors at the North. While it shall boldly advocate emancipation for our enslaved brethren, it will omit no opportunity to gain for the nominally free, complete enfranchisement. Every effort to injure or degrade you or your cause—originating wheresoever, or with whomsoever—shall find in it a constant, unswerving and inflexible foe.

We shall energetically assail the ramparts of Slavery and Prejudice, be they composed of church or state, and seek the destruction of every refuge of lies, under which tyranny may aim to conceal and protect itself.

Among the multitude of plans proposed and opinions held, with reference to our cause and condition, we shall try to have a mind of our own, harmonizing with all as far as we can, and differing from any and all where we must, but always discriminating between men and measures. We shall cordially approve every measure and effort calculated to advance your sacred cause, and strenuously oppose any which in our opinion may tend to retard its progress. In regard to our position, on questions that have unhappily divided the friends of freedom in this country, we shall stand in our paper where we have ever stood on the platform. Our views written shall accord with our views spoken, earnestly seeking peace with all men, when it can be secured without injuring the integrity of our movement, and never shrinking from conflict or division when summoned to vindicate truth and justice.

While our paper shall be mainly Anti-Slavery, its columns shall be freely opened to the candid and decorous discussion of all measures and topics of a moral and humane character, which may serve to enlighten, improve, and elevate mankind. Temperance, Peace, Capital Punishment, Education—all subjects claiming the attention of the public mind may be freely and fully discussed here.

While advocating your rights, the *North Star* will strive to throw light on your duties: while it will not fail to make known your virtues, it will not shun to discover your faults. To be faithful to our foes it must be faithful to ourselves, in all things.

Remember that we are one, that our cause is one, and that we must help each other, if we would succeed. We have drunk to the dregs the bitter cup of slavery; we have worn the heavy yoke; we have sighed beneath our bonds, and writhed beneath the bloody lash—cruel mementoes of our oneness are indelibly marked in our living flesh. We are one with you under the ban of prejudice and proscription—one with you under the slander of inferiority—one with you in social and political disfranchisement. What you suffer, we suffer; what you endure, we endure. We are indissolubly united, and must fall or flourish together.

We feel deeply the solemn responsibility which we have now assumed. We have seriously considered the importance of the enterprise, and have now entered upon it with full purpose of heart. We have nothing to offer in the way of literary ability to induce you to encourage us in our laudable undertaking. You will not expect or require this at our hands. The most that you can reasonably expect, or that we can safely promise, is, a paper of which you need not be ashamed. Twenty-one years of severe bondage at the South, and nine years of active life at the North, while it has afforded us the best possible opportunity for storing our mind with much practical and important information, has left us little time for literary pursuits or attainments. We have yet to receive the advantage of the first day's schooling. In point of education, birth and rank, we are one with yourselves, and of yourselves. What we are, we are not only without help, but against trying opposition. Your knowledge of our history for the last seven years makes it unnecessary for us to say more on this point. What we have been in your cause, we shall continue to be; and not being too old to learn, we may improve in many ways. Patience and Perseverance shall be our motto.

We shall be the advocates of learning, from the very want of it, and shall most readily yield the deference due to men of education among us; but shall always bear in mind to accord most merit to those who have labored hardest, and overcome most, in the praiseworthy pursuit of knowledge, remembering "that the whole need not a physician, but they that are sick," and that "the strong ought to bear the infirmities of the weak."

Brethren, the first number of the paper is before you. It is dedicated to your cause. Through the kindness of our friends in England, we are in possession of an excellent printing press, types, and all other materials necessary for printing a paper. Shall this gift be blest to our good, or shall it result in our injury? It is for you to say. With your aid, co-operation and assistance, our enterprise will be entirely successful. We pledge ourselves that no effort on our part shall be wanting, and that no subscriber shall lose his subscription—"The *North Star* Shall Live." *The North Star,* December 3, 1847.

An Anti-Slavery Address by Theodore Parker

ह•

Theodore Parker (1810–1860) was probably the greatest American scholar of his day, and after the death of William Ellery Channing, the most widely known Unitarian minister. He was an outstanding and devoted Abolitionist leader. The following address was delivered before a convention of the

New England Anti-Slavery Society on May 31, 1848. It appears in The Collected Works of Theodore Parker, *edited by Frances Power Cobbe, London, 1863, Vol. V, pp. 93–102.*

SPEECH AT FANEUIL HALL,
Before
The New England Anti-Slavery
Convention, May 31, 1848.

The design of the abolitionists is this—to remove and destroy the institution of slavery. To accomplish this well, two things are needed, ideas and actions. Of the ideas first, and then a word of the actions.

What is the idea of the abolitionists? Only this, That all men are created free, endowed with unalienable rights; and in respect of those rights, that all men are equal. This is the idea of Christianity, of human nature. Of course, then, no man has a right to take away another's rights; of course, no man may use me for his good, and not my own good also; of course, there can be no ownership of man by man; of course, no slavery in any form. Such is the idea, and some of the most obvious doctrines that follow from it.

Now, the abolitionists aim to put this idea into the minds of the people, knowing that if it be there, actions will follow fast enough.

It seems a very easy matter to get it there. The idea is nothing new; all the world knows it. Talk with men, Democrats and Whigs, they will say they like freedom in the abstract, they hate slavery in the abstract. But you find that somehow they like slavery in the concrete, and dislike abolitionism when it tries to set free the slave. Slavery is the affair of the whole people; not Congress, but the nation, made slavery; made it national, constitutional. Not Congress, but the voters, must unmake slavery; make it un-constitutional, unnational. They say Congress cannot do it. Well, perhaps it is so; but they that make can break. If the people made slavery, they can unmake it.

You talk with the people; the idea of freedom is there. They tell you they believe the Declaration of Independence—that all men are created equal. But somehow they contrive to believe that negroes now in bondage are an exception to the rule, and so they tell us that slavery must not be meddled with, that we must respect the compromises of the Constitution. So we see that respect for the Constitution overrides respect for the inalienable rights of three millions of negro men.

Now, to move men, it is necessary to know two things—first, What they think, and next, Why they think it. Let us look a little at both.

In New England, men over twenty-one years old may be divided into two classes. First, the men that vote, and secondly, the men that choose the Governor. The voters in Massachusetts are some hundred and twenty thousand; the men that choose the Governor, who tell the people how to vote, whom to vote for, what laws to make, what to forbid, what policy to pursue—they are not very numerous. You may take one hundred men out of Boston, and fifty men from the other large towns in the State—and if you could get them to be silent till next December, and give no counsel on political affairs, the people would not know what to do. The Democrats would not know what to do, nor the Whigs. We are a very democratic people, and suffrage is almost universal; but it is a very few men who tell us how to vote, who make all the most important laws. Do I err in estimating the number at one hundred and fifty? I do not like to exaggerate—suppose there are six hundred men, three hundred in each party; that six hundred manage the political action of the State, in ordinary times.

I need not stop to ask what the rest of the people think about freedom and slavery. What do the men who control our politics think thereof? I answer, They are not opposed to slavery; to the slavery of three millions of men. They may not like slavery in the abstract, or they may like it, I do not pretend to judge; but slavery in the concrete, at the South, they do like; opposition to that slavery, in the mildest form, or the sternest, they do hate.

That is a serious charge to bring against the prominent rulers of the State. Let me call your attention to a few facts which prove it. Look at the men we send to Congress. There are thirty-one New England men in Congress. By the most liberal construction you can only make out five anti-slavery men in the whole number. Who ever heard of an anti-slavery Governor of Massachusetts in this century? Men know what they are about when they select candidates for election. Do the voters always know what they are about when they choose them?

Then these men always are in favour of a pro-slavery President.

The President must be a slave-holder. There have been fifteen presidential elections. Men from the free States have filled the chair twelve years, or three terms; men from the slave States fourty-four years, or eleven terms. During one term, the chair was filled by an amphibious presidency, by General Harrison, who was nothing but a concrete availability, and John Tyler, who was—John Tyler. They called him an accident; but there are no accidents in politics. A slave-holder presides over the United States forty-eight years out of sixty! Do those men who control the politics of New England not like it? It is no such thing. They love to have it so. We have just seen the Democratic party, or their leaders, nominate General Cass for their candidate—and General Cass is a Northern man; but on that account is he any the less a pro-slavery man? He did oppose the South once, but it was in pressing a war with England. Everybody knows General Cass, and I need say no more about him. But the Northern Whigs have their leaders—are they anti-slavery men? Not a whit more. Next week you will see them nominate, not the great Eastern Whig, though he is no opponent of slavery, only an expounder and defender of the Constitution; not the great Western Whig, the compromiser, though steeped to the lips in slavery; no, they will nominate General Taylor, a man who lives a little further South, and is at this moment dyed a little more scarlet with the sin of slavery.

But go a step further as to the proof. Those men who control the politics of Massachusetts, or New England, or the whole North, they have never opposed the aggressive movements of the slave power. The annexation of Texas, did they oppose that? No, they were glad of it. True, some earnest men came up here in Faneuil Hall, and passed resolutions, which did no good whatever, because it was well known that the real controllers of our politics thought the other way. Then followed the Mexican war. It was a war for slavery, and they knew it; they like it now—that is, if a man's likings can be found out by his doings, not his occasional and exceptional deeds, but his regular and constant actions. They knew that there would be a war against the currency, a war against the tariff, or a war against Mexico. They chose the latter. They knew what they were about.

The same thing is shown by the character of the press. No "re-spectable" paper is opposed to slavery; no Whig paper, no Demo-cratic paper. You would as soon expect a Catholic newspaper to oppose the Pope and his church, for the slave power is the pope of

America, though not exactly a pious pope. The churches show the same thing; they also are in the main pro-slavery, at least not anti-slavery. There are some forty denominations or sects in New England. Mr. President, is one of these anti-slavery? Not one! The land is full of ministers, respectable men, educated men—are they opposed to slavery? I do not know a single man, eminent in any sect, who is also eminent in his opposition to slavery. There was one such man, Dr. Channing; but just as he became eminent in the cause of freedom, he lost power in his own church, lost caste in his own little sect; and though men are now glad to make sectarian capital out of his reputation after he is dead, when he lived, they cursed him by their gods! Then, too, all the most prominent men of New England fraternize with slavery. Massachusetts received such an insult from South Carolina as no State ever before received from another State in this Union; an affront which no nation would dare offer another, without grinding its sword first. And what does Massachusetts do? She does—nothing. But her foremost man goes off there, "The schoolmaster that gives no lessons,"[1] to accept the hospitality of the South, to take the chivalry of South Carolina by the hand; the Defender of the Constitution fraternizes with the State which violates the Constitution, and imprisons his own constituents on account of the colour of their skin.

Put all these things together, and they show that the men who control the politics of Massachusetts, of all New England, do not oppose or dislike slavery.

So much for what they think; and now for the why they think so.

First, there is the general indifference to what is absolutely right. Men think little of it. The Anglo-Saxon race, on both sides of the water, have always felt the instinct of freedom, and often contended stoutly enough for their own rights. But they never cared much for the rights of other men. The slaves are at a distance from us, and so the wrong of this institution is not brought home to men's feelings as if it were our own wrong.

Then the pecuniary interests of the North are supposed to be connected with slavery, so that the North would lose dollars if the South lost slaves. No doubt this is a mistake; still, it is an opinion currently held. The North wants a market for its fabrics, freight for its ships. The South affords it; and, as men think, better than if she

[1] This was a sentiment offered at a public dinner given by the citizens of Charleston, S. C., to Hon. Daniel Webster.

had manufactures and ships of her own, both of which she could have, were there no slaves. All this seems to be a mistake. Freedom, I think, can be shown to be the interest of both North and South.

Yet another reason is found in devotion to the interests of a party. Tell a Whig he could make Whig capital out of anti-slavery, he would turn abolitionist in a moment, if he believed you. Tell a Democrat that he can make capital out of abolition, and he also will come over to your side. But the fact is, each party knows it would gain nothing for its political purposes by standing out for the rights of man. The time will come, and sooner too than some men think, when it will be for the interest of a party to favour abolition, but that time is not yet. It does seem strange, that while you can find men who will practise a good deal of self-denial for their sect or their party, lending, and hoping nothing in return, you so rarely find a man who will compromise even his popularity for the sake of mankind.

Then, again, there is the fear of change. Men who control our politics seem to have little confidence in man, little in truth, little in justice, and the eternal right. Therefore, while it is never out of season to do something for the tariff, for the moneyed interests of men, they think it is never in time to do much for the great work of elevating mankind itself. They have no confidence in the people, and take little pains to make the people worthy of confidence. So any change which gives a more liberal government to a people, which gives freedom to the slave, they look on with distrust, if not alarm. In 1830, when the French expelled the despotic king who encumbered their throne, what said Massachusetts, what said New England, in honour of the deed? Nothing. Your old men? Nothing. Your young men? Not a word. What did they care for the freedom of thirty millions of men? They were looking at their imports and exports. In 1838, when England set free eight hundred thousand men in a day, what did Massachusetts say about that? What had New England to say? Not a word in its favour from these political leaders of the land. Nay, they thought the experiment was dangerous, and ever since that it is with great reluctance you can get them to confess that the scheme works well. In 1848, when France again expels her king, and all the royalty in the kingdom is carted off in a one horse cab— when the broadest principles of human government are laid down, and a great nation sets about the difficult task of moving out of her old political house, and into a new one, without tearing down the old, without butchering men in the process of removal—why, what has Boston to say to that? What have the political leaders of Massachusetts, of New England, to say? They have nothing to say for liberty; they are sorry the experiment was made; they are afraid the French will not want so much cotton; they have no confidence in man, and fear every change.

Such are their opinions, to judge by what they do; such the reasons thereof, judging by what they say.

But how can we change this, and get the idea of freedom into men's minds? Something can be done by the gradual elevation of men, by schools and churches, by the press. The churches and colleges of New England have not directly aided us in the work of abolishing slavery. No doubt by their direct action they have retarded that work, and that a good deal. But indirectly they have done much to hasten the work. They have helped educate men; helped make men moral, in a general way; and now this moral power can be turned to this special business, though the churches say, "No, you shall not." I see before me a good and an earnest man,[2] who, not opening his mouth in public against slavery, has yet done a great service in this way: he has educated the teachers of the Commonwealth, has taught them to love freedom, to love justice, to love man and God. That is what I call sowing the seeds of anti-slavery. The honoured and excellent Secretary of Education,[3] who has just gone to stand in the place of a famous man, and I hope to fill it nobly, has done much in this way. I wish in his reports on education he had exposed the wrong which is done here in Boston, by putting all the coloured children in one school, by shutting them out of the Latin school and the English high school. I wish he had done that duty, which plainly belongs to him to do. But without touching that, he has yet done, indirectly, a great work towards the abolition of slavery. He has sown the seeds of education wide spread over the State. One day these seeds will come up; come up men, men that will both vote and choose the Governor; men that will love right and justice; will see the iniquity of American slavery, and sweep it off the continent, cost what it may cost, in spite of all compromises of the Constitution, and all compromisers. I look on that as certain. But that is slow work, this waiting for a general

[2] Rev. Cyrus Pierce, teacher of the Normal School at Newton.
[3] Hon. Horace Mann.

morality to do a special act. It is going without dinner till the wheat is grown for your bread.

So we want direct and immediate action upon the people themselves. The idea must be set directly before them, with all its sanctions displayed, and its obligations made known. This can be done in part by the pulpit. Dr. Channing shows how much one man can do, standing on that eminence. You all know how much he did do. I am sorry that he came so late, sorry that he did not do more, but thankful for what he did do. However, you cannot rely on the pulpit to do much. The pulpit represents the average goodness and piety; not eminent goodness and piety. It is unfair to call ordinary men to do extraordinary works. I do not concur in all the hard things that are said about the clergy, perhaps it is because I am one of them; but I do not expect a great deal from them. It is hard to call a class of men all at once to rise above all other classes of men, and teach a degree of virtue which they do not understand. But you may call them to be true to their own consciences.

So the pulpit is not to be relied on for much aid. If all the ministers of New England were abolitionists, with the same zeal that they are Protestants, Universalists, Methodists, Calvinists, or Unitarians, no doubt the whole State would soon be an anti-slavery State, and the day of emancipation would be wonderfully hastened. But that we are not to look for.

Much can be done by lecturers, who shall go to the people and address them, not as Whigs or Democrats, not as sectarians, but as men, and in the name of man and God present the actual condition of the slaves, and show the duty of the North and South, of the nation, in regard to this matter. For this business, we want money and men, the two sinews of war; money to pay the men, men to earn the money. They must appeal to the people in their primary capacity, simply as men.

Much also may be done by the press. How much may be done by these two means, and that in a few years, these men[4] can tell; all the North and South can tell. Men of the most diverse modes of thought can work together in this cause. Here on my right is Mr. Phillips, an old-fashioned Calvinist, who believes all the five points of Calvinism. I am rather a new-fashioned Unitarian, and believe only one of the

---

[4] Messrs. Garrison, Phillips and Quincy.

five points, the one Mr. Phillips has proved—the perseverance of the saints; but we get along without any quarrel by the way.

Some men will try political action. The action of the people, of the nation, must be political action. It may be constitutional, it may be unconstitutional. I see not why men need to quarrel about that. Let not him that voteth condemn him that voteth not, nor let not him that voteth not condemn him that voteth, but let every man be faithful to his own convictions.

It is said, the abolitionists waste time and wind in denunciation. It is partly true. I make no doubt it inspires the slave-holder's heart to see division amongst his foes. I ought to say his friends, for such we are. He thinks the day of justice is deferred, while the ministers thereof contend. I do not believe a revolution is to be baptized with rose-water. I do not believe a great work is to be done without great passions. It is not to be supposed that the Leviathan of American slavery will allow himself to be drawn out of the mire in which he has made his nest, and grown fat and strong, without some violence and floundering. When we have caught him fairly, he will put his feet into the mud to hold on by; he will reach out and catch hold of everything that will hold him. He has caught hold of Mr. Clay and Mr. Webster. He will catch hold of General Cass and General Taylor. He will die, though slowly, and die hard. Still it is a pity that men who essay to pull him out, should waste their strength in bickerings with one another, or in needless denunciation of the Leviathan's friends. Call slave-holding, slave-holding; let us tell all the evils which arise from it, if we can find language terrible enough; let us show up the duplicity of the nation, the folly of our wise men, the littleness of our great men, the baseness of our honourable men, if need be; but all that with no unkind feelings toward any one. Virtue never appears so lovely as when, destroying sin, she loves the sinner, and seeks to save him. Absence of love is absence of the strongest power. See how much Mr. Adams lost of his influence, how much he wasted of his strength, by the violence with which he pursued persons. I am glad to acknowledge the great services he performed. He wished to have every man stand on the right side of the anti-slavery line; but I believe there were some men whom he would like to have put there with a pitchfork. On the other hand, Dr. Channing never lost a moment by attacking a personal foe; and see what he gained by it! However, I must say this, that no great revolution of opinion and practice was ever brought about before with so little violence, waste of force, and denunciation. Consider the greatness of the work; it is to restore three millions to liberty; a work, in comparison with which the American Revolution was a little thing. Yet consider the violence, the denunciation, the persecution, and the long years of war, which that Revolution cost. I do not wonder that abolitionists are sometimes violent; I only deplore it. Remembering the provocation, I wonder they are not more so and more often. The prize is to be run for, "not without dust and heat."

Working in this way, we are sure to succeed. The idea is an eternal truth. It will find its way into the public mind, for there is that sympathy between man and the truth, that he cannot live without it and be blessed. What allies we have on our side! True, the cupidity, the tyranny, the fear, and the atheism of the land are against us. But all the nobleness, all the honour, all the morality, all the religion, are on our side. I was sorry to hear it said, that the religion of the land opposed us. It is not true. Religion never opposed any good work. I know what my friend meant, and I wish he had said it, calling things by their right names. It is the irreligion of the land that favours slavery; it is the idolatry of gold; it is our atheism. Of speculative atheism there is not much; you see how much of the practical!

We are certain of success; the spirit of the age is on our side. See how the old nations shake their tyrants out of the land. See how every steamer brings us good tidings of good things; and do you believe America can keep her slaves? It is idle to think so. So all we want is time. On our side are truth, justice, and the eternal right. Yes, on our side is religion, the religion of Christ; on our side are the hopes of mankind, and the great power of God.

Anti-Garrisonian Abolitionists Support the Liberty Party Candidates

ತಿ

The following statement by the executive committee of the American and Foreign Anti-Slavery Society highlights the difference in attitude toward political action between the Garrisonians, then represented in the American Anti-Slavery Society, and those who had seceded from the organization in 1840 and had formed the American and Foreign Anti-Slavery Society. While the Garrisonians, as we have seen in the statement by Wendell Phillips, were opposed to voting or holding office under the Constitution, their opponents were supporting the Liberty Party and its candidates and participating actively in the election. The statement reprinted here was published as a pamphlet, in twelve pages, under the title, "Address to the Friends of Liberty, by the Executive Committee of the American and Foreign Anti-Slavery Society," New York, July 4, 1848.

ADDRESS TO THE FRIENDS OF LIBERTY, BY THE EXECUTIVE COMMITTEE OF THE AMERICAN AND FOREIGN ANTI-SLAVERY SOCIETY.

———

In view of the approaching Presidential election, the undersigned, members of the Executive Committee of the American and Foreign Anti-slavery Society, beg leave to offer some considerations to the friends of impartial liberty. They do it, not in a spirit of dictation, but with the hope of preserving the unity, and promoting the efficient action, of those associated with them—of gaining the co-operation of all who prize the constitution of our country, who value our civil and religious institutions, and who desire to act on Christian principles, in the great work of overthrowing American slavery.

[209

It is a subject of devout thanksgiving to God that experience has demonstrated the soundness of the doctrines of a large majority of the abolitionists of Great Britain and the United States, that they are consistent with the best interests of mankind, in accordance with true philosophy and pure Christianity; that the measures adopted to communicate these important truths to the people of this country, with a view to bring about the peaceful abolition of slavery, have been so consistent with these principles; and that these doctrines and measures have been so signally overruled and blessed in furtherance of the cause of emancipation, republican liberty, and Christian freedom. Reflecting men can see that amidst all the opposition, violence, threats, and machinations of slaveholders, and their abettors, the cause of liberty has steadily advanced, and is about to be brought to a glorious consummation. And it ought to inspire the people of this country with gratitude, that such a momentous moral reformation, affecting the temporal and eternal welfare of millions of people, in this and coming generations, is to be achieved at no greater sacrifice. So deeply involved were the people of this country in the guilt of oppression and prejudice that probably nothing short of murders under Lynch law, profligate expenditures of life and property—war, robbery and conquest—and audacious attempts to defend, extend and perpetuate slavery, would have aroused the people of the free states to a consideration of impending danger, and inspired them with a determination to avert it. Much as the unconstitutional annexation of Texas, with the consequent war with Mexico, is deplored, this great calamity and ineffaceable national reproach will, we doubt not, be overruled for the downfall of the politicians who perpetrated the enormous evil, and for the arrestation and overthrow of American slavery, for which the annexation and war were perfidiously brought about. "HE TAKETH THE WISE IN THEIR OWN CRAFTINESS . . . SURELY THE WRATH OF MAN SHALL PRAISE THEE: THE REMAINDER OF WRATH SHALT THOU RESTRAIN."

Thanks to an overruling Providence, the great body of the people of the free states are beginning to see that their rights and their liberties are in jeopardy, and bands of patriotic and resolute men are standing aloof from their political parties, vowing eternal hostility to the extension of slavery. We see in these auspicious events, that the Almighty has been pleased to bless the instrumentality of those who early sounded the alarm, who have steadfastly advocated the cause of the oppressed, who have warned their countrymen of the encroachments of the slaveocracy, who have expended their property and hazarded their lives in defence of the rights of man, and the freedom inherited from their fathers. Had they faltered, had they prayed less, had they used less moral suasion, had they acted inconsistently at the ballot-box, the nation and sympathizing Europe might not have witnessed the revolution now in progress for the deliverance of our country from galling servitude to the slave aristocrats who have so long trampled upon their countrymen in chains, and been permitted for so many years to administer the affairs of this government.

Among the instrumentalities used to stay the progress, and put an end to the evils of slavery in this country, has been the consistent exercise of the elective franchise by the friends of human rights. They have inculcated the duty of electing good men to office, have rejected the unchristian sentiment that of two moral evils we may choose the least, have inculcated that the prayers of good men can be acceptable at the court of heaven only when they vote as they pray, that duties are ours and results are God's, that Christian electors are, morally speaking, always successful when they have truth, righteousness, and the divine approbation on their side; and that, sooner or later, it will be seen that fixedness of principle and unwavering adherence to right, result in success and triumph. The power of the ballot-box has been felt by venal politicians, and will be felt until, by the divine blessing, the friends of equal rights arise in their majesty, stop the extension of slavery, and by the exercise of moral and political power put an end to the accursed system.

In pursuance of this conviction, the representatives of the Liberty party in the United States assembled at Buffalo, in October last, and with unusual unanimity nominated the HON. JOHN P. HALE and the HON. LEICESTER KING for the offices of President and Vice President—fit representatives of the great principles for which we were contending, and well qualified to administer the government constitutionally, and for the general welfare. The consistent and manly conduct of MR. HALE in the Senate of the United States, since the nomination, has shown his constituents that their confidence was well placed, and has demonstrated that he is worthy to be the standard-bearer of the friends of liberty throughout the Union. If those who nominated him will stand by their principles and the man of their choice, preserve their unity, enlarge their operations, refuse to be diverted from the course they have themselves marked out, refrain from being submerged in other political parties, continue to use the light they have and seek for more; if they bear aloft the liberty standard; and if instead of forming alliances with the disaffected of other parties, who go no farther than to oppose the extension of slavery, they beckon their countrymen to higher and still higher principles and measures, we believe that they will not only do more good as members of the Liberty party, but exert increased influence over those who have avowed but a single anti-slavery principle. Non-extension is not abolition, though included in it; and it will be time to consider overtures of coalition from fellow-citizens who have recently awakened to see the disastrous policy of slavery extension when they shall have embraced the great anti-slavery principles we avow, viz.: the entire divorcement of the national government from slavery; the repeal of all the laws of Congress for its protection or continuance; the fulfilment of the treaty of Ghent, by which the United States agreed with Great Britain to co-operate to promote the entire abolition of the TRAFFIC IN SLAVES; the abolition of slavery in the District of Columbia; and the overthrow of slavery in this country by peaceful and constitutional means. It will be time enough for the Liberty party of the United States, who are not only for imposing limits, but for taking measures for the destruction of slavery, to relinquish their nominees when a more numerous body of anti-slavery men shall enrol themselves to restrain and annihilate slavery, with standard-bearers of equal honesty and independence, and superior wisdom, firmness, and discretion. Till then we owe it to our able and chosen candidates, and to our party, to be united; neither to propose nor listen to terms of affilation with any set of men, however patriotic or honest, who from policy or other cause, do not embrace the truth on the anti-slavery question, or will not fearlessly act out their convictions, or who content themselves with merely making efforts to stay the progress of an evil which we have banded together, in conjunction with the abolitionists of England and France, and the whole world, utterly to destroy.

An appeal is made to the friends of liberty to unite with those who have recently detached themselves from the two political parties with which they have hitherto acted, in elevating to the Presidency some citizen who has gone no farther in the great work of anti-slavery reform than to avow his resolution to oppose the farther extension of slavery—and this appeal, we regret to say, is endorsed by a few individuals in the Liberty party, who used strenuous efforts to bring about the nomination of Messrs. Hale and King. Permit us therefore in this exigenecy, to entreat you to be steadfast and unmovable, to adhere to the wise policy you have already marked out—the maintenance of which has made you so influential. Even many of those who censured you, at the last Presidential election, for voting for a third candidate, under the pretence that the nominee of either the whig or democratic party would certainly be elected, and therefore your votes would be thrown away, now commend your adherence to principle, by saying, "Because others do wrong, it is no reason for us to anticipate their crime."[1] They also imitate your past policy, forsake their old organizations, and are forming a distinct political party. Thus they bear testimony to the wisdom of your former course, while they solicit you to unite with them that your votes may swell the number that will be cast for the Wilmot proviso candidate. But while we approve this rising spirit of independence, let us not listen to such solicitations, let them proceed from whatever quarter they may. If you relinquish the high position you have attained, by so much toil and sacrifice, you will jeopard the cause. Nay, if, to accommodate those who profess to aim only at the non-extension of slavery, you postpone the great work of emancipation, and substitute a new issue for the glorious one already made, and which has been so successfully maintained, you will injure those who now seek your alliance. You have associated, to use the sentiments of the address of the Southern and Western convention of 1845, not as partizans, but for the purpose of subserving Truth and Right; to oppose not merely the extension of slavery but to bring about, by all lawful and righteous acts, its complete overthrow. Your association is founded upon the great cardinal principle of true Democracy and of true Christianity, the brotherhood of the human family; you have resolved on waging war against slaveholding as the direst form of oppression, and then against every other species of tyranny and injustice; you are aiming to carry out the principle of liberty in all its consequences, not as a mere Abolition party, but as a party that aims at the extinction of slavery because slaveholding is inconsistent with Christian and republican principles—aiming at it not as an ultimate end, but as an illustrious

---

[1] Hon. S. Hoar, President of the Worcester, Mass., Convention.

era in the advancement of society to be wrought out by its action and instrumentality.

By asserting and maintaining these high and uncompromising principles you have, with God's blessing, made a deep impression upon your countrymen, commanded the respect of mankind, and induced large numbers of the considerate and patriotic adherents to the other political parties to pause—resolve on new associations, and take the first step in withstanding the encroachments of the slave power. Be it your privilege to go forward in the great work of political regeneration, to aim at a still higher standard, and to lead forward the allies of freedom until liberty shall be proclaimed throughout the land to all the inhabitants thereof. Do not, we beseech you, retreat—under the pretence that you can thus urge on more effectually those who have just commenced the march of liberty. This is not the way to influence men nor to preserve your own integrity. Sound philosophy and political experience show that those worthy to conquer must lead, and that they who are feeling the first aspirations of freedom will follow those who bear the loftiest standard.

Is it said, this is a "crisis"—a "special case"—"unite this once," and the Liberty party hereafter can act as efficiently as before? This is the stereotyped declaration on the eve of every Presidential election. You have, with but few exceptions, refused to listen to it heretofore. Refuse compliance with it now. At every election temptations will be presented to postpose action on the great objects of your association, to carry some collateral issue, and thus friends or foes essay to make you instrumental in achieving inferior good at the expense of fundamental principles. You ought not to enter into compromises, barters, or substitutions. Profit by experience. Never risk the success of the cause by making an issue on a minor point. Adherence to principle has been your tower of strength. Instead of lowering your standard you have elevated it. Thus you have infused courage into your ranks, and gained the respect of other parties. Is it said, by uniting with the disaffected of the other political parties, you may inspire them with your sentiments, and induce them, if successful now with your aid, to take hold of the work of emancipation? Numerically you are the smallest portion, and would be in danger of losing your identity as well as your influence. It is only in moral principle that you are now superior to others. Besides, what will be your position if the party with which you are invited to merge yourselves should be unsuccessful? Like that of Samson in the prison-house.

We cannot believe that any voter, entitled to the appellation of a friend to liberty—we wish we could say we do not believe that any professing Christian—will, under any consideration, vote for a belligerent demagogue and aristocrat, or be carried away by popular excitement to aid in elevating to the highest office in the country a warrior destitute of civil qualifications, and whose reputation is derived from his success as a practitioner in "the science of human butchery," in a war that his own partizans have styled "unconstitutional," "unnecessary," "disgraceful," and "barbarous." Neither is it to be imagined that a single individual who prizes liberty and abhors slavery, who loves peace and values our Christian institutions, will vote for a slaveholder or one who is the creature of slaveholders, and who for personal aggrandizement, and the power to distribute the offices and treasure of the nation on political partizans, would plunge his country into a war with any nation with which a quarrel could be provoked. Should this be the case, however, and a man answering either description be elevated to the chief magistracy, a lesson never to be forgotten will have been given to the young men of this country, teaching them that time-serving, office-seeking, and flattering demagogueism, or successful fighting for territory and slavery are the tests of merit, and the qualifications for civil office, in the estimation of the people of the United States.

Neither can we believe that any Liberty party man will cast his vote for a politician who has, when in power, proffered his aid to the slaveocracy of the country and the world, and who has not evinced any desire that the record should be expunged. Though ready to award due praise to him who has repeatedly and ably advocated the doctrine of the non-extension of slavery, we cannot believe that while he rests there, and is "decidedly opposed" to any important principle of the Liberty party, you will be instrumental in elevating him again to the Presidential chair.

But there are apprehensions that not a few disaffected whigs and democrats; men who refuse to bow the knee to party dictation; men who have independence and conscience; men who are opposed to the extension of slavery, to the elevation of a warrior and a slaveholder, or a demagogue; men who profess to abhor slavery, nay, who avow their belief in the truth of anti-slavery doctrines, will, after all,

nominate and vote for some mere Wilmot proviso man—*this once*—
rather than meet the crisis manfully, and unite with the friends of
liberty in voting for one who goes not only for the non-extension but
for the non-existence of slavery on the American continent. Will not
such listen to the voice of expostulation and entreaty? A true-hearted
friend and advocate of liberty stands before you as the nominated
representative of the anti-slavery sentiment of the country. He has
shown that he is honest, capable, and independent. Why not, then,
unite with the friends of liberty in giving him the entire anti-slavery
vote of the country? He might be elected; but, if not, the demonstration made in favor of "Liberty—Equality—Fraternity" would be an
electric shock to arouse the slumbering energies of our countrymen,
and vibrate among the liberty-loving and liberty-achieving people of
Europe. Is there a man in your ranks whose position at the present
moment entitles him to more general favor and confidence, and who
is more acceptable to the anti-slavery electors of the country, than
JOHN P. HALE? We think not, and are fully persuaded that it is
more reasonable that we call upon you patriotically to vote with us,
than it is for you to invite our co-operation. "Principles, not men"
should be the motto. It is time that the friends of liberty were united
in one great confederation, not only to withstand and oppose the
extension of American slavery, but to deliver the nation from its
blight and curse. Any thing short of this is below the demands of the
age and the hopes of the world. Republican freemen in Europe have
set a noble example. Do not lag behind, and thus dishearten them in
their efforts to "form a more perfect union, establish justice, ensure
domestic tranquillity, provide for the common defence, promote the
general welfare, and secure the blessings of liberty" to themselves and
their posterity.

Uniting with our friends throughout the Union, in a hearty recom-
mendation of Mr. Hale, "we earnestly commend him to all whigs and
democrats who wish to vote against slavery, as the man of the hour,
possessing in an eminent degree the purity, wisdom, firmness, and
ability which the country now needs at the helm; one whom they can
honestly and consistently vote for, and thus secure all the advantages
of unity, without a sacrifice of principle from any."[2]

[2] Resolution of Liberty party in Massachusetts.

Friends of the slave! The eyes of Europe are upon us. They call our country the Model Republic. We are so, with one great exception. Let that stain be wiped from our national escutcheon. It was said by the departed statesman, JOHN QUINCY ADAMS, "the preservation, propagation, and perpetuation of slavery has been the vital and animating spirit of the national government." It might be so still, even if the Wilmot proviso is adopted, and Oregon and the vast Mexican territories continue free from slavery. Let us aim higher, and while we oppose the spread of the leprosy, effect a cure of this most revolting and consuming disease upon the body politic. "Let us not suffer a knot of slave-holders for ever to give law and prescribe the policy of the country."³ Rather "let virtuous men unite on the ground of *universal moral principle*, and the tyranny of party will be crushed."⁴ To this end be firm, united, progressive, unflinching, and persevere in the course marked out, "unangered and unawed." Continue to use moral suasion; cover the land, as with autumnal leaves, with anti-slavery publications, and with the speeches of the champions of freedom in Congress; "preach, print, and pray;" organize in school districts, in towns and villages; hold frequent meetings; go to other political meetings to proselyte and not to be proselyted; abandon not an inch of ground already acquired, but make aggressive movements. Invoke the aid of the pulpit, the press, the lyceum; above all, invoke the God of the oppressed—the God of our fathers—that he will indeed make this a Model Republic, where all men may rejoice in equal rights. Let your acts infuse new enthusiasm into liberty-loving men across the Atlantic, until Europe, regenerated and disenthralled, shall echo the sublime language of our revolutionary patriots: "All men are created equal, and are endowed by their Creator with certain inalienable rights: among these are life, liberty, and the pursuit of happiness."

In conclusion, brethren and friends, let it be your solemn and unalterable determination that while you oppose no man who is, in any way, friendly to the anti-slavery cause, you will not be instrumental in his election to office, unless he adopts the distinguishing principles of the Liberty party; and, especially, that you will not go backward in the great anti-slavery reform, but, according to the

³ John Quincy Adams.
⁴ President Wayland.

ability given you, do all in your power to uphold the doctrines and measures, to the maintenance and diffusion of which you have pledged yourselves before God and man.

ARTHUR TAPPAN
S. S. JOCELYN
WILLIAM JAY
GEORGE WHIPPLE
LEWIS TAPPAN
S. W. BENEDICT
J. WARNER
LUTHER LEE
J. W. C. PENNINGTON
S. WILDE
WILLIAM JOHNSTON
C. B. RAY
THOMAS RITTER

NEW YORK, July 4, 1848.

Wendell Phillips, "Philosophy of the Abolition Movement"

ॐ

In this address, delivered on January 27, 1853, before the Massachusetts Anti-Slavery Society, Wendell Phillips summarizes the philosophy and contributions of the Abolitionists to American history and thought. It was later included in a volume entitled Speeches, Lectures, and Letters, *by Wendell Phillips, first published in 1863 and reprinted in 1884, pp. 98–153.*

PHILOSOPHY OF THE ABOLITION MOVEMENT

. . . I wish, Mr. Chairman, to notice some objections that have been made to our course ever since Mr. Garrison began his career, and which have been lately urged again, with considerable force and emphasis, in the columns of the London Leader, the able organ of a very respectable and influential class in England. . . .

The charges to which I refer are these: that, in dealing with slaveholders and their apologists, we indulge in fierce denunciations, instead of appealing to their reason and common sense by plain statements and fair argument; that we might have won the sympathies and support of the nation, if we would have submitted to argue this question with a manly patience; but, instead of this, we have outraged the feelings of the community by attacks, unjust and unnecessarily severe, on its most valued institutions, and gratified our spleen by indiscriminate abuse of leading men, who were often honest in their intentions, however mistaken in their views; that we have utterly neglected the ample means that lay around us to convert the nation, submitted to no discipline, formed no plan, been guided by no foresight, but hurried on in childish, reckless, blind, and hotheaded zeal— bigots in the narrowness of our views, and fanatics in our blind fury of invective and malignant judgment of other men's motives.

The article in the Leader to which I refer is signed "Ion," and may be found in the *Liberator* of December 17, 1852. . . .

I claim, before you who know the true state of the case—I claim for the antislavery movement with which this society is identified, that, looking back over its whole course, and considering the men connected with it in the mass, it has been marked by sound judgment, unerring foresight, the most sagacious adaptation of means to ends, the strictest self-discipline, the most thorough research, and an amount of patient and manly argument addressed to the conscience and intellect of the nation, such as no other cause of the kind, in England or this country, has ever offered. I claim, also, that its course has been marked by a cheerful surrender of all individual claims to merit or leadership—the most cordial welcoming of the slightest effort, of every honest attempt, to lighten or to break the chain of the slave. I need not waste time by repeating the superfluous confession that we are men, and therefore do not claim to be perfect. Neither would I be understood as denying that we use denunciation, and ridicule, and every other weapon that the human mind knows. We must plead guilty, if there be guilt in not knowing how to separate the sin from the sinner. With all the fondness for abstractions attributed to us, we are not yet capable of that. We are fighting a momentous battle at desperate odds—one against a thousand. Every weapon that ability or ignorance, wit, wealth, prejudice, or fashion can command, is pointed against us. The guns are shotted to their lips. The arrows are poisoned. Fighting against such an array, we cannot afford to confine ourselves to any one weapon. The cause is not ours, so that we might, rightfully, postpone or put in peril the victory by moderating our demands, stifling our convictions, or filing down our rebukes, to gratify any sickly taste of our own, or to spare the delicate nerves of our neighbor. Our clients are three millions of Christian slaves, standing dumb suppliants at the threshold of the Christian world. They have no voice but ours to utter their complaints, or to demand justice. The press, the pulpit, the wealth, the literature, the prejudices, the political arrangements, the present self-interest of the country, are all against us. God has given us no weapon but the truth, faithfully uttered, and addressed, with the old prophets' directness, to the conscience of the individual sinner. The elements which control public opinion and mould the masses are against us. We can but pick off here and there a man from the triumphant majority. We have facts for those who think, arguments for those who reason; but he who cannot be reasoned out of his prejudices must be laughed out of them; he who cannot be argued out of his selfishness must be shamed out of it by the mirror of his hateful self held up relentlessly before his eyes. We live in a land where every man makes broad his phylactery, inscribing thereon, "All men are created equal,"—"God hath made of one blood all nations of men." It seems to us that in such a land there must be, on this question of slavery, sluggards to be awakened, as well as doubters to be convinced. Many more, we verily believe, of the first than of the last. There are far more dead hearts to be quickened, than confused intellects to be cleared up—more dumb dogs to be made to speak, than doubting consciences to be enlightened. [Loud cheers.] We have use, then, sometimes, for something beside argument.

What is the denunciation with which we are charged? It is endeavoring, in our faltering human speech, to declare the enormity of the sin of making merchandise of men—of separating husband and wife

—taking the infant from its mother, and selling the daughter to prostitution—of a professedly Christian nation denying, by statute, the Bible to every sixth man and woman of its population, and making it illegal for "two or three" to meet together, except a white man be present! What is this harsh criticism of motives with which we are charged? It is simply holding the intelligent and deliberate actor responsible for the character and consequences of his acts. Is there anything inherently wrong in such denunciation or such criticism? This we may claim—we have never judged a man but out of his own mouth. We have seldom, if ever, held him to account, except for acts of which he and his own friends were proud. All that we ask the world and thoughtful men to note are the principles and deeds on which the American pulpit and American public men plume themselves. We always allow our opponents to paint their own pictures. Our humble duty is to stand by and assure the spectators that what they would take for a knave or a hypocrite is really, in American estimation, a Doctor of Divinity or Secretary of State.

The South is one great brothel, where half a million of women are flogged to prostitution, or, worse still, are degraded to believe it honorable. The public squares of half our great cities echo to the wail of families torn asunder at the auction-block; no one of our fair rivers that has not closed over the negro seeking in death a refuge from a life too wretched to bear; thousands of fugitives skulk along our highways, afraid to tell their names, and trembling at the sight of a human being; free men are kidnapped in our streets, to be plunged into that hell of slavery; and now and then one, as if by miracle, after long years, returns to make men aghast with his tale. The press says, "It is all right"; and the pulpit cries, "Amen." They print the Bible in every tongue in which man utters his prayers; and get the money to do so by agreeing never to give the book, in the language our mothers taught us, to any negro, free or bond, south of Mason and Dixon's line. The press says, "It is all right"; and the pulpit cries, "Amen." The slave lifts up his imploring eyes, and sees in every face but ours the face of an enemy. Prove to me now that harsh rebuke, indignant denunciation, scathing sarcasm, and pitiless ridicule are wholly and always unjustifiable; else we dare not, in so desperate a case, throw away any weapon which ever broke up the crust of an ignorant prejudice, roused a slumbering conscience, shamed a proud sinner, or changed, in any way, the conduct of a human being. Our aim is to alter public opinion. Did we live in a market, our talk should be of dollars and cents, and we would seek to prove only that slavery was an unprofitable investment. Were the nation one great, pure church, we would sit down and reason of "righteousness, temperance, and judgment to come." Had slavery fortified itself in a college, we would load our cannons with cold facts, and wing our arrows with arguments. But we happen to live in the world—the world made up of thought and impulse, of self-conceit and self-interest, of weak men and wicked. To conquer, we must reach all. Our object is not to make every man a Christian or a philosopher, but to induce every one to aid in the abolition of slavery. We expect to accomplish our object long before the nation is made over into saints or elevated into philosophers. To change public opinion, we use the very tools by which it was formed. That is, all such as an honest man may touch.

All this I am not only ready to allow, but I should be ashamed to think of the slave, or to look into the face of my fellow-man, if it were otherwise. It is the only thing, which justifies us to our own consciences, and makes us able to say we have done, or at least tried to do, our duty.

So far, however you distrust my philosophy, you will not doubt my statements. That we have denounced and rebuked with unsparing fidelity will not be denied. Have we not also addressed ourselves to that other duty, of arguing our question thoroughly—of using due discretion and fair sagacity in endeavoring to promote our cause? Yes, we have. Every statement we have made has been doubted. Every principle we have laid down has been denied by overwhelming majorities against us. No one step has ever been gained but by the most laborious research and the most exhausting argument. And no question has ever, since Revolutionary days, been so thoroughly investigated or argued here, as that of slavery. Of that research and that argument, of the whole of it, the old-fashioned, fanatical, crazy Garrisonian antislavery movement has been the author. From this band of men has proceeded every important argument or idea which has been broached on the antislavery question from 1830 to the present time. [Cheers.] I am well aware of the extent of the claim I make. I recognize, as fully as any one can, the ability of the new laborers—the eloquence and genius with which they have recommended this cause to the nation, and flashed conviction home on the conscience of the community. I do not mean, either, to assert that they have in every instance borrowed from our treasury their facts and arguments. Left to themselves, they would probably have looked up the one and originated the other. As a matter of fact, however, they have generally made use of the materials collected to their hands. But there are some persons about us, sympathizers to a great extent with "Ion," who pretend that the antislavery movement has been hitherto mere fanaticism, its only weapon angry abuse. They are obliged to assert this, in order to justify their past indifference or hostility. At present, when it suits their purpose to give it some attention, they endeavor to explain the change by alleging that now it has been taken up by men of thoughtful minds, and its claims are urged by fair discussion and able argument. My claim, then, is this: that neither the charity of the most timid of sects, the sagacity of our wisest converts, nor the culture of the ripest scholars, though all have been aided by our twenty years' experience, has yet struck out any new method of reaching the public mind, or originated any new argument or train of thought, or discovered any new fact bearing on the question. When once brought fully into the struggle, they have found it necessary to adopt the same means, to rely on the same arguments, to hold up the same men and the same measures to public reprobation, with the same bold rebuke and unsparing invective that we have used. All their conciliatory bearing, their painstaking moderation, their constant and anxious endeavor to draw a broad line between their camp and ours, have been thrown away. Just so far as they have been effective laborers, they have found, as we have, their hands against every man, and every man's hand against them. The most experienced of them are ready to acknowledge that our plan has been wise, our course efficient, and that our unpopularity is no fault of ours, but flows necessarily and unavoidably from our position. "I should suspect," says old Fuller, "that his preaching had no salt in it, if no galled horse did wince." Our friends find, after all, that men do not so much hate us as the truth we utter and the light we bring. They find that the community are not the honest seekers after truth which they fancied, but selfish politicians and sectarian bigots, who shiver, like Alexander's butler, whenever the sun shines on them. Experience has driven these new laborers back to our method. We have no quarrel with them—would not steal one wreath of their laurels. All we claim is, that, if they are to be complimented as prudent, moderate, Christian, sagacious, statesmanlike reformers, we deserve the same praise; for they have done nothing that we, in our measure, did not attempt before. [Cheers.]

I claim this, that the cause, in its recent aspect, has put on nothing but timidity. It has taken to itself no new weapons of recent years; it has become more compromising—that is all! It has become neither more persuasive, more learned, more Christian, more charitable, nor more effective than for the twenty years preceding. Mr. Hale, the head of the Free Soil movement, after a career in the Senate that would do honor to any man—after a six years' course which entitles him to the respect and confidence of the antislavery public—can put his name, within the last month, to an appeal from the city of Washington, signed by a Houston and a Cass, for a monument to be raised to Henry Clay! If that be the test of charity and courtesy, we cannot give it to the world. [Loud cheers.] Some of the leaders of the Free Soil party of Massachusetts, after exhausting the whole capacity of our language to paint the treachery of Daniel Webster to the cause of liberty, and the evil they thought he was able and seeking to do— after that, could feel it in their hearts to parade themselves in the funeral procession got up to do him honor! In this we allow we cannot follow them. The deference which every gentleman owes to the proprieties of social life, that self-respect and regard to consistency which is every man's duty—these, if no deeper feelings, will ever prevent us from giving such proofs of this newly invented Christian courtesy. [Great cheering.] We do not *play* politics; antislavery is no half-jest with us; it is a terrible earnest, with life or death, worse than life or death, on the issue. It is no lawsuit, where it matters not to the good feeling of opposing counsel which way the verdict goes, and where advocates can shake hands after the decision as pleasantly as before. When we think of such a man as Henry Clay, his long life, his mighty influence cast always into the scale against the slave—of that irresistible fascination with which he moulded every one to his will; when we remember that, his conscience acknowledging the justice of our cause, and his heart open on every other side to the gentlest impulses, he could sacrifice so remorsely his convictions and the welfare of millions to his low ambition; when we think how the slave trembled at the sound of his voice, and that, from a multitude of breaking hearts there went up nothing but gratitude to God when it pleased him to call that great sinner from this world—we cannot find it in our hearts, we could not shape our lips to ask any man to do him honor. [Great sensation.] No amount of eloquence, no sheen of official position, no loud grief of partisan friends, would ever lead us to ask monuments or walk in fine processions for pirates; and the sectarian zeal or selfish ambition which gives up, deliberately and in full knowledge of the facts, three million of human beings to hopeless ignorance, daily robbery, systematic prostitution, and murder, which the law is neither able nor undertakes to prevent or avenge, is more monstrous, in our eyes, than the love of gold which takes a score of lives with merciful quickness on the high seas. Haynau on the Danube is no more hateful to us than Haynau on the Potomac. Why give mobs to one, and monuments to the other?

If these things be necessary to courtesy, I cannot claim that we are courteous. We seek only to be honest men, and speak the same of the dead as of the living. If the grave that hides their bodies could swallow also the evil they have done and the example they leave, we might enjoy at least the luxury of forgetting them. But the evil that men do lives after them, and example acquires tenfold authority when it speaks from the grave. History, also, is to be written. How shall a feeble minority, without weight or influence in the country, with no jury of millions to appeal to—denounced, vilified, and contemned— how shall we make way against the overwhelming weight of some colossal reputation, if we do not turn from the idolatrous present, and appeal to the human race, saying to your idols of to-day, "Here we are defeated; but we will write our judgment with the iron pen of a century to come, and it shall never be forgotten, if we can help it, that you were false in your generation to the claims of the slave!" [Loud cheers.]

. . . I have claimed that the antislavery cause has, from the first, been ably and dispassionately argued, every objection candidly examined, and every difficulty or doubt anywhere honestly entertained treated with respect. Let me glance at the literature of the cause, and try not so much, in a brief hour, to prove this assertion, as to point out the sources from which any one may satisfy himself of its truth.

I will begin with certainly the ablest and perhaps the most honest statesman who has ever touched the slave question. Any one who will examine John Quincy Adams's speech on Texas, in 1838, will see that he was only seconding the full and able exposure of the Texas plot, prepared by Benjamin Lundy, to one of whose pamphlets Dr. Channing, in his "Letter to Henry Clay," has confessed his obligation. Every one acquainted with those years will allow that the North owes its earliest knowledge and first awakening on that subject to Mr. Lundy, who made long journeys and devoted years to the investigation. His labors have this attestation, that they quickened the zeal and strengthened the hands of such men as Adams and Channing. I have been told that Mr. Lundy prepared a brief for Mr. Adams, and furnished him the materials for his speech on Texas.

Look next at the right of petition. Long before any member of Congress had opened his mouth in its defence, the Abolition presses and lecturers had examined and defended the limits of this right with profound historical research and eminent constitutional ability. So thoroughly had the work been done, that all classes of the people had made up their minds about it long before any speaker of eminence had touched it in Congress. The politicians were little aware of this. When Mr. Adams threw himself so gallantly into the breach, it is said he wrote anxiously home to know whether he would be supported in Massachusetts, little aware of the outburst of popular gratitude which the Northern breeze was even then bringing him, deep and cordial enough to wipe away the old grudge Massachusetts had borne him so long. Mr. Adams himself was only in favor of receiving the petitions, and advised to refuse their prayer, which was the abolition of slavery in the District. He doubted the power of Congress to abolish. His doubts were examined by Mr. William Goodell, in two letters of most acute logic, and of masterly ability. If Mr. Adams still retained his doubts, it is certain at least that he never expressed them afterward. When Mr. Clay paraded the same objections, the whole question of the power of Congress over the district was treated by Theodore D. Weld in the fullest manner, and with the widest research—indeed, leaving nothing to be added: an argument which Dr. Channing characterized as "demonstration," and pronounced the essay "one of the ablest pamphlets from the American press." No answer was ever attempted. The best proof of its ability is, that no one since has presumed to doubt the power. Lawyers and statesmen have tacitly settled down into its full acknowledgment.

The influence of the Colonization Society on the welfare of the colored race was the first question our movement encountered. To the close logic, eloquent appeals, and fully sustained charges of Mr. Garrison's Letters on that subject no answer was ever made. Judge

Jay followed with a work full and able, establishing every charge by the most patient investigation of facts. It is not too much to say of these two volumes, that they left the Colonization Society hopeless at the North. It dares never show its face before the people, and only lingers in some few nooks of sectarian pride, so secluded from the influence of present ideas as to be almost fossil in their character.

The practical working of the slave system, the slave laws, the treatment of slaves, their food, the duration of their lives, their ignorance and moral condition, and the influence of Southern public opinion on their fate, have been spread out in a detail and with a fulness of evidence which no subject has ever received before in this country. Witness the works of Phelps, Bourne, Rankin, Grimké, the "Antislavery Record," and, above all, that encyclopaedia of facts and storehouse of arguments, the *Thousand Witnesses* of Mr. Theodore D. Weld. He also prepared that full and valuable tract for the World's Convention called "Slavery and the Internal Slave-Trade in the United States," published in London, 1841. Unique in anti-slavery literature is Mrs. Child's *Appeal*, one of the ablest of our weapons, and one of the finest efforts of her rare genius.

The *Princeton Review*, I believe, first challenged the Abolitionists to an investigation of the teachings of the Bible on slavery. That field had been somewhat broken by our English predecessors. But in England, the proslavery party had been soon shamed out of the attempt to drag the Bible into their service, and hence the discussion there had been short and somewhat superficial. The proslavery side of the question has been eagerly sustained by theological reviews and doctors of divinity without number, from the half-way and timid faltering of Wayland up to the unblushing and melancholy recklessness of Stuart. The argument on the other side has come wholly from the Abolitionists; for neither Dr. Hague nor Dr. Barnes can be said to have added anything to the wide research, critical acumen, and comprehensive views of Theodore D. Weld, Beriah Green, J. G. Fee, and the old work of Duncan.

On the constitutional questions which have at various times arisen —the citizenship of the colored man, the soundness of the "Prigg" decision, the constitutionality of the old Fugitive Slave Law, the true construction of the slave-surrender clause—nothing has been added, either in the way of fact or argument, to the works of Jay, Weld, Alvan Stewart, E. G. Loring, S. E. Sewall, Richard Hildreth, W. I.

Bowditch, the masterly essays of the *Emancipator* at New York and the *Liberator* at Boston, and the various addresses of the Massachusetts and American Societies for the last twenty years. The idea of the antislavery character of the Constitution—the opiate with which Free Soil quiets its conscience for voting under a proslavery government—I heard first suggested by Mr. Garrison in 1838. It was elaborately argued that year in all our antislavery gatherings, both here and in New York, and sustained with great ability by Alvan Stewart, and in part by T. D. Weld. The antislavery construction of the Constitution was ably argued in 1836, in the *Antislavery Magazine,* by Rev. Samuel J. May, one of the very first to seek the side of Mr. Garrison, and pledge to the slave his life and efforts—a pledge which thirty years of devoted labors have nobly redeemed. If it has either merit or truth, they are due to no legal learning recently added to our ranks, but to some of the old and well-known pioneers. This claim has since received the fullest investigation from Mr. Lysander Spooner, who has urged it with all his unrivalled ingenuity, laborious research, and close logic. He writes as a lawyer, and has no wish, I believe, to be ranked with any class of antislavery men.

The influence of slavery on our government has received the profoundest philosophical investigation from the pen of Richard Hildreth, in his invaluable essay on "Despotism in America"—a work which deserves a place by the side of the ablest political disquisitions of any age.

Mrs. Chapman's survey of "Ten Years of Antislavery Experience," was the first attempt at a philosophical discussion of the various aspects of the antislavery cause, and the problems raised by its struggles with sect and party. You, Mr. Chairman [Edmund Quincy, Esq.], in the elaborate Reports of the Massachusetts Antislavery Society for the last ten years, have followed in the same path, making to American literature a contribution of the highest value, and in a department where you have few rivals and no superior. Whoever shall write the history either of this movement, or any other attempted under a republican government, will find nowhere else so clear an insight and so full an acquaintance with the most difficult part of his subject.

Even the vigorous mind of Rantoul, the ablest man, without doubt, of the Democratic party, and perhaps the ripest politician in New England, added little or nothing to the storehouse of antislavery argument. The grasp of his intellect and the fulness of his learning every one will acknowledge. He never trusted himself to speak on any subject till he had dug down to its primal granite. He laid a most generous contribution on the altar of the antislavery cause. His speeches on our question, too short and too few, are remarkable for their compact statement, iron logic, bold denunciation, and the wonderful light thrown back upon our history. Yet how little do they present which was not familiar for years in our antislavery meetings!

Look, too, at the last great effort of the idol of so many thousands, Mr. Senator Sumner—the discussion of a great national question, of which it has been said that we must go back to Webster's reply to Hayne, and Fisher Ames on the Jay Treaty, to find its equal in Congress—praise which we might perhaps qualify, if any adequate report were left us of some of the noble orations of Adams. No one can be blind to the skilful use he has made of his materials, the consummate ability with which he has marshalled them, and the radiant glow which his genius has thrown over all. Yet, with the exception of his reference to the antislavery debate in Congress, in 1817, there is hardly a train of thought or argument, and no single fact in the whole speech, which has not been familiar in our meetings and essays for the last ten years.

Before leaving the halls of Congress, I have great pleasure in recognizing one exception to my remarks, Mr. Giddings. Perhaps he is no real exception, since it would not be difficult to establish his claim to be considered one of the original Abolition party. But whether he would choose to be so considered or not, it is certainly true that his long presence at the seat of government, his whole-souled devotedness, his sagacity and unwearied industry, have made him a large contributor to our antislavery resources.

The relations of the American Church to slavery, and the duties of private Christians—the whole casuitry of this portion of the question, so momentous among descendants of the Puritans—have been discussed with great acuteness and rare common-sense by Messrs. Garrison, Goodell, Gerrit Smith, Pillsbury, and Foster. They have never attempted to judge the American Church by any standard except that which she has herself laid down—never claimed that she should be perfect, but have contented themselves by demanding that she should be consistent. They have never judged her except out of her own mouth, and on facts asserted by her own presses and leaders. The sundering of the Methodist and Baptist denominations, and the universal agitation of the religious world, are the best proof of the sagacity with which their measures have been chosen, the cogent arguments they have used, and the indisputable facts on which their criticisms have been founded.

In nothing have the Abolitionists shown more sagacity or more thorough knowledge of their countrymen than in the course they have pursued in relation to the Church. None but a New-Englander can appreciate the power which church organizations wield over all who share the blood of the Puritans. The influence of each sect over its own members is overwhelming, often shutting out, or controlling, all other influences. We have Popes here, all the more dangerous because no triple crown puts you on your guard. The Methodist priesthood brings the Catholic very vividly to mind. That each local church is independent of all others, we have been somewhat careful to assert, in theory and practice. The individual's independence of all organizations which place themselves between him and his God, some few bold minds have asserted in theory, but most even of those have stopped there.

In such a land, the Abolitionists early saw, that, for a moral question like theirs, only two paths lay open: to work through the Church —that failing, to join battle with it. Some tried long, like Luther, to be Protestants, and yet not come out of Catholicism; but their eyes were soon opened. Since then we have been convinced that, to come out from the Church, to hold her up as the bulwark of slavery, and to make her shortcomings the main burden of our appeals to the religious sentiment of the community, was our first duty and best policy. This course alienated many friends, and was a subject of frequent rebuke from such men as Dr. Channing. But nothing has ever more strengthened the cause, or won it more influence; and it has had the healthiest effect on the Church itself. British Christians have always sanctioned it, whenever the case has been fairly presented to them. Mr. John Quincy Adams, a man far better acquainted with his own times than Dr. Channing, recognized the soundness of our policy. I do not know that he ever uttered a word in public on the delinquency of the churches; but he is said to have assured his son, at the time the Methodist Church broke asunder, that other men might be more startled by the *éclat* of political success, but nothing, in his opinion, promised more good, or showed more clearly the real strength of the antislavery movement, than that momentous event.

In 1838, the British Emancipation in the West Indies opened a rich

field for observation, and a full harvest of important facts. The Abolitionists, not willing to wait for the official reports of the government,
sent special agents through those islands, whose reports they scattered, at great expense and by great exertion, broadcast through the
land. This was at a time when no newspaper in the country would
either lend or sell them the aid of its columns to enlighten the nation
on an experiment so vitally important to us. And even now, hardly a
press in the country cares or dares to bestow a line or communicate
a fact toward the history of that remarkable revolution. The columns
of the *Antislavery Standard, Pennsylvania Freeman,* and *Ohio Bugle*
have been for years full of all that a thorough and patient advocacy
of our cause demands. And the eloquent lips of many whom I see
around me, and whom I need not name here, have done their share
toward pressing all these topics on public attention. There is hardly
any record of these labors of the living voice. Indeed, from the nature
of the case, there cannot be any adequate one. Yet, unable to command a wide circulation for our books and journals, we have been
obliged to bring ourselves into close contact with the people, and to
rely mainly on public addresses. These have been our most efficient
instrumentality. For proof that these addresses have been full of perti-
nent facts, sound sense, and able arguments, we must necessarily
point to results, and demand to be tried by our fruits. Within these
last twenty years it has been very rare that any fact stated by your
lecturers has been disproved, or any statement of theirs successfully
impeached. And for evidence of the soundness, simplicity, and perti-
nency of their arguments we can only claim that our converts and
co-laborers throughout the land have at least the reputation of being
specially able "to give a reason for the faith that is in them."

I remember that when, in 1845, the present leaders of the Free Soil
party, with Daniel Webster in their company, met to draw up the
Anti-Texas Address of the Massachusetts Convention, they sent to
Abolitionists for antislavery facts and history, for the remarkable
testimonies of our Revolutionary great men which they wished to
quote. [Hear! Hear!] When, many years ago, the Legislature of
Massachusetts wished to send to Congress a resolution affirming the
duty of immediate emancipation, the committee sent to William Lloyd
Garrison to draw it up, and it stands now on our statute-book as he
drafted it.

How vigilantly, how patiently, did we watch the Texas plot from its commencement! The politic South felt that its first move had been too bold, and thenceforward worked underground. For many a year, men laughed at us for entertaining any apprehensions. It was impossible to rouse the North to its peril. David Lee Child was thought crazy, because he would not believe there was no danger. His elaborate "Letters on Texan Annexation" are the ablest and most valuable contribution that has been made towards a history of the whole plot. Though we foresaw and proclaimed our conviction that annexation would be, in the end, a fatal step for the South, we did not feel at liberty to relax our opposition, well knowing the vast increase of strength it would give, at first, to the Slave Power. I remember being one of a committee which waited on Abbott Lawrence, a year or so only before annexation, to ask his countenance to some general movement, without distinction of party, against the Texas scheme. He smiled at our fears, begged us to have no apprehensions; stating that his correspondence with leading men at Washington enabled him to assure us annexation was impossible, and that the South itself was determined to defeat the project. A short time after, Senators and Representatives from Texas took their seats in Congress!

. . . So far from the antislavery cause having lacked a manly and able discussion, I think it will be acknowledged hereafter that this discussion has been one of the noblest contributions to a literature really American. Heretofore, not only has our tone been but an echo of foreign culture, but the very topics discussed and the views maintained have been too often pale reflections of European politics and European philosophy. No matter what dress we assumed, the voice was ever "the voice of Jacob." At last we have stirred a question thoroughly American; the subject has been looked at from a point of view entirely American; and it is of such deep interest, that it has called out all the intellectual strength of the nation. For once, the nation speaks its own thoughts, in its own language, and the tone also is all its own. It will hardly do for the defeated party to claim that, in this discussion, all the ability is on their side.

We are charged with lacking foresight, and said to exaggerate. This charge of exaggeration brings to my mind a fact I mentioned, last month, at Horticultural Hall. The theatres in many of our large cities bring out, night after night, all the radical doctrines and all the startling scenes of "Uncle Tom." They preach immediate emancipation, and slaves shoot their hunters to loud applause. Two years ago, sitting in this hall, I was myself somewhat startled by the assertion of my friend, Mr. Pillsbury, that the theatres would receive the gospel of antislavery truth earlier than the churches. A hiss went up from the galleries, and many in the audience were shocked by the remark. I asked myself whether I could indorse such a statement, and felt that I could not. I could not believe it to be true. Only two years have passed, and what was then deemed rant and fanaticism, by seven out of ten who heard it, has proved true. The theatre, bowing to its audience, has preached immediate emancipation, and given us the whole of "Uncle Tom"; while the pulpit is either silent or hostile, and in the columns of the theological papers the work is subjected to criticism, to reproach, and its author to severe rebuke. Do not, therefore, friends, set down as extravagant every statement which your experience does not warrant. It may be that you and I have not studied the signs of the times quite as accurately as the speaker. Going up and down the land, coming into close contact with the feelings and prejudices of the community, he is sometimes a better judge than you are of its present state. An Abolitionist has more motives for watching and more means of finding out the true state of public opinion, than most of those careless critics who jeer at his assertions to-day, and are the first to cry, "Just what I said," when his prophecy becomes fact to-morrow.

Mr. "Ion" thinks, also, that we have thrown away opportunities, and needlessly outraged the men and parties about us. Far from it. The antislavery movement was a patient and humble suppliant at every door whence any help could possibly be hoped. If we now repudiate and denounce some of our institutions, it is because we have faithfully tried them, and found them deaf to the claims of justice and humanity. Our great Leader, when he first meditated this crusade, did not "At once, like a sunburst, his banner unfurl." O no! he sounded his way warily forward. Brought up in the strictest reverence for church organizations, his first effort was to enlist the clergymen of Boston in the support of his views. On their aid he counted confidently in his effort to preach immediate repentance of all sin. He did not go, with *malice prepense,* as some seem to imagine, up to that "attic" where Mayor Otis with difficulty found him. He did not court hostility or seek exile. He did not sedulously endeavor to cut himself off from the sympathy and countenance of the community about him. O no! A fervid disciple of the American Church, he conferred with some of the leading clergy of the city, and laid before them his convictions on the subject of slavery. He painted their responsibility, and tried to induce them to take from his shoulders the burden of so mighty a movement. He laid himself at their feet. He recognized the colossal strength of the Clergy; he knew that against their opposition it would be almost desperate to attempt to relieve the slave. He entreated them, therefore, to take up the cause. But the Clergy turned away from him! They shut their doors upon him! They bade him compromise his convictions—smother one half of them, and support the colonization movement, making his own auxiliary to that, or they would have none of him. Like Luther, he said: "Here I stand; God help me; I can do nothing else!" But the men who joined him were not persuaded that the case was so desperate. They returned, each to his own local sect, and remained in them until some of us, myself among the number—later converts to the antislavery movement—thought they were slow and faltering in their obedience to conscience, and that they ought to have cut loose much sooner than they did. But a patience, which old sympathies would not allow to be exhausted, and associations, planted deeply in youth, and spreading over a large part of manhood, were too strong for any mere argument to dislodge them. So they still persisted in remaining in the Church. Their zeal was so fervent, and their labors so abundant, that in some towns large societies were formed, led by most of the clergymen, and having almost all the church members on their lists. In those same towns now you will not find one single Abolitionist, of any stamp whatever. They excuse their falling back by alleging that we have injured the cause by our extravagance and denunciation, and by the various other questions with which our names are associated. This might be a good reason why they should not work with us, but does it excuse their not working at all? These people have been once awakened, thoroughly instructed in the momentous character of the movement, and have acknowledged the rightful claim of the slave on their sympathy and exertions. It is not possible that a few thousand persons, however extravagant, could prevent devoted men from finding some way to help such a cause, or at least manifesting their interest in it. But they have not only left us, they have utterly deserted the slave, in the hour when the interests of their sects came across his cause. Is it uncharitable to conjecture the reason? At the early period, however, to which I have referred, the Church was much exercised by the persistency of the Abolitionists in not going out from her. When I joined the antislavery ranks, sixteen years ago, the voice of the clergy was: "Will these *pests* never leave us? Will they still remain to trouble us? If you do not like us, there is the door!" When our friends had exhausted all entreaty, and tested the Christianity of that body, they shook off the dust of their feet, and came out of her.

At the outset, Mr. Garrison called on the head of the Orthodox denomination—a man compared with whose influence on the mind of New England that of the statesman whose death you have just mourned was, I think, but as dust in the balance—a man who then held the Orthodoxy of Boston in his right hand, and who has since taken up the West by its four corners, and given it so largely to Puritanism—I mean the Rev. Dr. Lyman Beecher. Mr. Garrison was one of those who bowed to the spell of that matchless eloquence which then fulmined over our Zion. He waited on his favorite divine, and urged him to give to the new movement the incalculable aid of his name and countenance. He was patiently heard. He was allowed to unfold his plans and array his facts. The reply of the veteran was, "Mr. Garrison, I have too many irons in the fire to put in another." My friend said, "Doctor, you had better take them all out and put this one in, if you mean well either to the religion or to the civil liberty of our country." [Cheers.]

The great Orthodox Leader did not rest with merely refusing to put another iron in his fire; he attempted to limit the irons of other men. As President of Lane Theological Seminary, he endeavored to prevent the students from investigating the subject of slavery. The result, we all remember, was a strenuous resistance on the part of a large number of the students, led by that remarkable man, Theodore D. Weld. The right triumphed, and Lane Seminary lost her character and noblest pupils at the same time. She has languished ever since, even with such a President. Why should I follow Dr. Beecher into those ecclesiastical conventions where he has been tried, and found wanting, in fidelity to the slave? He has done no worse, indeed he has done much better, than most of his class. His opposition has always been open and manly.

But, Mr. Chairman, there is something in the blood which, men tell us, brings out virtues and defects, even when they have lain dormant for a generation. Good and evil qualities are hereditary, the physicians

say. The blood whose warm currents of eloquent aid my friend so-
licited in vain in that generation has sprung voluntarily to his assistance in the next—both from the pulpit and the press—to rouse the
world by the vigor and pathos of its appeals. [Enthusiastic cheers.]
Even on that great triumph I would say a word. Marked and unequalled as has been that success, remember, in explanation of the
phenomenon—for *Uncle Tom's Cabin* is rather an event than a book
—remember this: if the old antislavery movement had not roused
the sympathies of Mrs. Stowe, the book had never been written; if
that movement had not raised up hundreds of thousands of hearts to
sympathize with the slave, the book had never been read. [Cheers.]
Not that the genius of the author has not made the triumph all her
own; not that the unrivalled felicity of its execution has not trebled,
quadrupled, increased tenfold, if you please, the number of readers;
but there must be a spot even for Archimedes to rest his lever upon,
before he can move the world [cheers], and this effort of genius,
consecrated to the noblest purpose, might have fallen dead and un-
noticed in 1835. It is the antislavery movement which has changed
1835 to 1852. Those of us familiar with antislavery literature know
well that Richard Hildreth's *Archy Moore,* now *The White Slave,*
was a book of eminent ability; that it owed its want of success to no
lack of genius, but only to the fact that it was a work born out of
due time; that the antislavery cause had not then aroused sufficient
numbers, on the wings of whose enthusiasm even the most delightful
fiction could have risen into world-wide influence and repute. To the
cause which had changed 1835 to 1852 is due somewhat of the influence of *Uncle Tom's Cabin.*

The Abolitionists have never overlooked the wonderful power
which the wand of the novelist was yet to wield in their behalf over
the hearts of the world. Fredrika Bremer only expressed the common
sentiment of many of us, when she declared that "the fate of the
negro is the romance of our history." Again and again, from my
earliest knowledge of the cause, have I heard the opinion, that in the
debatable land between Freedom and Slavery, in the thrilling incidents of the escape and sufferings of the fugitive, and the perils of his
friends, the future Walter Scott of America would find the "border-
land" of his romance, and the most touching incidents of his "sixty
years since"; and that the literature of America would gather its
freshest laurels from that field.

So much, Mr. Chairman, for our treatment of the Church. We clung to it as long as we hoped to make it useful. Disappointed in that, we have tried to expose its paltering and hypocrisy on this question, broadly and with unflinching boldness, in hopes to purify and bring it to our aid. Our labors with the great religious societies, with the press, with the institutions of learning, have been as untiring, and almost as unsuccessful. We have tried to do our duty to every public question that has arisen, which could be made serviceable in rousing general attention. The Right of Petition, the Power of Congress, the Internal Slave-Trade, Texas, the Compromise Measures, the Fugitive Slave Law, the motions of leading men, the tactics of parties, have all been watched and used with sagacity and effect as means to produce a change in public opinion. Dr. Channing has thanked the Abolition party, in the name of all the lovers of free thought and free speech, for having vindicated that right, when all others seemed ready to surrender it—vindicated it at the cost of reputation, ease, property, even life itself. The only blood that has ever been shed, on this side the ocean, in defence of the freedom of the press, was the blood of Lovejoy, one of their number. . . .

No one, Mr. Chairman, deserves more of that honor than he whose chair you now occupy. Our youthful city can boast of but few places of historic renown; but I know of no one which coming time is more likely to keep in memory than the roof which Francis Jackson offered to the antislavery women of Boston, when Mayor Lyman confessed he was unable to protect their meeting, and when the only protection the laws could afford Mr. Garrison was the shelter of the common jail.

Sir, when a nation sets itself to do evil, and all its leading forces, wealth, party and piety, join in the career, it is impossible but that those who offer a constant opposition should be hated and maligned, no matter how wise, cautious, and well planned their course may be. We are peculiar sufferers in this way. The community has come to hate its reproving Nathan so bitterly, that even those whom the relenting part of it is beginning to regard as standard-bearers of the antislavery host think it unwise to avow any connection or sympathy with him. I refer to some of the leaders of the political movement against slavery. They feel it to be their mission to marshal and use as effectively as possible the present convictions of the people. They cannot afford to encumber themselves with the odium which twenty years of angry agitation have engendered in great sects sore from

unsparing rebuke, parties galled by constant defeat, and leading men
provoked by unexpected exposure. They are willing to confess, pri-
vately, that our movement produced theirs, and that its continued
existence is the very breath of their life. But, at the same time, they
would fain walk on the road without being soiled by too close contact
with the rough pioneers who threw it up. They are wise and honorable, and their silence is very expressive.

When I speak of their eminent position and acknowledged ability,
another thought strikes me. Who converted these men and their distinguished associates? It is said we have shown neither sagacity in
plans, nor candor in discussion, nor ability. Who, then, or what,
converted Burlingame and Wilson, Sumner and Adams, Palfrey and
Mann, Chase and Hale, and Phillips and Giddings? Who taught the
Christian Register, the *Daily Advertiser,* and that class of prints, that
there were such things as a slave and a slaveholder in the land, and
so gave them some more intelligent basis than their mere instincts to
hate William Lloyd Garrison? [Shouts and laughter.] What magic
wand was it whose touch made the toadying servility of the land start
up the real demon that it was, and at the same time gathered into the
slave's service the professional ability, ripe culture, and personal integrity which grace the Free Soil ranks? We never argue! These men,
then, were converted by simple denunciation! They were all converted
by the "hot," "reckless," "ranting," "bigoted," "fanatic" Garrison,
who never troubled himself about facts, nor stopped to argue with an
opponent, but straightway knocked him down! [Roars of laughter
and cheers.] My old and valued friend, Mr. Sumner, often boasts that
he was a reader of the *Liberator* before I was. Do not criticise too
much the agency by which such men were converted. That blade has
a double edge. Our reckless course, our empty rant, our fanaticism,
has made Abolitionists of some of the best and ablest men in the land.
We are inclined to go on, and see if even with such poor tools we
cannot make some more. [Enthusiastic applause.] Antislavery zeal
and the roused conscience of the "godless come-outers" made the
trembling South demand the Fugitive Slave Law, and the Fugitive
Slave Law "provoked" Mrs. Stowe to the good work of "Uncle Tom."
That is something! [Cheers.] Let me say, in passing, that you will
nowhere find an earlier or more generous appreciation, or more flowing eulogy, of these men and their labors, than in the columns of the

Liberator. No one, however feeble, has ever peeped or muttered, in any quarter, that the vigilant eye of the Pioneer has not recognized him. He has stretched out the right hand of a most cordial welcome the moment any man's face was turned Zionward. [Loud cheers.]

I do not mention these things to praise Mr. Garrison, I do not stand here for that purpose. You will not deny—if you do, I can prove it—that the movement of the Abolitionists converted these men. Their constituents were converted by it. The assault upon the right of petition, upon the right to print and speak of slavery, the denial of the right of Congress over the District, the annexation of Texas, the Fugitive Slave Law, were measures which the antislavery movement provoked, and the discussion of which has made all the Abolitionists we have. The antislavery cause, then, converted these men; it gave them a constituency; it gave them an opportunity to speak, and it gave them a public to listen. The antislavery cause gave them their votes, got them their offices, furnished them their facts, gave them their audience. If you tell me they cherished all these principles in their own breasts before Mr. Garrison appeared, I can only say, if the antislavery movement did not give them their ideas, it surely gave them the courage to utter them.

In such circumstances, is it not singular that the name of William Lloyd Garrison has never been pronounced on the floor of the United States Congress linked with any epithet but that of contempt! No one of those men who owe their ideas, their station, their audience, to him, have ever thought it worth their while to utter one word in grateful recognition of the power which called them into being. When obliged, by the course of their argument, to treat the question historically, they can go across the water to Clarkson and Wilberforce—yes, to a safe salt-water distance. [Laughter.] As Daniel Webster, when he was talking to the farmers of Western New York, and wished to contrast slave labor and free labor, did not dare to compare New York with Virginia—sister States, under the same government, planted by the same race, worshipping at the same altar, speaking the same language—identical in all respects, save that one in which he wished to seek the contrast; but no; he compared it with Cuba [cheers and laughter]—the contrast was so close! [Renewed cheers.] Catholic—Protestant; Spanish—Saxon; despotism—municipal institutions; readers of Lope de Vega and of Shakespeare; mutterers of the

Mass—children of the Bible! But Virginia is too near home! So is
Garrison! One would have thought there was something in the human
breast which would sometimes break through policy. These noble-
hearted men whom I have named must surely have found quite
irksome the constant practice of what Dr. Gardiner used to call "that
dispicable virtue, prudence"! [Laughter.] One would have thought,
when they heard that name spoken with contempt, their ready eloquence would have leaped from its scabbard to avenge even a word
that threatened him with insult. But it never came—never! [Sensa-
tion.] I do not say I blame them. Perhaps they thought they should
serve the cause better by drawing a broad black line between themselves and him. Perhaps they thought the Devil could be cheated;
I do not think he can. [Laughter and cheers.]

We are perfectly willing—I am, for one—to be the dead lumber
that shall make a path for these men into the light and love of the
people. We hope for nothing better. Use us freely, in any way, for the
slave. When the temple is finished, the tools will not complain that
they are thrown aside, let who will lead up the nation to "put on the
topstone with shoutings." But while so much remains to be done,
while our little camp is beleaguered all about, do nothing to weaken
his influence, whose sagacity, more than any other single man's, has
led us up hither, and whose name is identified with that movement
which the North still heeds, and the South still fears the most. After
all, Mr. Chairman, this is no hard task. We know very well, that, notwithstanding this loud clamor about our harsh judgment of men and
things, our opinions differ very little from those of our Free Soil
friends, or of intelligent men generally, when you really get at them.
It has even been said, that one of that family which has made itself
so infamously conspicuous here in executing the Fugitive Slave Law,
a judge, whose earnest defence of that law we all heard in Faneuil
Hall, did himself, but a little while before, arrange for a fugitive to
be hid till pursuit was over. I hope it is true—it would be an honorable inconsistency. And if it be not true of him, we know it is of
others. Yet it is base to incite others to deeds, at which, whenever
we are hidden from public notice, our own hearts recoil! But thus we
see that when men lay aside the judicial ermine, the senator's robe, or
the party collar, and sit down in private life, you can hardly distin-
guish their tones from ours. Their eyes seem as anointed as our own.
As in Pope's day:

At all we laugh they laugh, no doubt;
The only difference is, we dare *laugh out.*

Caution is not always good policy in a cause like ours. It is said that, when Napoleon saw the day going against him, he used to throw away all the rules of war, and trust himself to the hot impetuosity of his soldiers. The masses are governed more by impulse than conviction; and even were it not so, the convictions of most men are on our side, and this will surely appear, if we can only pierce the crust of their prejudice or indifference. I observe that our Free Soil friends never stir their audience so deeply as when some individual leaps beyond the platform, and strikes upon the very heart of the people. Men listen to discussions of laws and tactics with ominous patience. It is when Mr. Sumner, in Faneuil Hall, avows his determination to disobey the Fugitive Slave Law, and cries out, "I was a man before I was a Commissioner"—when Mr. Giddings says of the fall of slavery, quoting Adams, " 'Let it come; if it must come in *blood,* yet I say let it come!' "—that their associates on the platform are sure they are wrecking the party—while many a heart beneath beats its first pulse of antislavery life.

. . . In 1831, Mr. Garrison commenced a paper advocating the doctrine of immediate emancipation. He had against him the thirty thousand churches and all the clergy of the country—its wealth, its commerce, its press. In 1831, what was the state of things? There was the most entire ignorance and apathy on the slave question. If men knew of the existence of slavery, it was only as a part of picturesque Virginia life. No one preached, no one talked, no one wrote about it. No whisper of it stirred the surface of the political sea. The Church heard of it occasionally, when some colonization agent asked funds to send the blacks to Africa. Old school-books tainted with some antislavery selections had passed out of use, and new ones were compiled to suit the times. Soon as any dissent from the prevailing faith appeared, every one set himself to crush it. The pulpits preached at it; the press denounced it; mobs tore down houses, threw presses into the fire and the stream, and shot the editors; religious conventions tried to smother it; parties arrayed themselves against it. Daniel Webster boasted in the Senate, that he had never introduced the subject of slavery to that body, and never would. Mr. Clay, in 1839, makes a speech for the Presidency, in which he says, that to discuss the subject of slavery is moral treason, and that no man has a right to introduce the subject into Congress. Mr. Benton, in 1844, laid down his platform, and he not only denies the right, but asserts that he never has and never will discuss the subject. Yet Mr. Clay, from 1839 down to his death, hardly made a remarkable speech of any kind, except on slavery. Mr. Webster, having indulged now and then in a little easy rhetoric, as at Niblo's and elsewhere, opens his mouth in 1840, generously contributing his aid to both sides, and stops talking about it only when death closes his lips. Mr. Benton's six or eight speeches in the United States Senate have all been on the subject of slavery in the Southwestern section of the country, and form the basis of whatever claim he has to the character of a statesman, and he owes his seat in the next Congress somewhat, perhaps, to antislavery pretensions! The Whig and Democratic parties pledged themselves just as emphatically against the antislavery discussion—against agitation and free speech. These men said: "It sha'n't be talked about, it won't be talked about!" These are *your statesmen*—men who understand the present, that is, and mould the future! The man who understands his own time, and whose genius moulds the future to his views, he is a statesman, is he not? These men devoted themselves to banks, to the tariff, to internal improvements, to constitutional and financial questions. They said to slavery: "Back! no entrance here! We pledge ourselves against you." And then there came up a humble printer-boy, who whipped them into the traces, and made them talk, like Hotspur's starling, nothing BUT slavery. He scattered all these gigantic shadows—tariff, bank, constitutional questions, financial questions—and slavery, like the colossal head in Walpole's romance, came up and filled the whole political horizon! [Enthusiastic applause.] Yet you must remember he is not a statesman; he is a "fanatic." He has no discipline—Mr. "Ion" says so; he does not understand the "discipline that is essential to victory"! This man did not understand his own time—he did not know what the future was to be—he was not able to shape it—he had no "prudence"—he had no "foresight"! Daniel Webster says, "I have never introduced this subject, and never will"—and died broken-hearted because he had not been able to talk enough about it. Benton says, "I will never speak of slavery," and lives to break with his party on this issue! Mr. Clay says it is "moral treason" to introduce the subject into Congress, and lives to see Congress turned into an antislavery debating-society, to suit the purpose of one "too powerful individual"!

These were statesmen, mark you! Two of them have gone to their graves covered with eulogy; and our national stock of eloquence is all insufficient to describe how profound and far-reaching was the sagacity of Daniel Webster! Remember who it was that said, in 1831, "I am in earnest—I will not equivocate—I will not excuse—I will not retreat a single inch—*and I will be heard!*" [Repeated cheers.] That speaker has lived twenty-two years, and the complaint of twenty-three millions of people is, "Shall we never hear of anything but slavery?" [Cheers.] I heard Dr. Kirk, of Boston, say in his own pulpit, when he returned from London—where he had been as a representative to the "Evangelical Alliance"—"I went up to London, and they asked me what I thought of the question of immediate emancipation. They examined us all. Is an American never to travel anywhere in the world but men will throw this troublesome question in his face?" Well, it is all HIS fault [pointing to Mr. Garrison]. [Enthusiastic cheers.]

Now, when we come to talk of statesmanship, of sagacity in choosing time and measures, of endeavor, by proper means, to right the public mind, of keen insight into the present and potent sway over the future, it seems to me that the Abolitionists, who have taken—whether for good or for ill, whether to their discredit or to their praise—this country by the four corners, and shaken it until you can hear nothing but slavery, whether you travel in railroad or steamboat, whether you enter the hall of legislation or read the columns of a newspaper—it seems to me that such men may point to the present aspect of the nation, to their originally avowed purpose, to the pledges and efforts of all your great men against them, and then let you determine to which side the credit of sagacity and statesmanship belongs. Napoleon busied himself, at St. Helena, in showing how Wellington ought not to have conquered at Waterloo. The world has never got time to listen to the explanation. Sufficient for it that the Allies entered Paris. In like manner, it seems hardly the province of a defeated Church and State to deny the skill of measures by which they have been conquered.

It may sound strange to some, this claim for Mr. Garrison of a profound statesmanship. Men have heard him styled a mere fanatic so long, that they are incompetent to judge him fairly. "The phrases men are accustomed," says Goethe, "to repeat incessantly, end by becoming convictions, and ossify the organs of intelligence," I cannot accept you, therefore, as my jury. I appeal from Festus to Caesar; from the prejudice of our streets to the common sense of the world, and to your children.

Every thoughtful and unprejudiced mind must see that such an evil as slavery will yield only to the most radical treatment. If you consider the work we have to do, you will not think us needlessly aggressive, or that we dig down unnecessarily deep in laying the foundations of our enterprise. A money power of two thousand millions of dollars, as the prices of slaves now range, held by a small body of able and desperate men; that body raised into a political aristocracy by special constitutional provisions; cotton, the product of slave labor, forming the basis of our whole foreign commerce, and the commercial class thus subsidized; the press bought up, the pulpit reduced to vassalage, the heart of the common people chilled by a bitter prejudice against the black race; our leading men bribed, by ambition, either to silence or open hostility; in such a land, on what shall an Abolitionist rely? On a few cold prayers, mere lip-service, and never from the heart? On a church resolution, hidden often in its records, and meant only as a decent cover for servility in daily practice? On political parties, with their superficial influence at best, and seeking ordinarily only to use existing prejudices to the best advantage? Slavery has deeper root here than any aristocratic institution has in Europe; and politics is but the common pulse-beat, of which revolution is the fever-spasm. Yet we have seen Europeon aristocracy survive storms which seemed to reach down to the primal strata of European life. Shall we, then, trust to mere politics, where even revolution has failed? How shall the stream rise above its fountain? Where shall our church organizations or parties get strength to attack their great parent and moulder, the Slave Power? Shall the thing formed say to him that formed it, Why hast thou made me thus? The old jest of one who tried to lift himself in his own basket, is but a tame picture of the man who imagines that, by working solely through existing sects and parties, he can destroy slavery. Mechanics say nothing but an earthquake, strong enough to move all Egypt, can bring down the Pyramids.

Experience has confirmed these views. The Abolitionists who have acted on them have a "short method" with all unbelievers. They have but to point to their own success, in contrast with every other man's failure. To waken the nation to its real state, and chain it to the consideration of this one duty, is half the work. So much we have done. Slavery has been made the question of this generation. To startle the South to madness, so that every step she takes, in her blindness, is one step more toward ruin, is much. This we have done. Witness Texas and the Fugitive Slave Law. To have elaborated for the nation the only plan of redemption, pointed out the only exodus from this "sea of troubles," is much. This we claim to have done in our motto of IMMEDIATE, UNCONDITIONAL EMANCIPATION ON THE SOIL. The closer any statesmanlike mind looks into the question, the more favor our plan finds with it. The Christian asks fairly of the infidel, "If this religion be not from God, how do you explain its triumph, and the history of the first three centuries?" Our question is similar. If our agitation has not been wisely planned and conducted, explain for us the history of the last twenty years! Experience is a safe light to walk by, and he is not a rash man who expects success in future from the same means which have secured it in times past.

William Lloyd Garrison's Farewell to the Readers of the Liberator--*Valedictory*

THE LAST NUMBER OF THE *Liberator*

The last! the last! the last!
O, by that little word
How many thoughts are stirred—
That sister of THE PAST!

The present number of the *Liberator* is the completion of its thirty-fifth volume, and the termination of its existence.

Commencing my editorial career when only twenty years of age, I have followed it continuously till I have attained my sixtieth year— first, in connection with *The Free Press,* in Newburyport, in the spring of 1826; next, with *The National Philanthropist,* in Boston, in 1827; next, with the *Journal of The Times,* in Bennington, Vt., in 1828–9; next, with the *Genius of Universal Emancipation,* in Baltimore, in 1829–30; and, finally, with the *Liberator,* in Boston, from the 1st of January, 1831, to the 1st of January, 1866; at the start, probably the youngest member of the editorial fraternity in the land, now, perhaps, the oldest, not in years, but in continuous service—unless Mr. Bryant, of the New York *Evening Post,* be an exception.

Whether I shall again be connected with the press, in a similar capacity, is quite problematical; but, at my period of life, I feel no prompting to start a new journal at my own risk, and with the certainty of struggling against wind and tide, as I have done in the past.

I began the publication of the *Liberator* without a subscriber, and I end it—it gives me unalloyed satisfaction to say—without a farthing as the pecuniary result of the patronage extended to it during thirty-five years of unremitted labors.

From the immense change wrought in the national feeling and sentiment on the subject of slavery, the *Liberator* derived no advantage at any time in regard to its circulation. The original "disturber of the peace," nothing was left undone at the beginning, and up to the hour of the late rebellion, by Southern slaveholding villany on the one hand, and Northern pro-slavery malice on the other, to represent it as too vile a sheet to be countenanced by any claiming to be Christian or patriotic; and it always required rare moral courage or singular personal independence to be among its patrons. Never had a journal to look such opposition in the face—never was one so constantly belied and caricatured. If it had advocated all the crimes forbidden by the moral law of God and the statutes of the State, instead of vindicating the sacred claims of oppressed and bleeding humanity, it could not have been more vehemently denounced or more indignantly repudiated. To this day—such is the force of prejudice—there are multitudes who cannot be induced to read a single number of it, even on the score of curiosity, though their views on the slavery question are now precisely those which it has uniformly advocated. Yet no journal has been conducted with such fairness and impartiality; none has granted such freedom in its columns to its opponents; none has so scrupulously and uniformly presented all sides of every question discussed in its pages; none has so readily and exhaustively published, without note or comment, what its enemies have said to its disparagement, and the vilification of its editor; none has vindicated primitive Christianity, in its spirit and purpose—"the higher law," in its supremacy over nations and governments as well as individual conscience—the Golden Rule, in its binding obligation upon all classes—the Declaration of Independence, with its self-evident truths—the rights of human nature, without distinction of race, complexion or sex—more earnestly or more uncompromisingly; none has exerted a higher moral or more broadly reformatory influence upon those who have given it a careful perusal; and none has gone beyond it in asserting the Fatherhood of God and the brotherhood of man. All this may be claimed for it without egotism or presumption. It has ever been "a terror to evil-doers, and a praise to them that do well."

It has excited the fierce hostility of all that is vile and demoniacal in the land, and won the affection and regard of the purest and noblest of the age. To me it has been unspeakably cheering, and the richest compensation for whatever of peril, suffering and defamation I have been called to encounter, that one uniform testimony has been borne, by those who have had its weekly perusal, as to the elevating and quickening influence of the *Liberator* upon their character and lives; and the deep grief they are expressing in view of its discontinuance is overwhelmingly affecting to my feelings. None of these date their subscription from the commencement of the paper, and they have allowed nothing in its columns to pass without a rigid scrutiny. They speak, therefore, experimentally, and "testify of that which they have seen and do know." Let them be assured that my regret in the separation which is to take place between us, in consequence of the discontinuance of the *Liberator,* is at least as poignant as their own; and let them feel, as I do, comforted by the thought that it relates only to the weekly method of communicating with each other, and not to the principles we have espoused in the past, or the hopes and aims we cherish as to the future.

Although the *Liberator* was designed to be, and has ever been, mainly devoted to the abolition of slavery, yet it has been instrumental in aiding the cause of reform in many of its most important aspects.

I have never consulted either the subscription list of the paper or public sentiment in printing, or omitting to print, any article touching any matter whatever. Personally, I have never asked any one to become a subscriber, nor any one to contribute to its support, nor presented its claims for a better circulation in any lecture or speech, or at any one of the multitudinous anti-slavery gatherings in the land. Had I done so, no doubt its subscription list might have been much enlarged.

In this connection, I must be permitted to express my surprise that I am gravely informed, in various quarters, that this is no time to retire from public labor; that though the chains of the captive have been broken, he is yet to be vindicated in regard to the full possession of equal civil and political rights; that the freedmen in every part of the South are subjected to many insults and outrages; that the old slaveholding spirit is showing itself in every available form; that there is imminent danger that, in the hurry of reconstruction and readmission to the Union, the late rebel States will be left free to work any amount of mischief; that there is manifestly a severe struggle yet to come with the Southern "powers of darkness," which will require the utmost vigilance and the most determined efforts on the part of the friends of impartial liberty—&c., &c., &c. Surely, it is not meant by all this that I am therefore bound to continue the publication of the *Liberator*; for that is a matter for me to determine, and no one else. As I commenced its publication without asking leave of any one, so I claim to be competent to decide when it may fitly close its career.

Again—it cannot be meant, by this presentation of the existing state of things at the South, either to impeach my intelligence, or to impute to me a lack of interest in behalf of that race, for the liberation and elevation of which I have labored so many years! If, when they had no friends, and no hope of earthly redemption, I did not hesitate to make their cause my own, is it to be supposed that, with their yokes broken, and their friends and advocates multiplied indefinitely, I can be any the less disposed to stand by them to the last—to insist on the full measure of justice and equity being meted out to them—to retain in my breast a lively and permanent interest in all that relates to their present condition and future welfare?

I shall sound no trumpet and make no parade as to what I shall do for the future. After having gone through with such a struggle as has never been paralleled in duration in the life of any reformer, and for nearly forty years been the target at which all poisonous and deadly missiles have been hurled, and having seen our great national iniquity blotted out, and freedom "proclaimed throughout all the land to all the inhabitants thereof," and a thousand presses and pulpits support-

REMARKS OF THEODORE D. WELD

Friends, you have just heard the lines, written perhaps to-day, perhaps yesterday, by our own beloved poet, Whittier. I have in my hand a poem which he wrote almost fifty years ago, in the darkest hour of the midnight which brooded over our country. You are most of you, perhaps all, familiar with it. It is addressed to Mr. Garrison. Shall I read a single stanza? I do it to illustrate a point strongly put by our brother who has just taken his seat; that is, the power of a single soul, *alone,* of a single soul touched with sacred fire, a soul all of whose powers are enlisted—the thought, the feeling, the susceptibility, the emotion, the indomitable will, the conscience that never shrinks, and always points to duty—I say, the power which God has lodged in the human mind, enabling it to do and to dare and to suffer everything, and thank God for the privilege of doing it. To show also how, when one soul is thus stirred in its innermost and to its uttermost, it is irresistible; that wherever there are souls, here and there, and thick and fast, too, not merely one, and another, and another, of the great mass, but multitudes of souls are ready to receive the truth and welcome it, to incorporate it into their thought and feeling, to live and die for it. That was the effect of Garrison upon the soul of Whittier. He here gives us his testimony. The date of this is 1833—almost fifty years ago. He says in the third stanza:

> I love thee with a brother's love,
>   I feel my pulses thrill
> To mark thy spirit soar above
>   The cloud of human ill.
> My heart hath leaped to answer thine,
>   And echo back thy words,
> As leaps the warrior's at the shine
>   And flash of kindred swords!

Friends, in recounting the multiform cords upon which our great brother struck, and in following out those vibrations until we see them rouse the nation's heart—in doing this we come to a point where we stand amazed beyond our belief; we have seen nothing like it; we have thought of nothing like it; we know of nothing like it in the history of the world; where, on moral grounds, through the dictate of conscience, through the grasp of the intuitions, such force has been given to a single soul as to make it omnipotent. No wonder that the old prophet broke out, "I said, Ye are gods!" When God pulsates in a human soul, God is there. Not the Infinite God, the eternal existence, but the power of God; that which Jesus felt when He said, "To this end was I born, and for this cause came I into the world, to bear witness unto the truth;" and "the words I speak unto you, they are spirit and they are life." Think for a moment of Garrison, through his paper and by his speech, traversing the country, uttering words which fell with such force as to break the spell that was upon souls, rouse the latent and dormant and bring them to life, gird them with power, and put weapons into their hands, arming them from head to foot, to go forth and fight in the moral warfare!

It has been said by those who have preceded me, that we are not here to mourn. In looking over this congregation, I do not see a single face that seems to mourn. It is no hour for mourning. Why should we mourn here when they are exulting *there*? When they are receiving him with greetings and with songs of joy upon their lips, and putting the crown upon his head! "Well-dones" and "Welcomes" are echoing there: Why should be wailing here? We cannot wail. We are here to rejoice. We are here to make this a solemn and glorious festival of the spirit. We are here to thank God and take courage that such a man has lived. In devout gratitude we bow before him, saying: "Blessing, and honor, and glory, and thanksgiving to Him that sitteth upon the throne, that He hath given us, given this nation, given the world, so precious a thing as a human soul such as animated that form which lies motionless there."

Let us rejoice! Tears will come to our eyes, but they are not tears of bereavement. If we have grief, it is the joy of grief. They are tears of love; they are tears of sympathy; they are tears of exultation. Blessed are we that we have lived at the same time when there walked the earth such a man as WILLIAM LLOYD GARRISON. We did not know him. Those that knew him best did not know his innermost and his uttermost. The world around did not know him, even those who most appreciated him. Fifty years hence there will be something written about Garrison that will show what no one has exhibited or can exhibit now, for then time enough will have elapsed for his influence, the power of his soul, for those vast pulsations, so far-reaching—time enough to trace out all those lines of influence and show how they stamped hearts innumerable, and how they can be traced in vast and manifold effects. Great as the direct influence of the life of Garrison was, great as it is to the multitudes of the freedmen of the South who rise up to testify, great as is the direct influence which outpoured from his life, the indirect influences seem almost greater. He saw, at one of the main points of the human circle, something which compelled his attention, something which could not be ignored, which should not be left any longer; and he lifted up his voice and cried out against it, beseeched, appealed, and summoned up help from every quarter, and touched with such force as no man else could the springs that could accomplish his object—the abolition of slavery.

But that was only one point in the great circle of human interests, human rights, and human well-being. Now, indirectly, this line being traversed as he traversed it—all the light thrown upon rights that he threw—why, it led to other points of the circle; and then, as has been alluded to by our sister here, in considering the question of rights, what they are, it was seen that self-right is the foundation of all right, the nucleus, the centre, from which all other rights radiate; that it is really the trunk of the tree of all rights, and that every other right is a mere relative right to self-right, in the centre; and that the great heart that animates that right in the centre is *myself*. Take away the right to *myself*, and where is my right to my coat, or my book, or my anything else? It is nothing; it is uprooted and cast away to wither! He brought his mind to a focus upon the fundamental right, the intrinsic, the absolute, the eternal, the ineradicable right—*self-right*. And that was the reason why he uttered what are called such hard words about slaveholding. It was the same conviction that fired the soul of old John Wesley—blessings on him—when he said, "Slavery is the sum of all villanies!" No wonder he used words that sounded hard to those very soft and shrinking people who loved smooth things, and to those who sympathized with slavery. Why, when he saw the slaveholder not merely asserting his right to a man as a piece of property, but when he saw him stalking over all this New England and claiming the right to absorb into himself the self-right of another self and call it his, make it an article of property, and send it to the auction-block, no wonder he roused at length the North, no wonder the slaveholders put a price upon his head, because there he touched the apple of their eye. He had struck the very heart of the monster. It was a death-blow, and that must be fended off, or all must be given up.

Friends, you have been detained long already. I ought not to keep you from those words to which you are waiting to listen, from our brother who, more than any one else, struck blows and uttered words such as no other could except the great leader—uttered words, gave a testimony, and stamped an impression upon the nation's heart. You want to hear him, and not to hear me. But let me ask your patience for a moment longer. Some have said, we are not here to eulogize our brother. It really seems as though words were very weak in eulogy of WILLIAM LLOYD GARRISON. The truth is, we are shut up to the necessity of praising him. We cannot speak his name but it is the highest praise that can be given him. Who does not recognize that? Who can speak of a single one of his acts without that act rising up and testifying to what he was, to what he is, to what he has done, and what no other man did or could do? No, it is all around, from centre to circumference alike! See how the whole land is strewn with his deeds! See how the very air breathes of them! See how the very tones of the wind, as they go through the forest, shout them! The fact is, nothing that he has done can be spoken of that is not a eulogy. And yet, if those cold lips could move and utter words, it seems to me they would say, "In this hour let eulogy be dumb!" Blessed brother! We would let eulogy be dumb, if it were possible. But then we must stand dumb ourselves. We can say nothing at such a time as this if we cannot speak of what he has done, and every act is a eulogy. Why, those words that were repeated by our brother who has addressed you—what marvelous words they were! Marvelous they will be forever.

Let us for a moment look back fifty years. We see a church dead! Not merely blind and palsied, but dead to the sin of slavery. Whatever life it had, there was no pulsation indicating that it realized the sin of slavery. Look back there! What do we see? A great bank of darkness, in which the church lies dead; and as we look, we see a single hand unshrinkingly thrust out from the thickest of that darkness and writing a dozen simple words, little fireside words; writing them so large that they can be seen and read from far. We see those words take on a glow in the midst of the very darkness. We see those letters every one turned to a letter of fire. And what was written there? You have heard them already; you know them by heart: "*I am* *in earnest. I will not equivocate—I will not excuse—I will not retreat a single inch—*AND I WILL BE HEARD!" Take the circumstances and conditions of the time in which they were uttered, consider the great soul that propelled them forth, consider that he felt the necessity upon him and a woe unto him if he did not utter them—consider all this, and then tell me whether such words have ever been uttered by other mortal lips! Those words were the passwords of Liberty. They were the keynote, struck by him so loud that they startled the nation. Thank God that there was one man in those times who could utter them; who had a soul large enough, deep enough, strong enough, fired enough, godlike enough, to utter them!

Index